ManageFirst
PROGRAM™

ManageFirst®
Hospitality and
Restaurant Management
Competency Guide

PEARSON
Prentice
Hall

Upper Saddle River, New Jersey 07458

NATIONAL
RESTAURANT
ASSOCIATION
S O L U T I O N S ™

Disclaimer

Table of Contents

A Message from the National Restaurant Association

Founded in 1919, the National Restaurant Association is the leading business association for the restaurant industry. Together with the National Restaurant Association Educational Foundation (NRAEF) and National Restaurant Association Solutions (NRA Solutions) our goal is to lead America's restaurant industry into a new era of prosperity, prominence, and participation, enhancing the quality of life for all we serve.

As one of the nation's largest private-sector employers, the restaurant, hospitality and foodservice industry is the cornerstone of the American economy, of career-and-employment opportunities, and of local communities. The overall impact of the restaurant industry is astounding. The restaurant industry is expected to add 1.8 million jobs over the next decade, with employment reaching 14.8 million by 2019. At the National Restaurant Association, we are focused on enhancing this position by providing the valuable tools and resources needed to educate our current and future professionals.

For more information on the National Restaurant Association, please visit our Web site at www.restaurant.org.

What is the ManageFirst Program™?

The ManageFirst Program is a management-training certificate program that exemplifies our commitment to developing materials by the industry, for the industry. The program's most powerful strength is that it is based on a set of competencies defined by the restaurant, foodservice, and hospitality industry as critical for success. For more information on the ManageFirst Program, visit www.managefirst.restaurant.org.

ManageFirst Program Components

The ManageFirst Program includes a set of Competency Guides, exams, Instructor Resources, certificates, a credential, and support activities and services. By participating in the program, you are demonstrating your commitment to becoming a highly qualified professional either preparing to begin or to advance your career in the restaurant, hospitality, and foodservice industry.

The Competency Guides cover the range of topics listed in the chart at right.

Competency Guide/Exam Topics

ManageFirst Core Credential Topics

Controlling Foodservice Costs

Hospitality and Restaurant Management

Human Resources Management and Supervision

ServSafe® Food Safety

ManageFirst Elective Topics

Customer Service

Food Production

Inventory and Purchasing

Managerial Accounting

Menu Marketing and Management

Nutrition

Restaurant Marketing

ServSafe Alcohol® Responsible Alcohol Service

Within the guides, you will find the essential content for the topic as defined by industry, as well as learning activities, assessments, case studies, suggested field projects, professional profiles, and testimonials. You can also find an answer sheet or an online exam voucher for a NRA Solutions exam written specifically for each topic. The exam can be administered either online or in a paper and pencil format (see inside front cover for a listing of ISBNs), and it will be proctored. Upon successfully passing the exam, you will be issued a customized certificate from NRA Solutions. The certificate is a lasting recognition of your accomplishment and a signal to the industry that you have mastered the competency covered within the particular topic.

To earn the ManageFirst Professional™ (MFP™) credential, you will be required to pass four core exams and one elective exam (to be chosen from the remaining program topics) and to document your work experience in the restaurant and foodservice industry. Earning the MFP credential is a significant accomplishment.

We applaud you as you either begin or advance your career in the restaurant, hospitality, and foodservice industry. Visit *www.managefirst.restaurant.org* to learn about additional career-building resources offered through the National Restaurant Association, including scholarships for college students enrolled in relevant industry programs.

ManageFirst Program Ordering Information

Review copies or support materials:
FACULTY FIELD SERVICES
800.526.0485

Domestic orders and inquiries:
PEARSON CUSTOMER SERVICE
Tel: 800.922.0579
www.prenhall.com

International orders and inquiries:
U.S. EXPORT SALES OFFICE
Pearson Education International Customer Service Group
200 Old Tappan Road
Old Tappan, NJ 07675 USA
Tel: 201.767.5021
Fax: 201.767.5625

For corporate, government and special sales (consultants, corporations, training centers, VARs, and corporate resellers) orders and inquiries:
PEARSON CORPORATE SALES
Phone: 317.428.3411
Fax: 317.428.3343
Email: managefirst@prenhall.com

For additional information regarding other Prentice Hall publications, instructor and student support materials, locating your sales representative and much more, please visit *www.prenhall.com/managefirst.*

Acknowledgements

The National Restaurant Association Educational Solutions is grateful for the significant contributions made to this competency guide by the following individuals.

John A. Drysdale, MS, FMP

Cynthia Mayo, PhD

In addition, we are pleased to thank our many other advisors, subject matter experts, reviewers, and contributors for their time, effort, and dedication to this program.

Teresa Marie Gargano Adamski

Ernest Boger

Robert Bosselman

Jerald Chesser

Cynthia Deale

Fred DeMicco

Johnathan Deustch

Gene Fritz

John Gescheidle

Thomas Hamilton

John Hart

Thomas Kaltenecker

Ray Kavanaugh

John Kidwell

Carol Kizer

Holly Ruttan Maloney

Fred Mayo

Patrick Moreo

Robert O'Halloran

Brian O'Malley

Terrence Pappas

James Perry

Patricia Plavcan

William N. Reynolds

Rosenthal Group

Mokie Steiskal

Karl Titz

Terry Umbreit

David Wightman

Deanne Williams

Mike Zema

Renee Zonka

Features of the ManageFirst® Competency Guides

We have designed the ManageFirst competency guides to enhance your ability to learn and retain important information that is critical to this restaurant and foodservice industry function. Here are the key features you will find within this guide.

Beginning Each Guide

Tuning In to You

When you open a ManageFirst competency guide for the first time, you might ask yourself: Why do I need to know about this topic? Every topic of these guides involves key information you will need as you manage a restaurant or foodservice operation. Located in the front of each review guide, "Tuning In to You" is a brief synopsis that illustrates some of the reasons the information contained throughout that particular guide is important to you. It exemplifies real-life scenarios that you will face as a manager and how the concepts in the book will help you in your career.

Professional Profile

This is your opportunity to meet a professional who is currently working in the field associated with a competency guide's topic. This person's story will help you gain insight into the responsibilities related to his or her position, as well as the training and educational history linked to it. You will also see the daily and cumulative impact this position has on an operation, and receive advice from a person who has successfully met the challenges of being a manager.

Beginning Each Chapter

Inside This Chapter

Chapter content is organized under these major headings.

Learning Objectives

Learning objectives identify what you should be able to do after completing each chapter. These objectives are linked to the required tasks a manager must be able to perform in relation to the function discussed in the competency guide.

Test Your Knowledge

Each chapter begins with some True or False questions designed to test your prior knowledge of some of the concepts presented in the chapter. The answers to these questions, as well as the concepts behind them, can be found within the chapter—see the page reference after each question.

Key Terms

These terms are important for thorough understanding of the chapter's content. They are highlighted throughout the chapter, where they are explicitly defined or their meaning is made clear within the paragraphs in which they appear.

Throughout Each Chapter

Exhibits

Exhibits are placed throughout each chapter to visually reinforce the key concepts presented in the text. Types of exhibits include charts, tables, photographs, and illustrations.

Think About It…

These thought-provoking sidebars reveal supportive information about the section they appear beside.

Activities

Apply what you have learned throughout the chapter by completing the various activities in the text. The activities have been designed to give you additional practice and better understanding of the concepts addressed in the learning objectives. Types of activities include case studies, role-plays, and problem solving, among others.

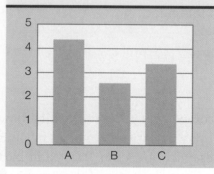

Exhibit

Exhibits are visuals that will help you learn about key concepts.

Think About It…

Consider these supplemental insights as you read through a chapter.

Activity

Activity

Types of activities you will complete include case studies, role-plays, and problem solving, among others.

At the End of Each Chapter

Review Your Learning

These multiple-choice or open- or close-ended questions or problems are designed to test your knowledge of the concepts presented in the chapter. These questions have been aligned with the objectives and should provide you with an opportunity to practice or apply the content that supports these objectives. If you have difficulty answering them, you should review the content further.

At the End of the Guide

Field Project

This real-world project gives you the valuable opportunity to apply many of the concepts you will learn in a competency guide. You will interact with industry practitioners, enhance your knowledge, and research, apply, analyze, evaluate, and report on your findings. It will provide you with an in-depth "reality check" of the policies and practices of this management function.

Tuning In to You

"I need to see the manager."

How many times does this sentence get spoken in a restaurant everyday? It might be said by a customer lodging a complaint, an employee needing a procedure explained, or a delivery driver reporting a few missing cases—just to name a few instances. No matter the speaker's situation, if you are the manager, you must be ready to deal with it.

Yet managing the fast pace of a restaurant isn't just about fixing problems, answering employees' questions, or simply being "the boss." Successful managers are leaders. Few organizations can survive nowadays without a leader who understands and lives its vision and its mission, acting as a role model for the company's staff.

Once you become a restaurant or foodservice manager, you will be called upon to define performance standards, conduct performance appraisals, and set wages, among other management duties. You must be prepared to approach all these functions with integrity. You will have the opportunity set an example of honesty, fairness, and caring that will affect how your employees approach their jobs.

Strong foodservice leaders know that the success of an organization is not possible without the efforts of its staff. Understanding the "people side" of management is critical. Every successful manager knows that results are achieved only through people, and recognizing and rewarding those who achieve the operation's goals are important for long-term success. Communicating effectively, establishing a harassment-free workplace, and building successful teams are also critical.

Finally, you must learn how to balance the needs of your employees with the needs of the operation, all while keeping the customers' needs in mind. Preparing yourself for the many facets and challenges of restaurant management will go a long way toward meeting all these needs. Solving problems will still be part of your job—there will always be someone who needs to see the manager—but the more prepared you are, the less often it will happen, and the smarter your decisions will be when it does.

Professional Profile
Your opportunity to meet someone working in the field

George Fiorile

General Manager
Dover Downs Hotel, a 4-Star Property
Dover, DE

At the age of five, the world of foodservice became my life. I assisted my uncles with their deliveries of freshly baked Italian bread to restaurants, bread stores, and local customers in New Jersey. The aroma of the bread stimulated my senses and my interest in becoming a foodservice entrepreneur. When I got older, I worked in the production area of my uncles' bakery from 3:00 a.m. until 12 noon where I made rolls and bread. I can remember waiting anxiously for the summer to come so I could work at the bakery—that was quite an experience!

Those summer experiences helped me to realize the importance of leadership skills. I had to learn how to work with a diverse group of people, some of whom were more interested in their paychecks than in achieving great results. While working for my uncles as a teenager, my job was to help their employees interpret the bakery recipes and make the products as required.

Many of the workers challenged me because of my age. My impression was that they thought I was too young to know anything. However, when they realized that my management style was very participatory, they became more responsive and more productive. I felt that it was important to communicate my expectations, but I also counted on their feedback, so that we could realize our goal of producing quality baked goods in the most efficient way. One thing I have always done, even at that early age, is to emphasize to the people I work with that I do not have all of the answers, that I need them to contribute their knowledge and experiences for us to be an effective team. I recall those summer experiences with such joy for two main reasons: I learned the benefits of working within a team environment, and I also felt great satisfaction because we made such positive contributions to my uncles' business.

I decided in high school that my career goal would be in some aspect of hospitality management. After high school, I attended James Madison University in Harrisonburg, Virginia, and graduated with a degree in hotel and restaurant management. To pay my tuition, I worked all four summers at casino operations in Atlantic City, New Jersey; I parked cars as a valet and I was a casino credit clerk.

The greatest lesson I learned in these positions is that "perseverance is the rent that must be paid" when you aspire to become a hospitality leader. As a valet, I received daily criticism and complaints from guests, many of whom had excessive demands. I realized that I couldn't take these comments personally. I learned that a friendly smile while greeting guests could set a pleasant tone, making their demands seem less intense. I was persistent in providing the best service possible. I learned quickly to make changes based on their criticism, and then to move on. Every encounter with guests and employees was a lesson learned. During those years, I kept a daily diary of these events and how I responded to them. I would ask myself the "so what" question, meaning: I had this encounter, so what did I learn from it?

The cumulative experiences I had over these summers taught me that the success of my job depended on the success of the people I worked with and supervised because the employee is also a guest. I learned that employees deserve and expect respectful treatment to help motivate them to perform at the highest levels. Early on, I implemented an open-door policy to encourage employees to come see me about their concerns or their ideas for improvement. Incorporating this policy worked well because the employees felt that I was willing to listen to them and accept their opinions.

Immediately after graduation, I returned to Atlantic City and began my career as a beverage supervisor. After a brief stint at the Trump Properties, I found my home at Caesars Casino and Hotel. I worked there for six years in beverages, restaurants, and then as the manager of the showroom. My challenge in the showroom position was to learn to use a combination of leadership, technical, and interpersonal skills to design a program that would boost productivity and sales. I developed training programs with the employees' input and provided incentive awards for results. Sales at the restaurant increased twofold due to the training in suggestive selling, service requirements, and incentive awards.

A promotion to beverage manager at Caesars in Lake Tahoe, Nevada, allowed me to broaden my experiences. I was then promoted to marketing director for Caesars, and although that position was based in New York City, I was responsible for the marketing for all three Caesars properties: Las Vegas, Atlantic City, and Lake Tahoe. Because I was managing from a remote location, I knew that I had to rely heavily on my staff to carry out the marketing goals for the organization. My passion for challenging employees intensified as I developed business plans that involved delegating many responsibilities. Distinct plans, employee suggestions, customer feedback, and my determination to succeed served as the tools for my success.

After six years in the casino business, I became the general manager of the fifth off-track wagering facility in Maryland, which broadcasted horse racing from across the country. For a short period after that, I owned and operated my own restaurant, and then I assumed the position of food services director at Dover Downs in Dover, Delaware. Dover Downs is the only casino and hotel property in the United States that offers casino events and horse, car, and hornet racing.

For seven years, I served as vice president and food and beverage director, supervising a team of 300 employees. Working in this position allowed me to expand my conceptual and visionary leadership skills because I had to view the organization from a holistic viewpoint. I analyzed our operations within this context for each of the events held at Dover Downs.

Over time, other areas that were critical to my development were planning employee training and developing programs, assessing operational costs, and designing menus "to sell." All of these opportunities added to my technical experience as well as my leadership confidence. As a result of meeting the goals in these areas and increasing profits, I was promoted in March, 2005, to vice president and general manager of Dover Downs Hotel and Conference Center.

My passion and dedication for operating foodservice facilities has had a tremendous impact on the organizations for which I have worked. I've applied that passion to the creation of new and novel events, such as the Dover Downs Cooking Show and the Wine and Jazz Festival, which have become two of the most popular and profitable events offered by Dover Downs.

I have learned many valuable lessons throughout my years in this industry, and one of the most important ones is, "You never know everything and there is nothing wrong with that!" Change is constant in the hospitality industry and it is impossible to know everything. I've learned not to hide what I do not know. I'll admit it, and I'll search for the answer or delegate it to one of my associates and make it a learning experience for both of us.

My advice to aspiring future managers is:

■ Do not manage by the moment. When making managerial decisions, ask yourself, "Is it the rule or the exception?" I have seen many managers make snap decisions—often poor ones—in reaction to something that only happens once a year.

■ Do not get bogged down in small matters. Learn how to delegate and develop employees. It is good for employees to learn as much as you know. It is a priceless reward. Employees will never forget you for helping develop them.

■ Employees are your most precious resource. You cannot be successful without their support of you and the organization. Since the hospitality industry is labor intensive and employees provide the services and experiences expected, extreme care of employees is required.

■ Celebrate employees in public and reprimand them in private; they make the business what it is.

■ Have passion for what you do. If you don't, find a field that better suits your passion. You will be much happier!

■ Celebrate the small accomplishments because sometimes the big accomplishments never come.

■ Stay current by being an active member and participant in professional organizations.

■ Stay focused, committed, and dedicated, whether you aspire to become a general manager of food services, or a position in any aspect of hospitality. I have, and I must say that my passion for what I do, along with my leadership skills, have paid off.

The Dynamics of Leadership in the Hospitality and Restaurant Industry

1

Inside This Chapter

- Managing in the Restaurant Industry
- Qualities of a Leader
- Workplace Ethics
- Setting the Right Course for Your Organization
- Keeping Things in Balance
- Professional Development and Leadership

After completing this chapter, you should be able to:

- Define these terms: workplace ethics, value statements, vision statement, mission statement, stress management, time management, delegation, and networking.
- Identify leadership behaviors.
- Discuss the importance of ethics in foodservice.
- Explain how to determine if a decision is ethical.
- Describe the relationship between vision, mission, values, and goals and job performance.
- Identify factors that contribute to stress and how stress can be minimized or prevented.
- Identify key elements of time management.
- Describe how a mentor contributes to a professional development plan.
- Identify career-building opportunities, professional organizations, and certification programs.

Test Your Knowledge

1 **True or False:** Initiating the right course of action requires the development of a vision statement that focuses on core values. *(See p. 7.)*

2 **True or False:** "To conduct annual customer surveys" is an example of a vision statement. *(See p. 8.)*

3 **True or False:** Goals and objectives serve as performance guidelines once the vision and mission statements are developed. *(See p. 11.)*

4 **True or False:** All stakeholders must provide input and feedback into the development of the vision and mission statements. *(See p. 9.)*

5 **True or False:** "Put the customer first" is a credible statement to be included as a vision or mission statement. *(See pp. 8–9.)*

6 **True or False:** Lack of planning creates unnecessary stress. *(See p. 13.)*

7 **True or False:** Time management is defined as balancing work activities based on the time you serve most customers. *(See p. 14.)*

Key Terms

Certification	Mission statement	Time management
Core values	Networking	Value statement
Delegation	Principles	Vision statement
Leadership	Professional development	Workplace ethics
Management	Stress	
Mentor	Stress management	

Introduction

Every successful restaurant and foodservice operation has managers who possess leadership qualities and skills that support the organization's vision and mission, setting the company on a course for achievement. There are many definitions of leadership and management, and the terms are sometimes confused with each other; however, a distinction between these two skills exists. Leadership often focuses on the "what" and "why" of the organization while management deals with the "how" to achieve the "what" and the "why."

Individuals who are effective as both managers and leaders are defined by their conduct and ethics. Today's foodservice operations can present daily ethical dilemmas, and a manager needs to be able to draw upon leadership attributes to deal effectively with them. Learning to handle constant stress and managing time well are also particularly important. Planning, for example, is one element of meeting these challenges effectively. Additionally, just as a manager creates daily, weekly, monthly, and yearly plans, career planning must be considered. Continuous improvements and certifications provide an effective leader the tools for maintaining relevant and up-to-date knowledge. Likewise, the need to establish and build relationships through mentoring activities and networking are important aspects for management development.

Managing in the Restaurant Industry

Management is the ability to plan, organize, direct, staff, control, and evaluate the many functions in a foodservice organization for the purpose of serving organizational goals. A manager's major task is to perform all these functions with the finite supply of resources available. These resources include:

- Labor
- Money
- Products
- Equipment
- Time
- Processes and tools
- Energy

While managing these many tasks, a restaurant manager may demonstrate different styles of management. Four common management styles are autocratic, bureaucratic, democratic, and laissez-faire, which are further described in *Exhibit 1a*. The most effective managers are those who can adapt their style to the situation and to their employees.

Exhibit 1a

Types of Management Styles

Management Style	Description	How It May Be Useful
Autocratic	Characterized by a domineering individual who has ultimate authority over workers.	Workers are new and performing relatively easy tasks.
Bureaucratic	Characterized by regularized procedures, division of responsibilities, hierarchy, and impersonal relationships.	Workers are performing standardized work, such as bookkeeping.
Democratic	Characterized by considering and treating others as equals; more participation in the tasks performed.	Workers are motivated and experienced; a collaborative environment is critical.
Laissez-faire	Characterized by noninterference; that is, letting people do as they decide.	Workers are consultants and subcontractors.

Exhibit 1b

Comparison of a Manager and a Leader

Manager

- Plans and budgets
- Oversees staffing
- Solves problems
- Maintains order
- Writes reports and other types of materials

Leader

- Charts a course that provides direction
- Offers guidance and counsel
- Motivates and inspires a call to action
- Creates an environment for change
- Trains and teaches

Think About It...

Do you think job satisfaction and commitment are low among many employees today? How does the manager play an important role in changing employees' views toward work?

Qualities of a Leader

Being an effective manager does not always mean being an effective leader. The roles are quite different. (See *Exhibit 1b*.) **Leadership** is the ability to inspire and motivate employees to behave in accordance with the vision of an organization and to accomplish the organization's goals. Good leaders demonstrate these behaviors:

- **Provide direction.** Leaders communicate clearly and ensure that employees know what is expected of them. One of the ways to accomplish this is to discuss roles and responsibilities with employees, verifying that they understand your directions.

- **Lead consistently.** Using the organization's vision, mission, and values as checkpoints, leaders maintain the organization's standards by holding themselves and others accountable for their actions. You must ensure fairness in employee treatment.

- **Influence others.** Gaining cooperation through caring acts, using persuasion to convince employees of appropriate behavior, and offering constructive feedback are ways that leaders influence others. Leaders also examine how to build consensus through a "give and take" dialogue as well as encouraging superior performance by relating employees' actions to the organization's vision.

- **Foster teamwork.** Leaders create functional work teams that build members' skills. They also establish cross-functional teams to monitor, standardize, and improve work processes across an organization. Assigning problems to temporary groups of selected employees is one way to begin developing these teams.

- **Motivate others.** The importance of communication cannot be overstated. Leaders give pep talks, ask their employees for advice, and vocally praise people's work. It is also vital to keep employees informed and provide them with a sense of belonging by allowing them to solve problems and contribute ideas.

- **Coach and develop employees.** Leaders instruct employees on better ways to perform a task, offer insights to high-potential workers, and ensure that every employee has a development plan. They also seek out learning opportunities for the staff and encourage them to enroll in these programs.

- **Champion change.** Anticipating the need for change, looking for better ways to do things, understanding the link between change and learning, and communicating the benefits of new processes and procedures are all actions of a leader. It is also crucial to help staff to embrace the change if it is to be successful.

Acquiring these leadership qualities is essential for restaurant and foodservice managers. To be successful at demonstrating them, it is also important to develop the skills and abilities listed in *Exhibit 1c*. Formal education combined with work experience and feedback is the ideal way to become an effective leader.

Exhibit 1c

Essential Leadership Skills and Abilities for Hospitality and Restaurant Managers

Interpersonal Skills	Employee Development	Organizational Responsibility
■ Listens well ■ Respects others ■ Defends civility and one's own company values ■ Has a sense of self-worth, responsibility, accountability, and equality ■ Values trust and human dignity ■ Keeps calm in a crisis	■ Takes responsibility for developing future leaders ■ Enables employees to realize their full potential—lets people grow ■ Teaches and mentors ■ Removes obstacles that prevent employees from doing their jobs ■ Encourages taking risks ■ Makes a meaningful difference in employees' lives	■ Provides stewardship of organizational value systems ■ Has industry expertise ■ Generates visionary ideas

Workplace Ethics

Not only are management skills and leadership traits critical to being an effective foodservice manager, but business ethics also serve as guiding principles for effective leaders to use in setting the professional tone and behavior in their operations. **Workplace ethics** refer to the standards of conduct or set of values and principles an individual or organization applies to work. **Principles** are guidelines for conduct that have enduring and lasting value to a society or organization. What distinguishes principles is that they are self-evident and unarguable. For example, the majority of people would agree that identifying unfairness, mediocrity, and deceitfulness as core principles for a long, happy, and successful life is ridiculous. The ethical behavior that is an outgrowth of principles is also influenced by many factors, including cultural background, religious belief, personal code of conduct, and personal experience.

Many establishments have created written codes of ethics, which are designed to remove the guesswork of what is right or wrong behavior. These codes act as a safety check for evaluating decisions before implementing them. An organization's code of ethics may include employee treatment, wages, benefits, working conditions, behavior of employees with reference to the use of company resources, acceptance of gifts from customers/vendors/suppliers, and other issues that impact organizational operations.

Think About It...

Ethics concern both the outcome of a situation and the character of the individual involved in it. Is a decision or action either good or bad? Is the individual or organization responsible for that decision or action either good or bad?

Upholding an organization's code of ethics can be directly related to the company's bottom line and profits. Ethical behavior encourages repeat business and a loyal customer base. In the foodservice industry, it becomes imperative to subscribe to a code of ethics because of the impact some decisions could have on the health and safety of others. For example, adhering to discard times for food to ensure food safety is one way of behaving ethically. Making certain that employees wash their hands before preparing food is another action that reflects ethical principles by which the operations of the restaurant are managed.

To determine whether a decision or action is based on sound ethics, a manager should ask the following questions:

- Is the action/behavior legal?
- Will the action/behavior hurt anyone?
- Does the action/behavior represent the company?
- Does the action/behavior make anyone uncomfortable?
- Does the action/behavior convey respect for others?
- Have I involved others by asking for their perspective on the situation?
- Is this decision essentially fair given all the circumstances?
- Does this decision uphold the core values of the organization?
- Could I tell my decision to my boss, family, or society as a whole?
- How would others regard the details of this decision if it were disclosed to the public?
- Am I confident that my position will be as valid over a long period of time as it seems now?

Additionally, effective managers know that they are the role models for many behaviors in the restaurant. Employees naturally look to their manager to set the example, and the ethics of a manager also build trust with his or her staff. Employees who see a manager applying principled leadership skills are more likely to want to behave in a similar manner.

Many of these ethical principles look toward corporate and personal values as the root for ethical decisions made by management. For example, "pride in oneself" is a personal value that contributes to how a manager represents the organization to the employees. By applying these principles and creating a work environment that exemplifies ethical leadership, a manager can ensure that employees understand the importance of making ethical decisions in foodservice.

Setting the Right Course for Your Organization

There is personal honor and excitement when foodservice managers set, plan, and initiate the right course of action for an organization. The right course is based on a clear and focused vision, which is developed through value statements and supported by a mission statement, goals, objectives, and ethical behavior. Knowing how to identify the value statements that serve as the foundation for these other elements is essential.

Identifying Value Statements for Your Organization

To identify value statements, first examine the core values of the organization. **Core values** are a company's key elements of operation, and they serve as the foundation for the development of both the vision statement and the mission statement. Core values are typically based on concepts of respect, caring, responsibility, and honesty. Some examples of core values are:

- Extraordinary customer service
- Serving quality, healthy food
- Respect for employees and customers

Value statements are developed with core values in mind. **Value statements** serve as a set of standards by which an organization operates. They dictate "what should be" in an organization and influence the choices that are made in determining vision, mission, and goals. Value statements also help to shape attitudes about the organization and to define acceptable and unacceptable employee behavior.

Organizations publish value statements along with other company information. Some examples of value statements include:

- Customers' opinions receive a high priority.
- Quality is our highest goal.
- Fair treatment of all employees is essential.
- Recognition of employees is our first priority.
- We respect employees' initiative and personal development.
- Teamwork results in high-quality products and services.

Think About It...

"Without a vision, the organization becomes extinct." This quote suggests that a vision is central to an organization's life. Why do you think a vision is important for an organization?

Activity

Ethical Dilemmas: What Should You Do?

You will be divided into four teams and assigned one of the ethical dilemmas from this list. Read the situation and then discuss it as a team to determine how you would resolve the situation. Develop a five-minute skit that explains the situation to the rest of the class and demonstrates the team's solution. There does not have to be verbal dialogue during the presentation, but the skit must convey the situation and resolution clearly.

1. RockFish, a seafood restaurant, prides itself on its merit-based pay system. One of your employees has done a tremendous job all year, thus deserving strong recognition. However, the person is already paid at the top of her salary range for the job's grade. Rockfish has too many people in the grade above her, so the organization cannot promote her either. What should you do?

2. Your boss tells you that one of your employees is among several others to be laid off soon, and that you are not to tell the employee yet or he might tell the whole organization, which would cause an uproar. Meanwhile, you hear from the employee that he plans to buy braces for his daughter and to add wood floors to his entire house. What should you do?

3. A fellow manager tells you that in two months she is going to quit the hotel chain that employs you both to start a new job, which has been guaranteed to her. Meanwhile, your boss tells you that you are being passed over for a new opportunity because he is going to give it to this fellow manager. What should you do?

4. The Great Steakhouse prides itself in serving the best martinis in town. As the manager on duty, you typically walk around the restaurant to check on your various employees. One night, you notice that a bartender is watering down a drink. Later in the evening, you talk with this person privately and find out that she was directed by the bar manager to do this with some of the drinks. What should you do?

Creating a Vision

An organization's vision is designed based on value statements, but managers must also take a leadership role to help shape an organization's vision and decide what the organization will promote and deliver to customers in order to generate profits. A **vision statement** describes what an organization wants to become and why it exists. Vision statements aim high, and are inspiring, stimulating, and exceptional.

A vision statement usually has terms and phrases that express "out of the ordinary aspects." Some examples are:

- Exceeds or excels
- Diversity
- Empowerment
- Delights or entertains
- Puts customers first
- Extraordinary
- Right the first time
- Preeminent
- Grand

Remember that the focus of a vision statement's development is the organization's core values. An example of a vision statement that reflects the core value of extraordinary customer service is: "An elegant restaurant where extraordinary service exceeds customer expectations." Once a vision statement has been crafted, it is refined further into a mission statement, goals, and objectives to assure that the vision is implemented through operational procedures. (See *Exhibit 1d*.)

Exhibit 1d

Development Flow of Values, Vision, and Goals

Core values → Vision statement → Mission statement → Goals

Mission Statements: Who You Are and What You Do

A **mission statement** refines the vision statement by stating the purpose of the organization to employees and customers. It should include the target market, target products and services, and sometimes the geographic region as well. One of the main benefits of a mission statement is that it provides a source of accountability for the organization. It communicates what the organization is striving to do each day. It needs to be written clearly, concisely, and in an interesting manner. Some examples of mission statements are:

■ To serve discriminating guests high-quality and tasty food

■ To serve the traveler meals prepared like home-cooking

■ To serve exceptional meals with elegant style

Creating the Organization's Vision and Mission Statements

While some organizations might already have well-defined vision statements and mission statements, at some time you may be responsible for the creation of one of these statements. Creating a vision or mission statement requires the input of all stakeholders. Stakeholders include the company executives, managers, directors, supervisors, and employees. Input from customer evaluations is also a source of information. The steps in *Exhibit 1e* on the next page demonstrate the right path for developing vision and mission statements that will serve as a solid foundation for an organization.

Exhibit 1e

Steps in Creating Vision and Mission Statements

1 Using the company's core values, reflect on the organization's purpose, and dream about the direction desired for the organization.

2 Begin writing some thoughts on paper.

3 Organize a team of interested individuals to help with the creation of these statements.

4 Seek input from stakeholders while winning the confidence of those who will be involved in implementing and supporting the vision and mission.

5 Work with the team, get their suggestions and ideas, and infuse these thoughts into the statements.

6 Write a draft of the vision statement.

7 Draft the mission statement based on the vision statement.

8 Review these statements with the team and the stakeholders.

9 Gain approval from the stakeholders.

10 Make copies of these statements and distribute to all stakeholders, including employees.

11 Post the vision and mission statements in a common area for the staff to see and reference as a constant reminder of why they are working for the organization.

Activity

Creating a Vision and Mission

Break into teams and create vision and mission statements for an Italian restaurant, Michelangelo's Italian Villa. The organization's core values are caring high quality, responsibility, and trust. Within your team, select a leader who will present your vision and mission statements to the class by writing them on a board or flip chart.

1 Mission Statement of Michelangelo's Italian Villa

_____

_____

_____

_____

2 Vision Statement of Michelangelo's Italian Villa

_____

_____

_____

_____

Leading and Living an Organization's Vision and Mission Statements

After creating these statements, the manager as the restaurant leader must focus, embrace, and demonstrate the vision and mission in his or her daily behavior. Consider some of the following actions to make the vision and mission of the organization come alive:

- Create an atmosphere that focuses on the vision, mission, and values of the organization.
- As part of daily planning, think about how some of the needed activities support the vision and mission.
- Focus each day on one specific aspect of the vision and mission statement.

Another way that a manager can reflect the organizational mission is to ensure that operational goals are directly linked to this statement. It is vital in today's competitive industry that managers do their best to understand this connection. Additionally, once this link has been verified, managers need to identify ways to communicate the mission and goals to their employees so the staff understands their importance and how they can support them as well.

Some things that a manager can do include:

- During orientation, ensure that new hires get information about the vision, mission, and goals of the organization. Communicate the expectation that everyone in the organization needs to support these statements.
- Ensure that all training materials align with and emphasize the importance of these statements.
- Post the statements in a prominent place for staff to see.
- Document these statements in employee handbooks to be presented during orientation.
- Discuss at employee meetings how operations are faring in terms of the mission and goals.

Since employee performance drives business performance, employee roles and responsibilities need to be based on the vision, mission, and goals of the organization as well. For example, if the mission statement of a restaurant is to prepare high-quality food, then ordering and purchasing functions need to include food quality criteria, such as requiring buyers to purchase only Grade A eggs. Managers also need to communicate and clarify to employees how their jobs support these statements and impact the success of the organization.

Performing jobs to standards and responsibilities that are specified in job descriptions and reflected in company values directly impacts the goals of the organization. For example, the Ritz Carlton's mission statement is "Ladies and Gentlemen serving Ladies and Gentlemen." This standard of quality is part of employee operational behavior statements. Not only should employees know the importance of this behavior and be able to recite the company's mission statement readily, but each employee should also be able to take appropriate action to exemplify this value to customers. This is just one way that an organization's employees understand how their jobs align with the company mission and goals and have real impact on the customer experience. Similarly, managers in any organization need to look for ways to confirm that employees are practicing the values and missions of the company on a daily basis.

Activity

What Would You Do?

You are employed as manager by M&M Restaurant in your hometown. The restaurant is a high-quality, upscale facility that provides entertainment choices for customers. It currently operates with a mission statement of, "Providing high-quality food and upscale entertainment." Upper management wants to change the statement to read, "Providing high-quality food and server entertainment." You are charged with the development of the recruitment and training program of servers who will sing and dance as part of their duties. You already have a staff of servers, but 50 percent of them have indicated they do not wish to entertain.

1 Why do you think some of the current staff objects to performing as entertainers?

_____

_____

_____

2 How would you get what is expected from your staff?

_____

_____

_____

Keeping Things in Balance

Although it is vital for a manager to develop and demonstrate leadership skills and be mindful of applying the company's vision, mission, and values, knowing how to balance the many objectives required to run an efficient and effective establishment is just as important. Far too often, managers feel intense daily pressures. Many feel that there is not enough time in the day to meet goals. At the same

Exhibit 1f

Stress affects all members of the team in an establishment.

time, everyone talks about wanting a balanced life. Your professional life can become stressful at times, but there are ways to manage it so that it does not overwhelm other aspects of your life. Two critical areas in which a manager and leader need to be effective are stress management and time management.

Stress Management

Stress is commonly defined as a condition or feeling experienced when a person perceives that demands exceed the resources he or she has available either personally or socially. Pressures related to stress can be categorized into three groups: system-imposed, employee-imposed and self-imposed. System-imposed pressures include anything related to the number of goals or activities that you are trying to accomplish, lack of equipment, malfunctioning equipment, or facility-related problems. Employee-imposed pressures can include things such as teams not functioning well, supervisors micromanaging, or employees not performing up to standards and requiring more supervision than expected. (See *Exhibit 1f.*) Self-imposed pressures result from a person having unrealistic expectations about what can be accomplished, such as the number of tasks that can be completed in a day. It can also be caused by lack of communication with immediate bosses so that false assumptions are made about activities.

Stress may be caused by such factors as time pressures, loss of a family member, divorce, constant changes, or failure to accept what cannot be changed. Workplace challenges, such as lack of planning or poor communication, also can contribute to stress levels. **Stress management** is a process managers use to identify what causes stress for them in the workplace as well as in their personal life, and then to apply various strategies to minimize its effects. The following are some stress indicators:

- General irritability
- Insomnia
- Headaches
- Indigestion
- Pain in neck and/or lower back
- Changes in appetite or sleep patterns

These indicators can help managers identify the actual root cause of stress. To identify and prevent stress, ask these questions:

- Is the stress due to planning or scheduling?
- Are tight timelines causing the stress?
- Is the pressure due to equipment-related problems (food prep, ventilation, etc.)?
- Is the pressure related to facility layout?
- Is the pressure related to employee performance?
- Is the pressure being caused by self-imposed, unrealistic expectations?
- Are personal problems interfering with work?

Once the causes have been determined, a stress-reduction plan can be designed and implemented. Seek input on the plan from people who you value and trust. Also consider incorporating some of these suggestions for coping with and preventing stress:

- Plan and evaluate daily activities to minimize any unanticipated situations.
- Involve employees in planning and scheduling the use of equipment based on menu needs.
- Delegate some work to responsible employees.
- Monitor activities by "walking around" and communicating with employees.
- Set daily realistic goals that can be accomplished by yourself or with your team.
- Identify company resources that can assist you with managing stress.

There are times when an individual needs to seek additional help in dealing with stress. A variety of resources in an organization are typically available to a manager or employee for learning how to cope with stress. These include employee assistance programs, stress management courses, and counseling. Outside resources can also be of assistance.

Being able to manage stress has another benefit worth mentioning: it creates a comfortable work environment for the staff. Managers who balance stress factors so they maintain a quality of life for themselves help foster that behavior in their employees.

Time Management

Time management generally refers to the execution of processes and the use of tools that increase a person's efficiency and productivity. To manage time effectively also means to know how to waste less time on noncritical, unimportant activities. Although there are

Think About It...

When it comes to time management, ask yourself this question: What is the most valuable use of my time right now?

several skills needed to be an effective time manager, two key skills are the ability to set priorities and the ability to concentrate on one activity at a time.

Other skills needed for effective time management include:

- Goal setting
- Delegating
- Planning
- Scheduling
- Decision making

There is an expression that states, "Practice what you plan and plan what you practice." Although you may have good intentions at the beginning of a day and write down what you plan to do, other things can get in the way. Being aware of all the things you do during a day can result in better planning, decision making, delegating, and goal setting, in order to use time more wisely.

One method that can improve the ability to plan time more effectively is to review the activities you need to complete on a daily or weekly basis and break these activities into smaller tasks. By dividing these activities into a controllable size, you can organize your work schedule more effectively. What may appear to be insurmountable tasks to complete in a day can actually become easier to handle when using this approach.

Once you have created this list of smaller tasks, it is important to follow through and act on the daily plan. Physically crossing tasks off your list also provides a visual sense of accomplishment. Evaluating later how the plans of daily and weekly activities actually worked is an additional way to improve your time management skills.

Many restaurant managers find that time management tools such as a PDA or time planner help them organize their time more effectively. These tools make it easier to schedule and monitor activities and appointments on a daily, weekly, and monthly basis.

Delegation

Delegation is another time management tool that a manager can leverage. **Delegation** is defined as handing a task over to a subordinate and assigning either authority, responsibility, or both to that person to carry out a specific activity. Delegation is often called the single most powerful leveraging activity a manager has in order to use time more effectively in the restaurant. Not only does delegation help with time management, but it also serves to enhance employee skills and provides a sense of accomplishment for them. Delegation contributes to the overall development and growth of your employees.

Activity

What Did I Do Today?

Think about a recent work or school day. Then, as close as you can remember, and without referring to any planning tool you might have, write down all the activities you had for that day on the form below. You should include all planned and unplanned things that occurred. Then answer the following questions:

1 What were the most important things for me to accomplish for the day?

_____

_____

2 What unexpected things got in the way of my accomplishing the important things?

_____

_____

3 How could I have managed the situation better so I could have used my time more effectively?

_____

_____

4 Did I create conditions prior to that day that supported getting my priorities done first?

_____

_____

Hour	Activity		Hour	Activity
7 am	00		3 pm	00
	30			30
8	00		4	00
	30			30
9	00		5	00
	30			30
10	00		6	00
	30			30
11	00		7	00
	30			30
12 pm	00		8	00
	30			30
1	00		9	00
	30			30
2	00		10	00
	30			30

Professional Development and Leadership

As daily tasks become more complex and you acquire more responsibility, you must also acquire new knowledge to keep pace with these changes. Continuous learning is key to professional development, and it is an integral part of a leader's growth.

The Need for Professional Development and Mentoring Plans

Professional development and mentoring plans with specific career goals and objectives are critical to career development. **Professional development** is the sum of activities a person performs to meet goals and/or to further his or her career. As a manager, you should know where you want to be in two years, five years, and even ten years. Unless you design a workable plan and take action, your goals will not be realized. A good development plan includes:

- Written plan illustrating where you want to be in two, five, and ten years
- Written assessment of your professional goals
- Assessment of what is needed to meet these goals
- Timeline establishing key milestones for achieving these goals

As part of your professional development plan, you should also take advantage of various self-evaluation instruments, such as DiSC and Meyers-Briggs, and request 360-degree feedback evaluations, if they are available. These tools help identify opportunities for improvement that can be included in your development program, as well as offer insights and perspective on your style of interaction, which could become a source of development opportunities as well. DiSC assesses your work productivity, teamwork, and interpersonal relationships, while Meyers-Briggs evaluates individual preferences within four personality traits.

Within a professional development plan is also the identification of a mentor. A **mentor** is someone who can play the role of a wise advisor for you. (See *Exhibit 1g.*) Ideally, this person should have a higher position in your company and be willing to serve in this capacity. A mentor should be available to offer insights, coach, be a sounding board, and provide feedback to you on your development plans and progress.

Exhibit 1g

Younger managers gain insight and valuable career advice from mentors.

Developing a Professional Relationship with Your Supervisor

Along with identifying a mentor who can help you in your professional development, you should also develop a sound relationship with your supervisor. Although much of your communication will be with your staff, upward and lateral communication is also very important to your professional development. Discussions with your supervisor should include discovering what kind of information he or she wants shared as well as how often the supervisor expects to receive it. The type of information determines the frequency. For example, sales numbers may be communicated on a daily, weekly, monthly, and quarterly basis, while team project goals may be shared only once a month.

Effective managers understand the importance of establishing situations that require interaction and approval from their supervisor. For example, an effective strategy to use is to set a weekly time to meet with your supervisor. At these meetings, topics for discussion should include progress on operational goals and a review of business performance. You should also ask for feedback on your own performance and ways to improve. Before the meeting, prepare discussion points and specific questions you want to ask. These discussion points might take the form of an agenda that you share with the supervisor. As your supervisor provides feedback on these various topics, be sure to listen attentively and follow up any points with additional questions for clarification.

Continuous Improvement: It's Essential

Continuous improvement or professional development is essential for success in restaurant management. (See *Exhibit 1h.*) Achieving certifications is one key way to improve yourself professionally. **Certification** indicates that you have demonstrated a high level of skill and have met specific performance requirements by participating in a rigorous process to become certified. Several certifications for foodservice managers include:

- Foodservice Management Professional (FMP)
- ServSafe Food Protection Manager Certification
- ServSafe Alcohol Certificate
- Certified Executive Chef (CEC)
- Certified Hospitality Executive (CHE)
- Master Certified Food Executive (MCFE)
- Certified Food Executive (CFE)
- Certified Food Manager (CFM)

Certifications are usually administered through professional organizations. Some organizations require that you become a member to become certified while others do not. Many certifications also may require work experience as a demonstration of competence in the field. Work experience counts as a part of the overall certification process.

Attending continuing education courses through either a local college or university also is essential for a manager to stay updated with the latest information in the industry. Many times, workshops are offered at conferences that provide continuing education credits as well.

Joining Professional Organizations

Professional organization membership is one way to stay on the "cutting edge" of the hospitality and restaurant industry. Weekly and/or monthly newsletters, workshops, and conferences are just some of the benefits of belonging to a professional organization. Some organizations you might want to consider joining include:

- National Restaurant Association (NRA)
- International Food Services Executive Association
- Council of Hotels, Restaurants, and Institutional Educators (CHRIE)

In addition, most national organizations have state and local chapters. There may also be specific State Restaurant Associations that you might want to join.

Exhibit 1h

Professional Development Opportunities

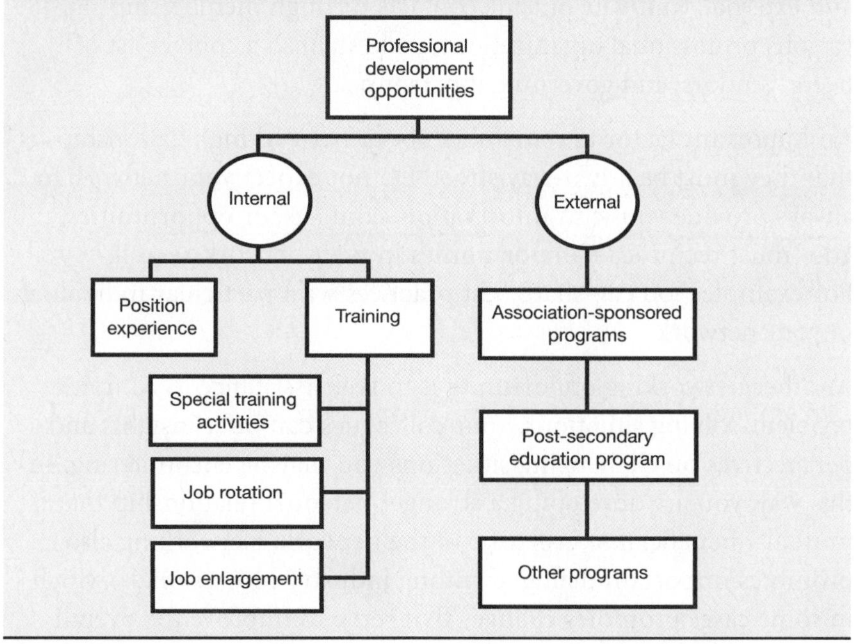

Other Resources

Other resources to consider for professional development opportunities include industry publications, such as *Nation's Restaurant News, Chain Leader, QSR Food Management,* and *Restaurant Business.* These publications provide the latest in industry information and should be part of your journal and magazine reading list. The Internet also provides a wealth of information for the foodservice professional, and a manager should keep up with a variety of Web-based resources to further their continuous education.

The Importance of Networking

Foodservice managers must stay connected to the industry. Staying connected means networking with industry professionals. The purpose of **networking** is to connect with several people to build relationships that may result in career advancement, industry updates, and knowledge or career enhancements. One method of networking is to attend trade shows and interact with people who are attending. Typically, a reception is held at the beginning or closing of the trade show. Other methods for networking include:

- Attending designated networking sessions during conventions, seminars, and conferences
- Participating in community events and sharing information about the organization
- Attending state and local restaurant association meetings and social events
- Participating in community career days, forums, charity events, and service projects
- Attending chamber of commerce meetings
- Volunteering as a community mentor and getting to know key community leaders
- Becoming an active member of a professional foodservice organization
- Visiting area competitors and other businesses to establish rapport and business opportunities

Networking is also valuable because it helps keep you current with industry trends. The network you develop should be both internal and external. Cultivate outside contacts through memberships in various professional organizations, and establish a contact list of peers, vendors, and government personnel.

An important factor to remember about networking relationships is that they must be a two-way street. Do not expect your network to always provide you with information, contacts, or opportunities. You must reciprocate opportunities in your network as well. For example, you can share best practices with particular individuals in your network.

Another networking opportunity is to seek assistance in complex problem-solving situations. Your colleagues can offer insights and perspectives on challenging situations you may be encountering. In this way, you are developing a stronger personal relationship that is mutually beneficial to everyone in the network. Networking also promotes important dialogue among industry professionals, which in some cases promotes changes that serve to improve the overall performance of the industry.

Summary

The development of a vision statement is the first step in planning a profitable organization that meets or exceeds guest expectations. Vision statements are statements of what the organization wants to become. High expectations should dominate the development of the vision statement. The organization's vision statement serves as a basis for developing the mission statement, and eventually for developing goals and objectives. The purpose of the mission statement is to communicate to everyone what the company is and what it strives to achieve.

The mission statement is designed as an outgrowth of the vision statement. All stakeholders and employees should embrace it. Business goals and specific objectives are developed after these two statements have been created. The mission statement should be posted in a place of prominence for customers and employees. It is important for a manager to reflect the vision and mission in his or her daily behavior so that employees are influenced and motivated to behave in this manner as well.

Stress and time management are key elements in becoming an effective restaurant manager and leader. Planning, prioritizing, and focusing on the most important tasks are essential to time management and to minimizing stress on the job. Evaluating your plan is also a part of improving your time management skills. Another method that can minimize stress is to delegate selected tasks to responsible employees. Delegation also provides assurance that an employee's contributions are valued and valuable.

Continuous learning and improvement are critical for a manager as they develop into an effective leader. Various memberships in professional organizations and certifications are essential in a management's development, as are continuous education courses and workshops. Other sources of industry information can be found in industry magazines and on the Internet.

Review Your Learning

1 An organization's vision statement serves to communicate

A. who the organization is serving.

B why the organization exists.

C. when the organization was created.

D. what key elements the organization has.

2 Without a vision, the organization will

A. prosper, and then perish.

B. become extinct.

C. have steady profits.

D. incur costs, not profits.

3 A mission statement is developed

A. congruently with goals.

B. after the development of goals.

C. after the vision statement.

D. developed after the stakeholders agree.

4 When developing initial vision and mission statements, stakeholders must

A. be informed of changes.

B. participate in their development.

C. only embrace the statements once developed.

D. assess their impact on individuals.

5 The mission statement is the prerequisite to the development of

A. the vision statement.

B. core values.

C. goals and objectives.

D. value systems.

6 "To make people happy and joyous" is an example of a(n)

A. vision statement.

B. mission statement.

C. objective.

D. core value.

7 Certification as a foodservice manager assures that the manager

A. meets minimum quality standards.

B. has a post-secondary degree.

C. has been a member of a professional organization.

D. has demonstrated a high level of skill and performance against set standards or requirements.

8 The most critical element of stress and time management is

A. knowing daily operational procedures.

B. taking reactionary steps after events.

C. planning yearly, monthly, and daily goals, based on vision and mission statements.

D. reviewing operational aspects from the customer's perspective.

9 Employee jobs and tasks are designed to

A. satisfy the CEO.

B. satisfy the employees' long-term goals.

C. meet the vision, mission, and goals of the organization.

D. meet everyday challenges to reduce organizational problems.

Goal Setting in the Hospitality and Restaurant Industry

2

Inside This Chapter

■ Why Goals Are Important

■ Setting Organizational Goals

■ Writing SMART Goals and Objectives

■ A Process for Achieving Organizational and Departmental Goals

After completing this chapter, you should be able to:

■ Define goals, benchmark, strategic priorities, accountability, objectives, and measurable results.

■ Identify and use different types of goals.

■ Describe factors that affect contribution levels by teams and individuals.

■ Write objectives that apply SMART criteria.

■ Explain and apply process steps in goal setting, managing, monitoring, and evaluating.

■ Explain the role of communications in the goal-setting process.

Test Your Knowledge

1　**True or False:** An organizational goal is the same as a mission statement. *(See p. 26.)*

2　**True or False:** Departments in an organization establish their own set of goals. *(See pp. 32–33.)*

3　**True or False:** Senior employees primarily act as reviewers in the goal-setting process. *(See pp. 28–30.)*

4　**True or False:** Goals define the purpose of the organization. *(See p. 25.)*

5　**True or False:** The relationship between business needs and departmental goals should vary widely in an organization. *(See p. 33.)*

6　**True or False:** Communicating goals to a team increases efficiency and productivity. *(See p. 37.)*

7　**True or False:** Goals vary in an organization from level to level. *(See p. 26.)*

8　**True or False:** A SWOT analysis helps create a framework for developing benchmarks. *(See p. 28.)*

Key Terms

Accountability

Benchmark

Departmental objectives

Goal

Individual performance
　objectives

Measurable results

Objective

Organizational goals

Strategic priority

SWOT analysis

Team objectives

Introduction

Every effort to achieve an organizational vision and mission needs specific, realizable, and measurable goals. This chapter reviews some of the basic concepts of organizational goal setting, which is an integral part of the planning function. Core values and the corporate vision and mission drive goals. The goals lay the foundation on which departmental and individual objectives are established.

Analyzing the strengths, weaknesses, opportunities, and threats that exist for your organization is a critical way to determine the goals that need to be set. This chapter also explores the types of goals that an organization creates and the difference between goals and objectives. You will learn that goals and objectives must be stated in measurable terms so they can be tracked, analyzed, and measured. You must learn, for example, how to write SMART goals and objectives for your organization.

Without setting, assigning, and communicating goals, employees lack direction. A process for defining goals and a plan to achieve them is presented. A central part of this process entails involving staff and determining contribution levels. Once these levels have been determined, staff accountabilities can be instituted. Additionally, communicating goals clearly throughout the organization is also critical to success.

Why Goals Are Important

Goals are statements of desired results. They are used to measure actual performance within an organization. In other words, goals are what people commit to do for an organization. They are achieved by a combination of employees' knowledge, skills, resources, attitudes, and tools. (See *Exhibit 2a*.) Without goals, an organization would never know if it has achieved its preferred situation.

Exhibit 2a

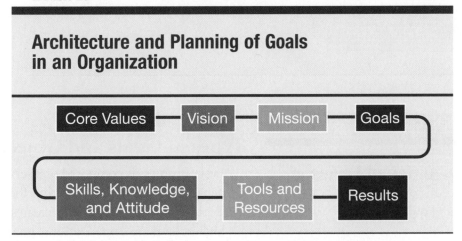

Architecture and Planning of Goals in an Organization

Core Values — Vision — Mission — Goals

Skills, Knowledge, and Attitude — Tools and Resources — Results

One of the characteristics of effective foodservice leaders is that they focus on results. Results focus on the end state or outcome, rather than the process or means to that end. Although an ineffective process will almost ensure that you do not reach your desired result, simply focusing on the means or process without achieving the end misses the critical feature of creating goals in the first place. Therefore, leaders and managers who do not concentrate on achieving desired outcomes are not leading or managing very effectively.

Managers must analyze results to determine whether the organization has properly focused on its goals. A **benchmark** is a standard by which something can be measured or judged. Benchmarks can help determine whether results are balanced, strategic, and long term.

Questions you should ask yourself to determine whether you are meeting benchmarks are (see *Exhibit 2b*):

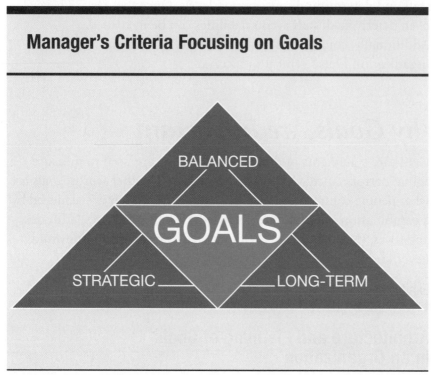

Manager's Criteria Focusing on Goals

■ **Balanced**—Do my results address and keep in balance the interests of these key components: organization, stakeholders, customers, and employees?

■ **Strategic**—Do my results align with the organizational strategies developed by the organization? How do they support the key drivers in the business, such as products, customers, and services? How do they support key customer desires, such as value, quality, service, cleanliness, and speed?

■ **Long term**—Have my results been sustainable over a period of time?

Different Levels of Goals within an Organization

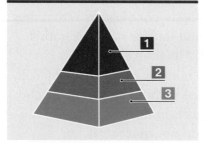

■ Organizational goals

② Departmental/team goals

③ Individual performance goals

Types of Goals and Objectives

Every business is composed of a series of levels that represent departments or functions within the organization. (See *Exhibit 2c.*) Typically, each of these levels creates goals for the organization. At the highest level are **organizational goals.** These goals focus on broad statements of what the organization as a whole wants to achieve. They are closely aligned with the vision and mission of the organization. Organizational goals need to reflect **strategic priorities,** which represent a select few of the highest concerns of the company. A strategic priority is linked to the company's vision and inspires employees to meet it.

The next level of goals is at the department, functional, or team level. These goals are referred to as **departmental** or **team objectives.** These objectives link to the organizational goals and help produce the desired outcomes. Departmental objectives may be assigned to either a team or an individual, while team objectives are specifically delegated to a team because of their scope or complexity.

Finally, there are **individual performance objectives.** These objectives further refine and divide the organizational goals and departmental objectives into smaller components that focus on an individual's contribution. These objectives should be identified as part of the staff development plan. It is important to make certain that employees understand how their objectives affect and add to the success of the organization.

The difference between a goal and an objective can be subtle at times. However, the clearest distinction is that goals tend to be grander, bigger picture aspirations that affect a broader section of the organization, while an objective tends to be a smaller component or enabler that can be linked to the larger goal. A goal is at a high level; objectives are typically stated for individuals.

Setting Organizational Goals

The expression, "The whole is greater than the sum of its parts," represents one aspect of what an organization does when setting goals for itself. The end results need to remain the focus as the organization moves ahead in trying to attain its goals. Looking at the different levels of goals and objectives and ensuring a balanced flow between them is a vital way to guarantee the whole will be greater than any subunit.

Traditionally, organizations review historical information and use it as one ingredient in the creation of goals. Comparisons of past activities allows the organization to forecast future activities. They also enable it to more accurately develop business plans that are focused on results. Other data, such as customer surveys, employee surveys, Human Resources data, financial data, and store-specific data, must be reviewed as well to get an overall snapshot of the organization's current state.

Once this data has been evaluated, goals can be written and used to establish performance levels and objectives for departments and employees. Goals are achieved by defining objectives that are specific. Some of the main reasons to set goals and objectives are:

- Provide direction
- Provide milestones to clearly tell you how far along on your plan you have gone and how far you still need to go
- Divide activities into smaller chunks of activities
- Clarify employee roles
- Motivate and challenge employees

An important task in setting goals is to align departmental efforts with organizational strategies. It is imperative for the manager to provide a clear understanding of what is expected of the department and how each employee has responsibility to contribute to the achievement of the goals. Managers must also decide whether a goal is too large and thus requires a team approach, taking into consideration the time and scope of the project.

A Method to Determine Which Goals to Set

A method that organizations use to help them determine which goals to establish at the organizational or department level is called a SWOT analysis. A **SWOT analysis** is a tool used to identify strengths and weaknesses and to examine opportunities and threats employees face in the organization. Conducting a SWOT analysis helps management to focus on activities and set goals for those areas where the organization is the strongest and has the greatest opportunities.

This type of analysis is best conducted by a team. Performing a SWOT analysis requires completion of three tasks:

1. Gathering facts

2. Reviewing facts

3. Sorting facts

Upon completion of these activities, the organization will need to answer questions about the strengths, weaknesses, opportunities, and threats listed in *Exhibit 2d*. Consider strengths from your point of view as well as from the points of view of the organization, customers, and key stakeholders. Also, think about the organization's strengths and weaknesses in relation to your competitors. For example, if all your competitors insist on having spotless restaurants, then a clean restaurant is a necessity, not a strength. One way to determine opportunity areas is to look at strengths with an eye for building upon them, or, alternatively, to look at weaknesses to determine whether eliminating any of them could create opportunity.

Contribution Levels

While managers need to evaluate and plan goals in the context of the larger strategic priorities set by the organization, they must also consider the capabilities of their staff. Understanding and leveraging your employees' capabilities helps you in setting and achieving goals. It also helps you determine the performance involvement and levels of various teams and individuals. Some questions to consider in assigning teams and/or individuals to various goals or objectives are:

■ What are this employee's strengths and weaknesses?

■ Where is the employee currently in his or her development?

■ Does this employee need a career development challenge?

Think About It...

Think of a time when you were asked to do something that had a certain element of struggle and challenge to it. How did it make you feel when you finally accomplished it? Why would it be important to create a goal or objective in which a person or team may need to struggle to achieve it?

- Will the employee do a good job?

- Can the employee work independently on this goal?

- Will the employee make a commitment to achieving the goal within parameters?

- Does this goal require more than one person to achieve it?

- Who should be part of the team assigned to this goal? How large should the team be?

- What qualities does each team member need to have to be part of this team?

- Will the team or individual be responsible for achieving the entire goal or are there smaller tasks that can be assigned?

Exhibit 2d

SWOT Questions

Strengths	
	■ What does our organization do well?
	■ What advantages do we have?
	■ What relevant resources can we access?
	■ What do we do for our customers that exceeds their expectations?
	■ What do we do better than our competition?
	■ What do other people see as our strengths?

Weaknesses	
	■ What does our organization do badly?
	■ What could we improve?
	■ What should we avoid?
	■ Where are we lacking in customer service?
	■ What does our competition do better than us?

Opportunities	
	■ What trends do we see that could boost demand for our products/services over the next five years?
	■ What opportunities do we think will emerge because of what is going on in the community?
	■ How might technology help us?
	■ What change could occur in the future that could benefit our organization?

Threats	
	■ What trends do we see that might hurt demand for our products/services over the next five years?
	■ What obstacles are we facing?
	■ Do we have cash flow problems?
	■ What might threaten us because of what is going on in the community?
	■ What change could occur in the future that would hurt our organization?

Think About It...

"The greatest danger for most of us lies not in setting our aim too high and falling short; but in setting our aim too low, and achieving our mark."
—*Michelangelo*

Think of someone you admire. How would you describe this person's success in terms of aiming high?

Once you have an understanding of the capabilities of your staff, four areas become leveraging points for determining contribution levels. All the following factors need to be considered in determining contribution levels by teams and individuals:

■ **Current skills and knowledge.** Individuals differ in the level of knowledge and the skills they possess. As part of the decision-making process, a manager must consider whether a goal requires a definite skill level or ability or if the goal could represent a developmental and growth opportunity for an employee. Whatever the manager's decision is on this point, it is essential that the employee understands how his or her developmental plan goals support the business and organizational goals. This awareness and appreciation by the employee of how he or she contributes to the business is essential in managing the employee's job performance, as well as creating a sense of commitment to working toward these goals.

■ **Ability to collaborate in teams.** Teamwork and cross-functional teams have increased the need for collaboration by staff. A manager needs to review goals in terms of the degree they will require a team approach. If a team is required to achieve a goal, the selection of team members becomes vital. A manager needs to understand a person's capacity to collaborate with others.

■ **Accountability.** When determining contribution levels, it is imperative for a manager to understand this factor. **Accountability** is the degree of responsibility an individual has to an activity. Managers must decide how much accountability they can give a team or individual. Factors to consider include how well an individual focuses on achieving goals as well as his or her commitment and ownership of the goals. Some questions a manager can use to evaluate the level of accountability staff members have are:

☐ Do they freely commit to projects?

☐ Are they focused on increasing revenue and decreasing expenses?

☐ Do they commit to quality work?

☐ How disciplined are they in following processes to get work completed?

☐ Do they accept responsibility readily?

■ **Responsiveness to change.** Change is inevitable. There is a certain degree of unpredictability to any goal. Some goals have a higher risk of change or ambiguity associated with them. A manager needs to examine how well staff can adjust and deal with uncertainty and change.

Activity

SWOT Analysis: Black Bear Restaurant

Black Bear Restaurant is located in a small, tourist community near the mountains of western North Carolina. It has been in business for just two years and has developed a solid, local customer base made up mostly of retirees. During the tourist season, the restaurant gets many referrals from various resorts in the area. The owner of the restaurant wants to set some goals so that Black Bear can move closer to its vision and mission statements: "To keep our customers always coming back for good food, attentive service, and a Southern welcoming atmosphere" and "Our mission is to provide customers quality, healthy Southern cuisine with superb and courteous service that exemplifies our heritage in the Smoky Mountains." The following information provides additional background on this establishment:

■ The chef was schooled at the Culinary Institute of America and has been a chef at several five-star hotels.

■ They have a small, select menu of healthy food, including game and fish.

■ They can create customized menu selections on request.

■ Because of housing development in the area, more restaurants are opening in the community.

■ They have a small staff.

■ Cash flow can be unreliable at times.

■ Several retirees have asked if the restaurant does catering.

■ The local chamber of commerce encourages local businesses to expand.

■ They do not have a lot of information about their competitors.

■ They are not sure of how the changing housing market will affect things.

■ A small influx of popular chain restaurants could wipe out the market.

As a team, identify and list what strengths, weaknesses, opportunities, and threats that Black Bear Restaurant may have. Once you have identified these factors, identify which three items your team would choose as their focus and be prepared to explain why.

Strengths

_____

_____

_____

Weaknesses

_____

_____

_____

continued on next page

Black Bear Restaurant *continued from previous page*

Opportunities

_____

_____

_____

Threats

_____

_____

_____

Top Three Areas

1 _____

2 _____

3 _____

Writing SMART Goals and Objectives

Once a manager has analyzed the opportunities present for the organization and created the framework for goals, he or she must determine specific objectives for the department or team. An **objective** is a specific description or statement of what a manager wants to achieve. The most effective goals and objectives are SMART:

■ **Specific.** The objective must be clearly stated. It must also communicate exactly what is expected, its completion date, and any other conditions that must be met in order to accomplish the goal.

■ **Measurable.** An objective needs to be quantifiable. **Measurable results** are outcomes that can be assessed by some means within the areas of performance, learning, and perception.

   ☐ Performance results refer to either system or financial results. An example of a system result is improvements to work processes. An example of a financial measure is increases to sales or cash flow units.

- ☐ Learning results include increased knowledge by individuals or by the overall organization as well as optimized efficiencies through employee behavior.

- ☐ Perception results can include customer or stakeholder perceptions of their interactions with organizational systems, processes, goods, or services.

- ■ **Achievable.** The objective must be realistic. The most effective goals are those that require an individual or team to strive to achieve them, but are not so unrealistic that employees lose motivation.

- ■ **Relevant.** Relatable goals and objectives are also important. Employees need to see and understand how an objective connects to the larger scheme of the organization. Goals and objectives that relate clearly to an organization's vision and mission have a much higher chance of being achieved.

- ■ **Timebound.** Objectives with dates for accomplishment also have a better chance for success. Just as most activities in life have a starting and ending point, goals need to be defined within parameters that fit into the rest of scheduled projects.

Writing SMART goals and objectives is an essential component of an effective management plan. SMART goals and objectives make for effective teams and individuals, which ultimately lead to an effective organization. Too often, goals end up being vague, unclear, unrealistic, unrelated to the organization's vision and mission, and/or immeasurable. By writing SMART goals and objectives, you and your employees can avoid these impediments and ensure progress for your department and organization.

Examples of SMART goals and objectives include:

- ■ Staff will decrease customer complaints by 5 percent over the next three months.

- ■ The management team will increase market share by 10 percent within the next eighteen months.

- ■ Managers and staff will use basic conversational phrases in English and Spanish before the end of the current fiscal year to make customers feel more welcome in our restaurant.

Keep in mind as you write SMART objectives and goals that these statements should not be longer than a sentence. They should also be concise, indicate any restrictions or conditions under which the goal or objective will be achieved, and be easy to read.

Activity

Writing SMART Organizational Goals

The Oasis is a four-star hotel with 560 rooms. It is a hotel and convention center located on the outskirts of a well-populated metropolitan gaming area near the desert. A new tower is under construction, which will provide 250 more sleeping rooms and a two-floor day spa. The day spa was included in the tower to capitalize on the expanding day spa trend in the industry. Customer surveys from a market analysis also indicated interest in a spa. The day spa will include the following services:

- Hair and color salon
- Manicure and pedicure stations
- Cosmetics
- Massages and body therapies
- Spa and "escape" packages

The Oasis's core values include listening to the customer, educating the customer on the latest techniques and beauty products, and providing ultimate service to customers. Its vision for the spa is "A place for guests to be treated to an extraordinary beauty experience." The spa's mission is "To provide guests with creative beauty solutions and indulgences that are personalized for them."

Create three SMART goals for the organization. Present your goals to the class and explain why they meet the criteria.

1 _____

   _____

2 _____

   _____

3 _____

   _____

A Process for Achieving Organizational and Departmental Goals

Knowing how to identify and write effective goals and objectives is a critical part of your role as a manager; however, that is only the first step in ensuring that goals will be achieved. An effective manager must have a process in place that will produce the desired results stated in the goals and objectives. There are four primary phases to this process: planning, incorporation, execution, and evaluation. *Exhibit 2e* illustrates the phases and steps that a manager should take toward achieving goals and objectives.

Exhibit 2e

Process Steps for Achieving Goals

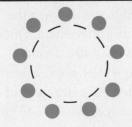

Plan

1	Select the most critical goals.
2	Develop a project plan for each goal.
3	Identify specific activities or tasks that need to be completed to achieve each goal.
4	Establish dates for milestones, follow up, and completion.
5	Determine who will be responsible for various tasks in the plan.
6	Identify any resources that may be needed to complete the plan.
7	Determine the measures you will use to evaluate results.
8	Engage your staff in developing the plan.
9	Communicate the final project plan and goals to your team and/or department.

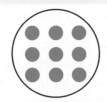

Incorporate

10	Work with your teams and employees to incorporate the goals and plan activities into their performance and development plans.
11	Gain commitment from the team and employees on completing the various activities assigned to them.

Execute

12	Implement the plan.
13	Monitor progress on the plan. Chart individual progress.
14	Review goals to ensure you stay on target. Follow up on issues that arise and interfere with achieving a goal.
15	Continue to communicate status to stakeholders on progress toward achieving the goal.
16	Revise and update plan if necessary.

Evaluate

17	Evaluate results.
18	Communicate the success.
19	Recognize and celebrate the accomplishments of the teams and individuals in meeting the goals and milestones.

Step 1: Planning

A project plan linked to each goal is the key to a manager's success. In the initial phase of planning, it is important not to be overwhelmed with tackling every objective immediately. One of the first things that a manager needs to consider is which goals are the most critical and have the greatest chance of having a positive impact on the organization. Remember to think in terms of the organization's strategic priorities when selecting the critical goals. A manager should then focus efforts on the chosen items by using a planning worksheet, which can be created using a spreadsheet, word processing software, or a form of your own design.

Taking the time to thoroughly scope out the logistics of achieving the selected goals will help your organization and team execute their assigned tasks. Each goal selected typically becomes a project. A plan needs to be developed for each project so you can monitor progress more efficiently. *Exhibit 2f* shows a sample worksheet for planning the details of a goal. Within the plan, you need to break down the goal into specific activities that contribute to its achievement. Once these smaller steps have been determined, you must decide such things as dates for completion, follow up, who will be responsible for various tasks, and what resources will be needed. A critical part of the planning process is understanding the resources available to you and your team. As you put the plan together, be sure to clearly identify the type of resource needed.

At this point, you must also determine the measures—or metrics—that will be used to evaluate the project and results. Metrics must be defined for each of the three critical business domains described previously in this chapter: performance, learning, and perception.

Additionally, be sure to engage your team in the planning process. Staff involvement offers many advantages. Besides leveraging the capabilities of everyone on your team, staff involvement in planning creates teams that are more self-motivated and committed to working for the desired results. Involvement also ensures vested interest and creates a sense of ownership.

Exhibit 2f

Sample Planning Worksheet for Goals

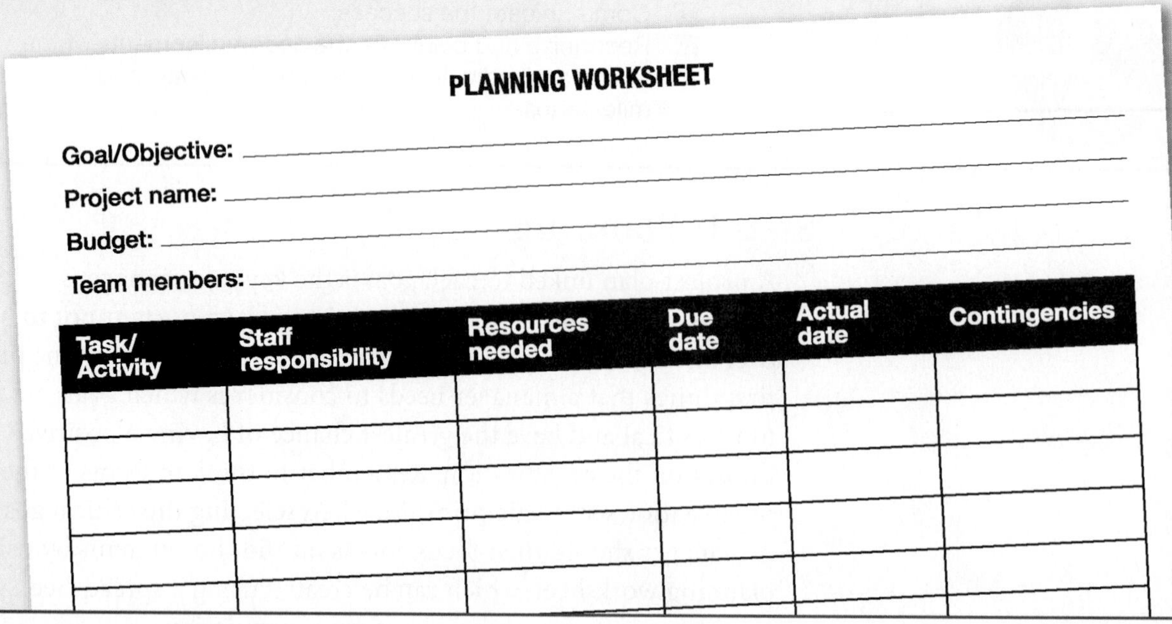

PLANNING WORKSHEET

Goal/Objective: _____

Project name: _____

Budget: _____

Team members: _____

Task/Activity	Staff responsibility	Resources needed	Due date	Actual date	Contingencies

Once a preliminary plan has been generated, communicate it. Communication includes not only the overall goal and plan but also any trade-offs or constraints related to meeting a goal. Discussions on priorities, contingencies, and/or potential sacrifices need to be part of open communication. A manager must be able to explain how the goal and plan support the core values, vision, and mission of the organization. At the same time, acknowledge the dynamic and changing aspects that any project may have. Being open and communicative about all aspects of what it will take to achieve the desired results is a necessary requirement for an effective manager.

Step 2: Incorporation

After completing the planning phase of goal achievement, you must ensure that the project aligns with management, team, and individual development plans. Incorporating business goals into these plans ensures that everyone is aligned with the critical objectives of the business. Take advantage of working with the team to incorporate task assignments into their development plans. As part of this routine, you must get the team or individual to commit to working on their assigned tasks and provide assurances that they will put in the needed effort to help achieve the goal. Individual performance goals must also tie into the departmental goals and business needs. In making these connections, employees understand how they contribute to the organizational goals.

Step 3: Execution

When the first two phases have been completed, you and your team are ready to execute the plan in order to achieve the desired results. This phase requires monitoring each activity listed on the project plan and charting individual progress. Goals must constantly be monitored to manage performance. Periodically, you also need to review goals to ensure that priorities and the project's status within the organization have not changed. Adjustments, revisions, and updates to the plan can be made by following this process. Use status meetings to continue communication on how your staff is performing and making progress toward achievement of the goal.

Step 4: Evaluation

When the project has been completed, you must evaluate the results. Earlier in the planning phase, organizational metrics for each goal were defined within three domains, focusing on systems results, financial data, volume of knowledge, or customer/stakeholder perceptions. Gathering statistics and feedback within these categories, which is then analyzed and reviewed to determine how successful the project was at achieving the goal, is a significant task for the manager to perform. Involving the individual or team in reviewing this information is beneficial. Using these earlier identified metrics helps you and the employees focus on results instead of other extraneous data.

Once you have reviewed and analyzed this data, communicate the success to your staff. It is important to recognize and celebrate these accomplishments. Whether this recognition is done during a staff meeting or during a performance review, people want to know how well they performed and whether their assignments contributed to the success of the organization. Consider avenues other than meetings to celebrate success, such as lunches and after-work gatherings.

Summary

Goals set the direction for an organization. Using historical data and identifying the organization's current strengths, weaknesses, opportunities, and threats contribute to the identification of a set of goals. Goals provide the basis for the creation of objectives for departments and individuals. Both goals and objectives need to be SMART: specific, measurable, achievable, relevant, and time bound. Putting a plan together to accomplish the goals requires a manager to consider the capabilities of the team. A four-step process that can be followed for achieving goals was also introduced with ways to ensure the success of a project. The role of communication in this process is particularly important. Periodic meetings can establish lines of communication throughout the process and allow for clarification of any ambiguities or changes in goal status. Results should be communicated and celebrated to both the team responsible for achieving the goals and the key stakeholders within the organization.

Activity

Planning and Writing Goals

The Spring Garden Hotel is a tropical resort paradise. The hotel is part of Majestic Resorts, an elite chain of hotels in the Caribbean, with annual sales of more than one billion dollars. Their motto is: "Where excellent service is no problem." The owners recently rolled out a new campaign to diversify their holdings. The thrust of the campaign was in retaliation to aggressive moves made by their primary competitor, Harbor View Hotels.

Majestic's goal is to increase holdings by having a presence within the next ten years in every major Caribbean tourist destination that caters to the rich and famous. Each hotel will have a distinct, unique theme and will actualize a minimum profit margin of 5 percent within its second year of business. The purpose of this move is to retain Majestic's dominance in the market and to become the largest, most profitable Caribbean-owned and -operated chain of resorts. By adding one resort per island, the company anticipates the addition of twenty-five hundred rooms—a 25 percent increase in the rooms' inventory. Plans are on target to open the first of the new "Majestic Resorts."

The new hotel will be the twentieth property for the organization and has a "couples only" theme. It will have 250 rooms, with a golf course nestled among the green mountain ranges. Each room will have a Jacuzzi on its small, private balcony. There will also be eighty private villas that feature two bedrooms, spacious living and dining facilities, and butler service.

You are part of the executive team of Majestic Resorts meeting to establish key strategic plans and goals for the new hotel.

Some of the success measures that the organization periodically uses are:

1 Increased occupancy percentage

2 Improved REVPAR (revenue per available room)

3 Lower unit cost

4 Increased GOP (gross operating profit)

5 Higher net income

6 Lower CPOR (cost per occupied room)

7 Increased average checks

8 Lower food cost

9 More favorable comment cards

10 Lower turnover rate

Listed below are facts that need to be considered as you develop these goals:

■ The budget is as follows: $5 million for marketing, $20 million for entertainment development, and $56 million for sports development.

■ At least 6 percent of future sales should be earmarked for marketing.

■ Creative revenue sources need to be identified for the hotel. Since it is a "couples only" resort, departments need to leverage this concept and take advantage of it for revenue.

■ The target market is couples between the ages of twenty-four and forty-five. They are either newly married or living together for several years.

■ Staff receives forty hours of company orientation, including skills training for their area.

■ Majestic has a strong reputation in the market. The hotel, however, does not have a market presence on this island.

■ Majestic has the latest technology for managing their hotels; the technology is also available in each hotel's suites.

continued on next page

Planning and Writing Goals *continued from previous page*

On each line provided, write one of the three goals you have developed for the new hotel.

1 _____

2 _____

3 _____

Now answer each question below.

1 Why do you think the goals your team created will be successful?

_____

_____

2 What trade-offs did you make?

_____

_____

3 What constraints will you try to control?

_____

_____

4 What departments will be key to obtaining the desired results?

_____

_____

5 What resources will you need to achieve the goals?

_____

_____

6 What methods will you use to monitor the progress toward achievement of the goals?

_____

_____

7 What kinds of internal communication will be instrumental in ensuring staff is committed to the goals?

_____

_____

Review Your Learning

1 Measurable goals allow the organization to

  A. determine production levels.

  B. create staffing schedules.

  C. forecast needs.

  D. identify progress towards achievement.

2 Which of these is a benefit of involving staff in the goal-setting process?

  A. Determines interest

  B. Benchmarks everyone's involvement

  C. Ensures vested interest

  D. Gets clarification from employees

3 The organization's goals are derived from

  A. mission statements and business needs.

  B. strategic priorities and employee feedback.

  C. employee demands and surveys.

  D. business plans and needs.

4 Individual performance goals must correlate to the organization goals in order to

  A. determine rate of pay.

  B. rank the department.

  C. ensure that the organization achieves its goals.

  D. obtain positive employee satisfaction.

5 When a manager has focused appropriately on goals, results are

  A. diverse.   C. communicated.

  B. long-term.   D. employee-based.

6 A strategic priority is an issue that is

  A. both linked to the vision and capable of gaining employee commitment.

  B. based on customer demands.

  C. central to the promotion of sales.

  D. both goal oriented and market driven.

7 One of the first things a manager needs to do in setting goals is

  A. gain management commitment.

  B. identify key stakeholders.

  C. review historical data.

  D. analyze team capabilities.

8 When determining contribution levels by staff members, managers must consider each employee's

  A. years of experience.

  B. variety of positions held.

  C. ability to respond quickly.

  D. current skill and knowledge.

9 What is a *specific* component of an effective management plan worksheet?

  A. Teamwork

  B. SMART goals

  C. Commitment by the department

  D. Leveraging schedules

10 Communicating with your team about project plans does *not* include telling them about

  A. deadlines.

  B. trade-offs.

  C. your concerns.

  D. performance reviews.

Notes

_____

_____

_____

_____

_____

_____

_____

_____

_____

_____

_____

_____

_____

_____

_____

_____

_____

_____

_____

_____

_____

_____

_____

_____

_____

_____

_____

Communicating Effectively as a Leader and a Manager

3

Inside This Chapter

- The Importance of Effective Communication
- The Communication Process Defined
- Effective Speaking
- The Importance of Listening
- The Telephone as a Communication Tool
- Effective Writing
- Organizational Communication

After completing this chapter, you should be able to:

- Define communication, information sender, encoding, information receiver, decoding, message, message channel, message context, environmental noise, informal and formal communication, listening, internal communication, nonverbal communication, and organizational communication.

- Describe and apply the communication process with various audiences.

- Identify obstacles to effective communication.

- Identify and demonstrate characteristics of effective speaking.

- Identify types of nonverbal communication.

- Describe characteristics of effective listening.

- Identify and use business-appropriate telephone skills.

- Describe and use a systematic process for developing a written message or speech.

- Identify common pitfalls to business writing.

- Identify various formats that a message can take for use with staff and external audiences.

Test Your Knowledge

1. **True or False:** Communicating effectively is typically a personal quality demanded by employers. *(See p. 44.)*

2. **True or False:** The information receiver is a passive receptor of information. *(See p. 47.)*

3. **True or False:** Understanding communication is verified through paraphrasing or asking questions. *(See p. 57.)*

4. **True or False:** Obstacles to effective communication include eye contact, repetition, and intent listening. *(See p. 50.)*

5. **True or False:** When answering the restaurant's telephone, identifying the restaurant followed by the call receiver's name is required. *(See p. 58.)*

6. **True or False:** One common pitfall in writing is the use of jargon and buzz words. *(See pp. 60–61.)*

7. **True or False:** One of the keys to effective writing is an assessment of the audience. *(See p. 61.)*

8. **True or False:** Business operating principles and goals are examples of external organizational communication. *(See p. 64.)*

9. **True or False:** Word of mouth is an effective way to promote a restaurant. *(See p. 65.)*

10. **True or False:** Welcoming customers to your restaurant has little to do with the vision or mission of the organization. *(See p. 46.)*

Key Terms

Communication	Informal communication	Message
Decoding	Information receiver	Message channel
Encoding	Information sender	Message context
Environmental noise	Internal communication	Nonverbal communication
Formal communication	Listening	Organizational communication

Introduction

Effective communication skills top the list of personal qualities and skills demanded by employers in the foodservice industry today. A manager who is an effective communicator knows how to build strong relationships, strong teams, and exceptional profits. In this chapter, you will be introduced to several key skills needed for communicating effectively with others inside and outside the foodservice establishment.

Today you have more ways to communicate than ever before. Not only is the communication you have with your staff critical in meeting goals of the organization, but the communication you undertake with customers and the media also have a significant impact on whether you achieve your goals as well. This chapter covers an array of communication types and methods available to managers. It also focuses on the importance of speaking, listening, and writing in building the key messages that will aid in achieving the mission and goals of the organization. In particular, one vital tool for the foodservice manager—the telephone—will be addressed. Communication with customers and the media will also be examined.

Exhibit 3a

A manager's ability to communicate can be the difference between a successful team and an ineffective team.

The Importance of Effective Communication

Ask yourself: "How many successful managers do you know who are poor communicators?" Remember that the key word in this question is "successful." You probably cannot think of very many. Being able to communicate is critical to your professional growth and to the growth and expansion of organizations.

In particular, your ability to communicate affects three groups. These include:

- **Employees.** Your ability to communicate with staff influences the work environment and the relationship and impact you have on the team. (See *Exhibit 3a.*)

- **Customers.** Your ability to communicate with customers and the public influences profits and organizational growth.

- **Yourself.** Your ability to communicate influences how well you reach your professional goals.

Employees have expectations of their managers, since a manager is the primary source of information for them. A manager communicates many things, including simple updates, changes in procedures, feedback on employee performance, and organizational changes in goals and missions. The regularity, consistency, and mode of delivery of these messages all affect the work environment. Good communication nurtures that environment, builds trust, and raises productivity. Bad communication does the opposite. Managers who communicate on a regular basis can actually curb and lower turnover rates, since employees feel they are more connected to what is happening in the organization. A manager's credibility with employees is also strengthened through these types of effective communication.

Customer interaction is also vital to the success of the organization. Without customers, an organization will not stay in business. The manager often is the customers' initial contact with the organization; it is important to welcome all guests with a warm and hospitable greeting. That greeting gives customers both a first impression and a lasting impression of the business. The manager's persona and communication skills drive the customers' perception of the establishment. How well a manager handles the positive and negative experiences that customers have can directly impact guest satisfaction, recurring sales, and profit. The effective manager establishes a strong and consistent presence with customers, and models behavior to reflect the organization's vision and mission. A manager who demonstrates effective communication and relationship-building skills during a guest's dining experience will ensure high guest satisfaction, an increase in sales, profitability, and return visits.

In addition to communicating well with employees and guests, you must also consider your own professional development. Take the time to build your networking skills, and explore ways to improve and fine-tune your communication skills. Career opportunities can arise for those managers who know how to network and are effective at communicating their needs and desires. To grow professionally, it is essential for a manager to become a confident speaker. As part of your professional development plan, consider participating in business communication courses that can help enhance your skills. Mentors can also provide feedback and advice on your ability to get ideas across clearly both in speaking and writing.

The Communication Process Defined

If communication is essential to developing strong relationships with your employees and customers, then understanding the dynamics of the communication process is important to your success. It is not only *what* you say that is important, but also *how* you say it that can influence whether your communication is well received by your audience.

Exhibit 3b

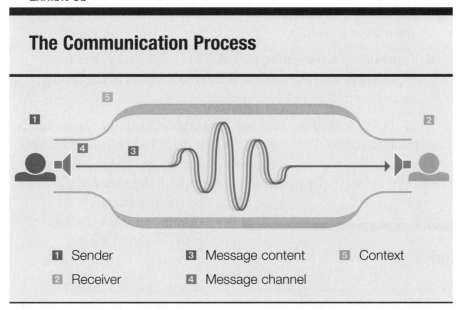

The Communication Process

- 1 Sender
- 2 Receiver
- 3 Message content
- 4 Message channel
- 5 Context

Communication is defined as the process of sending and receiving information by talk, gestures, or writing for some type of response or action. The communication process is composed of five parts: sender, receiver, message content, message channel, and context. (See *Exhibit 3b.*)

The **information sender** is the originator and developer of the information that will be communicated. Usually, the sender wants something done as a result of the communication. The process of developing the message to be sent is called **encoding.** Some of the things that the sender needs to answer before sending a message are:

- For whom is the communication intended? (receiver)

- What message do I want to send? (content)

- How should I construct the message? (channel)

- What environmental factors do I need to consider as I deliver the message? (context)

The **information receiver** is the person for whom the communication is intended. In most cases, this person is not just a passive receptor of the information. Some things an information receiver does are:

- Communicates understanding of the information

- Interprets the message

- Acts on it

- Makes decisions along the way to complete the act

The receiver's process of translating the sender's message into a meaningful form is called **decoding.**

The main connection between the sender and receiver is the **message,** or content that is being communicated. Typically, there are three kinds of messages sent by the information sender:

- **Historical information.** This is information that has already occurred, such as company history and orientation information, status updates, and management decisions. This information often requires no action, but is knowledge enhancing.

- **Action-oriented information.** This information has an expectation of an end result. The receiver will usually do something with it.

- **Impending-action information.** This information has an expectation that the receiver will do something in the future, such as complete tasks for someone on vacation.

Once the content of the message has been decided, the sender needs to think about how the message will be delivered and any inhibitors that may affect the clear delivery of the message. The **message channel** refers to the medium through which the message will be communicated. Communication can take many different forms:

- Words—verbal or written

- Graphic illustrations—pictures, diagrams, job aids

- Signs and symbols—gestures, nonverbal forms

Messages also have direction. Although downward communication from the manager is thought to be the dominant path of information, communication also occurs upward and laterally. (See *Exhibit 3c.*) Upward communication provides management with information on project results and goal attainment, but it also can be used for human resources issues such as grievances. Lateral communication can be a rich source of information for a manager in the form of casual insights and reality checks.

Exhibit 3c

Directional Communication

Upward
- Management reports
- Project completion meetings
- Suggestive systems
- Grievance procedures

Lateral
- Personal networking
- Team meetings
- Informal conversations

Downward
- Employee orientation
- Employee duties
- Performance reviews
- Management decisions
- Updates
- Training
- Annual reports
- Various new program

Upward

Lateral

Downward

Finally, there is a vast ocean between the sender and receiver, and many things can interfere with a message being received successfully. The environment that a message travels through is referred to as the **message context**. There are three levels to this contextual environment. (See *Exhibit 3d.*) The inner or core level of context deals with the immediate surroundings between you and the receiver. The middle, secondary circle refers to a broader function that affects or impacts the department, team, or restaurant surroundings. The outermost circle refers to the broadest effect the message may have, reaching the entire organization or the public. Each of these components, if not considered, can affect the success of any communication.

Exhibit 3d

Message Context Environment

Outer
entire organization, public

Middle
department, team, restaurant

Inner
sender/receiver environment

Exhibit 3e

Barriers to Communication

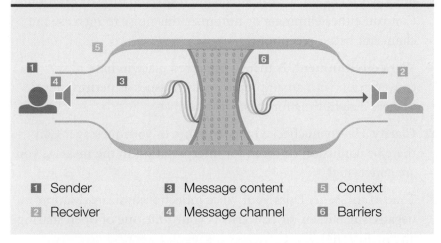

| **1** Sender | **3** Message content | **5** Context |
| **2** Receiver | **4** Message channel | **6** Barriers |

Noise, environment, language, cultural differences, tone of message, nonverbal communication, and lack of comprehension can be barriers to communication.

Barriers to Communication

Although it may sometimes seem that communicating is a fairly easy task, things can often get in the way, turning your plans for a successful sharing of information into a challenging experience for both parties. That vast ocean between the sender and receiver can cause a variety of breakdowns in the communication process. *Exhibit 3e* illustrates some of the hurdles that an effective communicator needs to consider to ensure that a message is correctly received and interpreted.

Confusion in any part of the communication process can cause a seemingly simple message to become an enormous challenge for the intended audience. Specifically, a manager needs to be aware of the following obstacles when crafting any communication to staff, customers, or the media:

- Semantics. Does the audience interpret your message as you intended? Does the intended audience have a deficiency with the language of the message? Do you have any language dialects that could interfere

Think About It...

Consider this section from Lewis Carroll's *Alice's Adventures in Wonderland*, in which the Mouse is conveying information to Alice.

"Mine is a long and sad tale" said the Mouse, turning to Alice, and sighing.

"It is a long tail, certainly," said Alice, looking down with wonder at the Mouse's tail, "but why do you call it sad?"

What are some of the breakdowns that can happen in your communication? Remember that a clever turn of phrase is no substitute for simplicity or clarity.

with the message? Do words or phrases mean one thing to you and another thing to the audience?

- **Jargon.** Have you reviewed your message to ensure that it does not contain buzzwords or technical language that your audience might not know?

  Have you asked someone to review or edit your longer speeches or written communication to check for jargon?

- **Gestures.** Do you exhibit too much body movement that interferes with listening? Do gestures convey the right message?

- **Cultural differences.** Are there any cultural perspectives that you need to consider?

- **Assumptions.** Do you assume your team knows how to solve a problem when it happens? Have you provided enough instruction to get the problem fixed?

- **Preconceptions about audience or situational characteristics.** Do you think some of your employees have a tendency not to listen? Do you repeat yourself to them—often resulting in the person losing even more interest? Are you afraid to confront employees?

- **Prejudices.** Do you carry certain biases based on experiences you have had? Do you have attitudes that influence the way you send your message? Are you sincere in your motives and attitudes?

- **Immediate environment.** Environmental noise is any sound that interferes with clear reception. Will machinery, loud-talking employees, or blaring radios interfere with clear reception of the message? Is the noise associated with a specific time or location? Can you either eliminate or minimize this noise to increase the chance of better reception?

- **Work environment.** Is there a preferred place to have a conversation with an employee on such issues as performance? Is there a right time for these discussions?

- **Clarity.** Have you checked the structure of your message? Can there be confusion or room for interpretation in the message you are conveying?

- **Tone of message.** Does your voice inflection indicate disapproval, negativism, elitism, or concern? Is your tone one of open sharing and inclusion?

- **Nonverbal boundaries.** Does the intended audience feel uncomfortable with invasion of their personal space when you have face-to-face meetings?

Environment Issues

Other obstacles to effective communication can be environmentally induced. If distractions such as noisy equipment or loud customers are apparent, then investigate moving to a different location that would eliminate these distractions. Other pressing issues that any manager typically handles on a daily basis can interfere with how well he or she communicates. For example, time commitments can seem overwhelming; using time management skills, however, can allow you to block time in your schedule to deal with necessary communication with your employees. Additionally, a demanding supervisor or manager may make numerous requests, and these things unavoidably take precedence over your messages to employees. No matter how imposing daily pressures can be, an effective manager should prevent these things from interfering with effective communication with employees.

Message Construction

Finally, if the actual construction of the message is too difficult to comprehend, employees might either misinterpret the message or not understand it at all. Reviewing the content of the actual message can help prevent these obstacles. Evaluate the content to be sure that you have minimized jargon, buzzwords, and any language barriers that might exist with your employees. In preparing to deliver your message, be sure to avoid using a tone that clouds the content message. Also avoid any particular dialect. Ways to prevent these obstacles include using a voice recorder to record your message before conveying it or asking someone to listen to your presentation and provide feedback on any apparent delivery barriers.

Ultimately, all of these obstacles can be prevented if you are willing to critically evaluate your messages and delivery style.

Managers must optimize each communication opportunity by considering the needs of their various audiences. Review these potential pitfalls and make certain you eliminate as many as you can.

Activity

What Is Causing the Communication Problem?

Gail is the manager of The Circle Restaurant. Gail has noticed that one of the employees, Mrs. Ross, refuses to communicate directly with her. Mrs. Ross tells other employees to go to Gail with her concerns. The other employees adhere to Mrs. Ross's wishes. They inform Gail that Mrs. Ross is afraid that Gail might speak harshly to her because she has seen Gail speak to the other staff in this manner. Mrs. Ross has also told some employees that Gail does not speak to her when she conducts her rounds. Mrs. Ross considers herself a very shy, timid person. She is, however, an excellent employee.

1 Why is Mrs. Ross unhappy about approaching Gail?

_____

_____

_____

2 Should Gail talk to Mrs. Ross about the situation?

_____

_____

_____

3 What could Gail do to make Mrs. Ross more comfortable in talking to her?

_____

_____

_____

4 Should Gail continue to accept messages from the other employees on Mrs. Ross's behalf?

_____

_____

_____

5 What next steps can Gail take to improve communications with Mrs. Ross?

_____

_____

_____

_____

_____

Activity

Identifying the Parts of the Communication Process

Fred has just started the evening shift at Chloe's Grill. He is told that a new crew member, Maria, is starting and it is his responsibility to show her how to use the fryers tonight. Fred is introduced to Maria, who just moved to the U.S. from Costa Rica nine months ago. While Fred takes Maria to the fryer area and begins to explain how to use the equipment, the restaurant becomes busy with an early rush for dinner. Several crew members are also talking nearby about last night's baseball game.

Fred goes through the standard operating procedure with Maria on how to make French fries. Halfway through his explanation, the assistant manager yells over to him to be sure to follow through on his shift checklist when he is done. Fred is feeling pressured to get back to his usual routine, so he quickly asks Maria if she has any questions. Maria shakes her head. Fred says, "Great, let's see you use the equipment!" Maria starts the process to fry a batch of French fries. She looks around and gives Fred a puzzled look. Fred notices that the storage bin for fries is empty. Obviously, Maria does not know where to get additional bags of fries. He points to where they are located, and she walks over to get a bag.

When Maria returns, she starts to make the fries, but Fred stops her once she has put them on the heating table. Fred tells her that she has forgotten to salt them properly. She simply stares at him. Fred begins to feel frustrated and asks Maria if she had heard him. She nods again. Fred asks why she did not salt the fries properly. Maria smiles. At this point, George, a fellow cook, stops by and whispers in Fred's ear that Maria does not understand English all that well and that Fred probably needs to show her again. George offers to translate what Fred is saying, since he also speaks Spanish. Fred accepts George's help, and Maria understands what she needs to do by both watching Fred and listening to George. Fred observes Maria frying several more batches of fries and feels she has caught on. He leaves to work on his shift checklist.

1 Using the diagram from *Exhibit 3e*, review this situation and label the parts of the communication process. Identify all of the barriers that may be involved in this situation.

1 _____   **5** _____

2 _____   **6** _____

3 _____

4 _____   _____

2 What type of message was the assistant manager conveying?

_____

3 How might you improve the communication process to eliminate some of the barriers that Fred faced?

_____

_____

4 Fred primarily used words to communicate with Maria. How could he have used other message channels to communicate?

_____

_____

Effective Speaking

Speaking is one of the most common ways for getting information out to an organization. In today's business environment, most managers engage in informal communication more often than formal communication. **Informal communication** includes all those opportunities that managers have to talk with their employees on a one-to-one basis or in small groups. Communicating messages through channels such as dialogue and discussion are excellent ways to ensure employees can share what they are thinking. **Formal communication** addresses those infrequent speeches, presentations, lengthy memos, or reports that require systematic planning and developments.

As the senders of these numerous types of information, managers need to choose and plan the words they will use as well as how they will deliver the message. Although there will be times when you must think on your feet, most often you will be able to prepare so that your verbal communication will have the impact and results you want.

When you plan the message, it is essential to articulate the key points in a concise manner. A method to ensure that your communication has covered all the vital information is to answer the five "Ws" and "how" questions. The five "Ws" and "how" questions are:

- Who?
- What?
- Where?
- When?
- Why?
- How?

As you further develop the communication, you must also think about how the audience will respond to the message and consider ways to personalize or customize it for them.

Once the speaker has a good sense of what content will be in the communication, he or she should take some time to rehearse the presentation. Things that speakers keep in mind when they are preparing for a speech include how their voice sounds and which nonverbal actions might hinder the audience's ability to hear the message. As the speaker fine-tunes the communication, awareness of audience interaction is also imperative, since an interactive communication is more engaging.

Message delivery is extremely important for a successful speaker. No matter the type of communication, a successful speaker exhibits certain characteristics while delivering a message that increases the likelihood that the receiver will be receptive and understand. (See *Exhibit 3f.*) As the speaker, you must verify understanding *and* listen to your audience. The communication process represents the dynamic interaction between sender and receiver, and what you thought was clearly communicated may not be what was received. Three techniques can be used to verify understanding by your audience:

Exhibit 3f

Characteristics of an Effective Speaker

Articulates points	Interacts with the audience
■ Concise message	■ Verifies understanding
■ Employs the five "Ws" and "how" in the message (who, what, where, when why, and how)	■ Repeats the message to ensure understanding
	■ Creates a comfortable and relaxing environment
■ Does not mispronounce words	■ Maintains eye contact

Personalizes the message to the audience	Uses suitable language
■ Cultural differences	■ Minimizes jargon and buzzwords
■ Language barriers	■ Defines technical terms
■ Age of audience	■ Eliminates sarcasm
■ Education level	■ Refrains from using slang
■ Disabilities—visible or otherwise	

Uses appropriate nonverbal communication	Varies speech patterns
■ Ensures body language does not interfere with the message	■ Varies the inflection of tone and pitch of the voice
■ Uses appropriate gestures	■ Enunciates clearly
■ Uses appropriate facial expressions	■ Minimizes any dialect in speech
■ Monitors nonverbal communication during speech	■ Eliminates mumbling or swallowing word endings
■ Exhibits appropriate demeanor	■ Speaks at a steady pace

■ Ask the receiver a question about the topic to see if he or she interpreted your message correctly.

■ Paraphrase the message by repeating the information in your own words.

■ Encourage the receiver to provide feedback on your message.

All of these methods can help finalize the communication process and ensure your audience receives the message correctly.

Additionally, listening to what your employees communicate is critical. Effective listening is not limited to simply the receiver of the message. Staff will listen more carefully to management if they believe that management is just as interested in hearing and understanding what they have to say. As part of the communication process, the manager must ensure that the dynamic give-and-take of speaking and listening is a two-way opportunity.

Exhibit 3g

What message is being sent by the manager and the employees?

Nonverbal Communication

Can you recall a time when someone who was delivering a message to you was saying one thing but his or her body language was saying something else? Words are not the only means of communicating with people. The impact that nonverbal communication such as gestures, facial expressions, and movement have on your audience can turn any message into a miscommunication. **Nonverbal communication** is the many expressions and movements of a speaker that convey additional information about the message being given. (See *Exhibits 3g* and *3h.*) One way that you can minimize nonverbal misinterpretation is to practice in front of a mirror or ask someone to give you feedback as you practice your delivery. For example: Do you raise your shoulders when you are unsure of the content reaction from your audience? Effective speakers make a conscious effort to know what nonverbal messages they may be conveying in a speech, and then try to eliminate them.

Some examples of specific nonverbal behavior that send an inappropriate message are:

■ Pursing lips as a sign of anger

■ Biting lips as a sign of nervousness

■ Slouching in a chair, showing disinterest

■ Raising eyebrows, indicating disbelief or amazement

■ Using vocal tones that signal aloofness and detachment

■ Gesturing with hands—can be annoying and distracting

■ Pointing your finger, indicating authority, acting like an expert, or lecturing

However, the following two nonverbal movements and expressions can have a positive effect on the audience:

■ Sitting on the edge of a chair and leaning forward is a sign of interest.

■ Smiling can be a sign of confidence and enthusiasm.

Exhibit 3h

Examples of Nonverbal Communication

Smiles

Facial expressions

Crossed arms

Gestures

Body language

Posture

Touching

Invasion of personal space

Clothing and appearance

Eye contact

The Importance of Listening

Although much of the responsibility for communicating effectively is placed on the sender, the act of communicating implies a two-way interaction. Therefore, the receiver has a responsibility to listen effectively. **Listening** is defined as the ability to attend closely to what another person is saying to capture the essence of a message being communicated. Occasionally, everyone has experienced this: they begin listening attentively, but find that their mind starts wandering. Instead of listening to what the person is saying, they are thinking about the mound of paperwork on their desk, the budget they have to get together by the end of the week, or the softball game tomorrow. All of these thoughts become the listener's interference with the message being communicated.

When the receiver does not pay attention to the sender, both of them are shortchanged. Not only do you miss the full intention of the message, but you also can convey the impression that you do not care what the person has to say. In addition, ill feelings might develop between the sender and receiver.

Skills of an Effective Listener

Effective listening requires actively engaging yourself in the communication process. Skills that an effective listener needs to develop include:

- Maintaining eye contact with the speaker
- Avoiding constantly interrupting the speaker
- Asking questions for clarity
- Occasionally rephrasing and repeating what the speaker has said to verify understanding
- Using effective body language to convey attentiveness
- Keeping hands at side and not folded
- Nodding to indicate approval or recognition
- Leaning toward the speaker to indicate interest in the content
- Showing empathy for the speaker
- Taking notes on the information
- Relaying the information to others if necessary, without losing meaning

By developing these listening skills, managers and employees will find it easier to acquire the essential information in a verbally communicated message.

Activity

Listening Attentively

Think of something that recently happened to you or an event which you heard about or read. This could be a positive or a stressful situation, but it must be one that you are willing to share with another classmate. Each person will take turns and communicate the story to his or her partner. The person who is the listener will retell what he or she heard. The communicator can then clarify any items necessary, and the listener will then retell the story one more time for accuracy.

Once both partners have completed the listening activity, answer the following questions in the space provided.

1 What parts of this activity were most difficult for you?

_____

_____

2 What got in the way of listening attentively?

_____

_____

Exhibit 3i

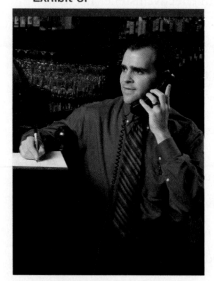

Procedures for talking with customers on the telephone help ensure good customer service.

The Telephone as a Communication Tool

Since the telephone is one of the most used communication tools in a foodservice establishment, how a manager and employees use it is very important to customer service. (See *Exhibit 3i.*) There are specific procedures that an effective manager needs to follow in answering the business phone. At the same time, the manager must also convey the importance of following these procedures with staff. Underlying these steps is the ability of the call receiver to be an effective listener.

The steps for proper business phone answering are:

1 Identify the name of the organization, followed by the call receiver's name and the question, "How may I assist you?"

2 Listen for the reason the caller has phoned your organization. Be sure to wait until the caller has finished before responding.

3 Maintain a positive, polite, and courteous attitude when speaking with the caller. Empathize with the caller.

4 If the caller has a large amount of information, take notes to be sure you have all the information. Be sure to ask the five "Ws" and "how" questions when taking a message.

5 Paraphrase or repeat what the caller has stated to ensure you have heard everything correctly.

6 Ask probing questions to get at the root of any issues or problems the caller may have.

7 Evaluate the reason for the call and whether you can provide the answer. If not, know who the "right" person is to answer the caller's issues and transfer the call to provide a quick resolution. Before transferring the call, it is a good practice to get the caller's name and phone number in case the call is lost during the transfer process. This will allow you to call the caller back and help them resolve their problem.

8 Explain to the caller any steps to be taken.

9 Close the conversation by asking the caller if there is anything else you can do to assist him or her.

10 End the call politely, perhaps by saying, "Thank you for calling (the name of the organization), and have a nice day."

Dealing with a Difficult Caller

At times, customers may become irate or rude during a phone conversation, yet calmness and politeness must be used at all times in dealing with the public. Applying effective listening skills and empathizing with the caller can help in dissipating any anger. As the manager, you might have the power to resolve the caller's issue. If so, inform the caller of what resolution you can provide. If you cannot resolve the issue, transfer the call to a person who can make a decision about solving the problem. If there is no one immediately available, either inform the customer that you will provide the information to another individual in authority who will call the customer back, or give the caller the contact name and phone number to call back at his or her convenience.

Effective Writing

Most of a manager's communication with staff, customers, and supervisors is done verbally, either in person or on the phone. However, written business communication is another means for a manager to share information. These types of messages include memos, faxes, emails, letters, and reports.

The success of any written communication is based on its structure and the process you use to develop the message. Written communication tends to be more formal than that which is spoken, so knowing the basic components of writing structure will help as you develop the

Why do you think that some of your written communication has failed to achieve its purpose? What does structure have to do with effective written communication?

content. In most written materials, the structure has several common parts. These include:

- **Introduction**—Used to capture the attention of the audience, state the purpose of the message, identify the topics of the materials, and establish the writer's point of view.

- **Body of the message**—Orderly arrangement and development of the content or topics presented in the introduction.

- **Conclusion**—Summarizes significant points, calls for action, and identifies the benefits and value of the message.

Many people find writing challenging. To make the task less daunting, you can take several steps to help organize your thoughts. Planning what you want to say makes the writing process easier. Using a systematic process to develop your ideas can enhance the writing experience and result in a clear, concise, and readable document. *Exhibit 3j* identifies steps you should follow to be an effective writer.

As you develop your written communication, keep in mind these pointers that will make writing easier to do:

Exhibit 3j

Systematic Process for Writing

1. Think about the audience.

2. Think about the purpose and what you want to accomplish.

3. Think about the situation and details. Ask yourself the five "Ws" and "how" questions, and write their answers.
   - Who?
   - Where?
   - Why?
   - What?
   - When?
   - How?

4. Record the action you want taken as a result of the written message.

5. Identify the benefits to the message. How will it help the company, the reader, your customers, and you?

6. Identify the topics and group the details underneath it.

7. Order the topics in a logical sequence.

8. Write the main body first, then the introduction, and then the conclusion.

9. Read through the draft, and edit and revise the content, grammar, flow, and readability.
   - Get another set of eyes to read your draft.
   - Ask a colleague to read your writing, and edit or make suggestions on how to improve it.

10. Write the final draft and distribute the communication.

- Be concise. A reader appreciates brevity. Long, drawn-out sentences add to complexity. The best written messages make the point and move on without inserting unnecessary words.

- Be clear and complete. Although conciseness is important, be sure that you do not sacrifice clarity or completeness. Review your writing to be sure your ideas are understandable and comprehensive. Using planning and organizing steps when writing will help you avoid missing information.

- Keep it simple. Complex sentences are hard to read. Use short sentences and simple words where possible. If you must use jargon, acronyms, or technical terms, define them so the reader understands what you are trying to say.

■ **Check your work.** Have another colleague read your materials to check for proper usage. If possible, use the grammar and spell check functions in your word processing program.

■ **Always convey an upbeat attitude.** Even if your message needs to deliver troubling news, frame it with long-term benefits. No one likes to read negative messages.

One other factor to consider in writing is the growth and use of technology as a means to communicate. Emails, faxes, and text messaging are just some ways that technology has influenced the written word. Although these formats are more casual, it is important to apply the same principles to their use as you do with other forms of written communication.

Roadblocks to Effective Writing

Despite every effort, all writers occasionally make mistakes. In addition to the pointers in the previous section, beware of these common pitfalls:

■ **Lack of planning.** Even if you think you do not have the time, take a few minutes to think through the message's purpose and main points before you write. (*See Exhibit 3k.*)

■ **Lack of purpose.** Reading impact decreases quickly if the reader does not understand the reason for the written communication.

Exhibit 3k

Take time to think about the purpose, audience, and style of the message before writing.

■ **Forgetting the audience.** Before you start writing, know who will be reading your words and if they have any preference for how the message should be structured. Writing for an audience can make them understand your message better.

■ **Use of incorrect style.** Although writing tends to be more formal in style, infusing some informal style to increase readability can be effective. Understanding the audience and purpose of the writing also influences what style you should use.

Writing challenges most managers and leaders. Understanding some of the writing traps that can befall any writer will help you revise drafts of your messages. If you thoughtfully use and master these concepts, you can capture your reader's attention and get your message across effectively.

Activity

Improving Sentence Content

Look at each of the sentences below. Think about what the person is trying to communicate. Rewrite a clearer version of the sentence in the space provided.

1 A big increase in market share was achieve by Taco Pete's.

_____

_____

2 The report suggested an increase in food toxins.

_____

_____

3 The meeting was held at the restaurant and the new menu item's marketing program was discussed but consensus was not reached and it was agreed that another meeting needs to be scheduled.

_____

_____

_____

4 The inconsistent and uncharacteristic results of the processes, which were conducted at the food labs in St. Louis, Missouri in the central region of the United States. by a team consisting of one senior food chemist and five sanctioned lab technicians and in conjunction with other tests completed in Germany as well as tests done in Mexico by a team of chemists from Costa Rica and which were analyzed using advanced computer technology electronically to the various sites, appeared to be the outcome of the different languages spoken by the food analysis teams.

_____

_____

_____

_____

_____

_____

_____

_____

Organizational Communication

Just as a manager's personal ability to communicate effectively builds his or her credibility and leadership reputation, organizational communication is vital to establishing the overall identity, brand, and operations of a foodservice establishment. **Organizational communication** is comprised of the numerous messages and information that convey operational procedures, policies, and announcements to a wide variety of audiences. **Internal communication** is any message presented to staff to create a cohesive and productive workforce. Internal communication should be timely, clear, concise, informative, and interesting.

Two primary groups receive communication from the organization. The internal audience is composed of staff and employees, colleagues and management, and other internal support resources. The other group is external, which can include guests or customers, media and press, community and city officials, law enforcement and regulative agencies, public relations groups, legal counsel and accountants, and vendors and suppliers. A third group to consider is potential employees who may be pursuing employment with your establishment. The information needs of each group can vary, as seen in *Exhibit 3l*.

Exhibit 3l

Comparison of Internal and External Audience Communication

Internal Audience Communication	External Audience Communication
Organizational vision and mission statements	Press releases
Organizational goals and objectives	Special events announcements
Organizational procedures, such as standardized recipes, opening and closing procedures, cash handling, food safety, and emergencies	Sponsorship of community activities, such as charity walks, scholarships for students, etc.
Announcements, such as changes to policies and procedures	New store openings and neighborly issues, such as construction
Dress code policies, job descriptions, and benefits	Crisis management
Special recognition and awards	Environmental, industry-related, and food-related issues

In particular, industry-related, environmental, and neighborhood issues should receive a high priority for organizational communication. Industrial and environmental issues impact every foodservice organization. Regulatory changes, such as pollution reduction caused by consumer demands for better air quality, affect foodservice establishments. Organizational communication is key to alerting the public about these changes and the restaurant's support of them.

Another external communication concern is messages about actions that may affect the establishment's neighborhood. For example, parking lot construction or renovations to the building need to be communicated in a timely manner so the customer will not be inconvenienced. New restaurant openings require an effective public communication strategy so any fears of increased traffic, noise, or other disturbance can be eliminated and avoided.

Understanding different audiences, their needs, and the process used to develop organizational messages requires a broad range of skills. From determining the initial need for various messages to following up on the communication, an effective manager must adhere to a consistent process for crafting these messages.

Process for Developing Organizational Communication

The process for developing an effective organizational communication is almost identical to the method used to develop your own written communication. Initially, the manager needs to evaluate the audience characteristics, which include:

- Need for information
- Language skills
- Reading levels
- Interest level and motivation
- Skill levels

Once you know the audience, your next step is to determine the most effective method for communicating the information. *Exhibit 3m* identifies numerous ways that the message can be communicated. In particular, public service announcements provide information about community events through local and cable television stations. These channels usually are free, especially if the organization is sponsoring a community service project. However, the budget for organizational communication can be the decisive factor in choosing which methods to use.

After you have evaluated the audience and determined the most effective method of communication, you are ready to develop the organizational message. Developing the message includes identifying its purpose, ensuring you have answered the five "Ws" and "how"

Exhibit 3m

Methods for Communicating Organizationally

Print

- Letters
- Press releases
- Company newsletters
- Billboards
- Posters and other signage
- Menu clip-ons or table tents
- Training materials
- Newspaper articles or advertisements
- Emails, text messaging, and other electronic methods

Television and Radio

- Public service announcements (PSAs)
- Commercials
- Videos

Direct Speaking

- Dialogue
- Discussion
- Word of mouth
- Meetings
- Training sessions

questions, organizing the content in a logical flow, and writing the message. As with other types of written communication, you must use clear and concise language. You must also make sure the tone and language are appropriate for the intended audience. You should also verify that the message is consistent with other organizational communication and that it upholds the company's vision and mission statements.

Following final revisions to the communication, you will send or execute the message using the delivery method you selected earlier. Subsequently, you should monitor the dissemination of the message and conduct any follow-up necessary to ensure the intended audience receives the message in a timely manner. You should also invite any questions or discussion from the audience to clarify points in the message. Solicit feedback from a cross section of the audience to discover the message's effectiveness. This feedback will complete the loop in the overall process for development of organizational communication, and will help you improve similar messages in the future. (See *Exhibit 3n*.)

Exhibit 3n

Development of Organizational Communication

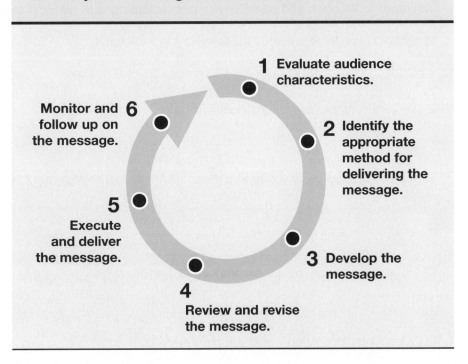

1 Evaluate audience characteristics.

2 Identify the appropriate method for delivering the message.

3 Develop the message.

4 Review and revise the message.

5 Execute and deliver the message.

6 Monitor and follow up on the message.

Activity

A Manager's Communication Opportunities

You will be grouped into teams to make recommendations on the managerial problem described in the following story. Read the situation, and then answer the questions at the end of the case as a team. Each team will make a short presentation on its evaluation of the situation and recommendations.

Sam, a manager at The Great American Grill Restaurant, is having problems relating to his employees. Sam feels that employees should perform their duties as they are told and without asking any questions. Sam is a veteran manager with over twenty years of experience. He has not participated in any continuing education courses in more than five years.

During his twenty years in the foodservice industry, many things have changed. The style of management has shifted from one of "control and command" to one of more collaboration and input. Sam feels that employees should not provide feedback, or any suggestions on their assignments. He feels that the daily meetings are sufficient for employees to hear what is expected of them. Sam rarely speaks to the employees other than during these meetings.

In protest of Sam's inability to communicate effectively with them, the employees stage a "sick-out" (half of the employees call in sick). The head cook, Walter, is responsible for the "sick-out." Walter informs the assistant cook that the plan is to hold the "sick-out" for at least a week. When this actually happens, Sam works as the head chef, and operations managers from other locations also fill in.

The Director of Operations, who supervises Sam, thinks that Sam has excellent technical skills and can learn to be open and effective at communicating with his employees—with some training.

1 What do you think is at the root cause of the "sick-out?"

_____

2 What should the Director of Operations do?

_____

3 As the director, would you have a meeting with the staff? What would you say?

_____

_____

4 What plan of study would you propose for Sam?

_____

5 What kind of follow-up would you do, if any?

_____

_____

Summary

Outstanding writing and speaking skills are characteristics of the most successful foodservice leaders. Developing these skills requires thoughtful application and determination to ensure that whatever you communicate is clear, concise, and complete. Effective communication is important to your career, employees, and customers. The communication process includes a connection between sender and receiver, as well as other components that need to be considered in the crafting of any business message. A number of impediments to the communication process must be considered, including semantics and jargon usage, voice intonation, nonverbal messages, and cultural and work environment issues. Informal and formal communication are two broad categories of messages a manager uses in daily activities. Planning either type of communication requires a systematic approach to the development of the message.

Other factors can interfere with an audience's ability to understand and act on a message. One of these factors includes personal experiences interfering with the development and execution of an effective message. However, underlying the effectiveness of a communicator is the ability to listen.

Organizing a written message before actually writing it is important, since many factors can hinder writing ability. Having someone else proofread communication is particularly important.

Through the application of the processes presented in this chapter, you can improve your writing and speaking skills, giving you more confidence in delivering messages to colleagues, staff, customers, and upper management.

Review Your Learning

1 Another name for developing a message is

A. decoding.

B. channeling.

C. encoding.

D. context setting.

2 Confidence is exhibited in managers and employees when

A. employees are proficient in operations.

B. effective communication dominates the operation.

C. customers are completely satisfied.

D. a professional plan has been developed.

3 Which is an example of nonverbal communication?

A. Hand gestures

B. Group thinking

C. Speed writing

D. Emphatic discussion

4 Seating oneself on the edge of a chair and leaning slightly forward is a sign of

A. passion.

B. enthusiasm.

C. interest.

D. intelligence.

5 When delivering a speech or communicating verbally, tone is defined as

A. feelings displayed in the voice.

B. behavior demonstrated when speaking.

C. the factor that determines the volume of the voice.

D. verbal and nonverbal behavior.

6 Internal organizational communication includes

A. procedures, job aids, and job descriptions.

B. sponsorship of community events.

C. messages for the public.

D. All of the above

7 When writing a speech or preparing a presentation, it is essential to

A. understand technical jargon.

B. check with upper management.

C. write using the five "Ws" and "how."

D. delegate parts of the writing for developmental reasons.

8 One common pitfall to effective writing is lack of

A. focus.

B. jargon.

C. planning.

D. complexity.

9 Messages that contain information such as status updates and management decisions are referred to as

A. impending action.

B. interpretive data.

C. action oriented.

D. historical.

10 When developing and delivering communication, a person needs to be aware of which personal factor?

A. Nervousness

B. Voice tone

C. Preconceptions

D. All of the above

Managing Compensation

4

Inside This Chapter
- Defining Compensation
- Establishing Policies and Procedures for Employee Wage and Compensation
- Merit Pay Policies and Guidelines
- Maintaining Confidentiality of Payroll Information

After completing this chapter, you should be able to:
- Define compensation, wage, merit pay, controllable costs, noncontrollable costs, salaries, bonuses, commissions, semivariable costs, payroll standards, Fair Labor Standards Act (FLSA), Equal Pay Act, collective bargaining agreement, performance standard, and performance review cycles.
- Establish a policy and procedure for determining employee compensation.
- Establish guidelines for merit increases.
- Maintain confidentiality of payroll information.

Test Your Knowledge

1 **True or False:** A minimum wage of $5.15 must be paid to all persons working in a restaurant or foodservice establishment. *(See p. 75)*

2 **True or False:** When there is both a state minimum wage and a federal minimum wage, the federal minimum wage takes precedence. *(See p. 76)*

3 **True or False:** Exceptions can be made to a company's policy regarding pay increases for employees. *(See pp. 81–82.)*

4 **True or False:** A collective bargaining agreement is between a business and a union that is representing the employees. *(See p. 79.)*

5 **True or False:** When managers are evaluated, one of the key items evaluated is their ability to maintain costs at the standard set by the company. *(See p. 82.)*

6 **True or False:** Rates of individual employees should be open to all to avoid dissension. *(See p. 83.)*

Key Terms

Bonuses

Collective bargaining
  agreement

Commissions

Compensation

Controllable costs

Fair Labor Standards Act
  (FLSA)

Merit pay

Noncontrollable costs

Payroll standards

Performance review cycles

Performance standard

Salaries

Semivariable costs

Wage

Introduction

In the world of management, some of the most challenging subjects are employee compensation and termination. How these are handled go a long way in determining the culture of the foodservice establishment and, ultimately, may affect the profitability of the operation.

In discussing compensation, several forces are at play—all pulling in opposite directions. Consider the players:

- **The employees.** They want maximum compensation for the work that they do. The more they do, the more they will want.

Think About It...

If you are presently working in the foodservice industry, how do you feel about the relationship between your pay and the operation's profit? What factors influence your feelings?

- **The owner.** Whether it is a single proprietor or a large corporation, profit is the ultimate goal. After all, it is profit that repays the investment, fuels expansion, and makes the risk worthwhile. If too much is spent on labor, profit suffers.

- **The manager.** Caught in the middle. The manager wants his or her employees, particularly the good ones, to be well paid. The manager works hard at training and building a team and does not want to lose it.

Because compensation is such a sensitive issue from all sides, it is important that policies and procedures are established so it can be handled correctly and fairly. Some factors that are linked to the proper development of compensation policies include analyzing gross sales and local and regional pay studies, investigating the competition in the sector of restaurant service you handle, and determining whether contract negotiations must be considered part of compensation.

Another challenging aspect of management is the subject of termination, particularly involuntary termination. It is probably the most unpleasant task that a manager has to perform. It is even worse for the employee, who is now without a job and, consequently, without an income. Policies and procedures must be in place to handle this situation effectively.

Defining Compensation

Labor costs are one of the most important considerations in a restaurant or foodservice establishment. Labor costs fall into three broad categories: compensation, wage, and merit pay. **Compensation** is all types of wages combined with other rewards or benefits that the employee receives as part of a package. **Wage** refers specifically to the pay that an employee receives as a result of working for the organization and is a subcategory to compensation. **Merit pay,** on the other hand, is defined as an additional sum paid to an employee whose work is superior and whose services are valued.

Since labor costs can devour a large part of an organization's sales, it is critical for a manager to understand the importance of establishing and following guidelines set for wage and merit pay. Although it is imperative to use job duties or classifications as the foundation for determining pay scales and yearly compensation, employee performance must also be examined as another factor that contributes to the employee's total compensation. These two factors will be examined in subsequent sections.

Establishing Policies and Procedures for Employee Wage and Compensation

If there is one key word for establishing employee compensation policies and procedures, it would have to be *fair*. The policy has to be fair to the employee, the employer, and management. It must be fairly and consistently administered with equal consideration for all parties. The policies should be open and known to all concerned. Problems arise when pay scales and how they are determined are kept secret. While an individual's pay rate is confidential information, the pay range for each position should be known. This is important because employees who wish to move up in the organization need to know what financial gain can be made by taking on more responsibility or performing a task that requires a higher skill level. Also, by knowing pay ranges for each position, employees are less likely to spread rumors about pay. For these reasons, it is important to have established and published compensation ranges for each job classification or position in the operation.

Policies and procedures for employee compensation fall under the category of a control function. A typical control process for compensation policies and procedures involves the six steps shown in *Exhibit 4a.*

Exhibit 4a

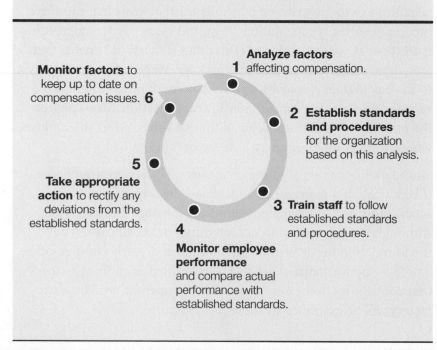

Typical Compensation Control Process

Monitor factors to keep up to date on compensation issues. **6**

1 **Analyze factors** affecting compensation.

2 **Establish standards and procedures** for the organization based on this analysis.

5

Take appropriate action to rectify any deviations from the established standards.

3 **Train staff** to follow established standards and procedures.

4

Monitor employee performance and compare actual performance with established standards.

Factors Affecting Compensation

The first step in the control process for compensation policies and procedures is to analyze the factors that affect compensation. There are several factors that need to be taken into consideration (see *Exhibit 4b*):

■ Controllable costs versus noncontrollable costs

■ The restaurant's sales level

■ Payroll standards

■ State and federal minimum wage laws

Exhibit 4b

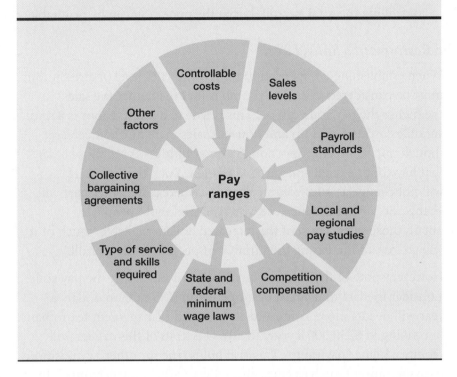

Factors Affecting Pay Ranges

- Local and regional pay studies
- The competition's compensation
- Type of service and skills required
- Collective bargaining agreements and contracts
- Other factors, such as benefits

The sections that follow will give a closer look at these factors and how they relate to establishing pay ranges for each position.

Total Controllable Costs versus Noncontrollable Costs

There are two types of costs in any business, including restaurants and foodservice operations: controllable and noncontrollable. **Controllable costs** are those costs that management can control and **noncontrollable costs** are those costs that management cannot control. Labor is a controllable cost. It include salaries, wages, tips, bonuses and merit pay, and commissions. **Salaries** tend to be associated with management positions since they are fixed dollar amounts for compensation. Hourly wages, on the other hand, are determined by the actual hours of work by an employee. Although not paid by the employer, tips are considered compensation by law. In fact, many workers in the industry make more in tips than they do from wages. **Bonuses** and merit pay are dollar amounts in addition to the regular wage and salary. These are given either for special projects or assignments, many times coming from discretionary funds. Merit pay is added to an employee's basic wage or salary. **Commissions** are usually associated with a sales function and are a percentage of the money taken in on various types of sales. For example, the sales group in a hotel resort may have commissions for booking a certain number or percentage of conferences or rooms. Commissions are typically additions to salary or wages.

Think About It...

It is often said that using money as the only motivator leads to a steady scarcity of quality products and services. Do you agree or disagree? Why?

In the restaurant and hospitality industry, labor is the highest or second highest cost that management has to control (the other being food cost). Having an established range of pay based on solid data for each position in the restaurant will assist management in controlling the total payroll so that the operation can be profitable.

The Restaurant's Sales Level

When establishing compensation ranges, the sales level of a restaurant must be considered. A rule of thumb is that the higher the sales, the higher the pay scale can be. This is true to a point. Labor is a semivariable cost that goes up and down as sales increase and decrease, though not in direct proportion. **Semivariable costs** are those costs that have both a fixed and variable element, such that one part will not change as sales volume changes, whereas the other part will change. So when sales increase, you will need more people to obtain those sales. Thus, of the increased dollars available, much of it will go toward increasing the number of people on the payroll.

However, some of the increase can go toward increasing the pay scale. Consider the fact that a restaurant taking in $2.5 million dollars a year will need a more astute and experienced management team than one taking in $250,000 a year. To attract a team of this caliber will require a higher pay range. This also holds true for other key positions in the restaurant, such as chefs, line cooks, and pantry personnel. In other words, increased sales will mean more payroll dollars available, most of which will go toward increasing the number of personnel, but some may also go toward increasing particular position pay ranges.

Payroll Standards

Any restaurant has, or should have, standards for each controllable cost in the operation. **Payroll standards** are set by management to ensure the operation's profitability. Since controllable costs are normally variable or semivariable, the payroll standards are expressed as a percentage of sales. For example, a restaurant could have a food cost standard of 35 percent, a payroll standard of 30 percent, and a supply cost standard of 4 percent. These standards would have to be met for the operation to achieve a profit. The payroll standard is a set number that could be anywhere from 15 to 50 percent depending on many variables; however, it is normally set between 20 to 35 percent of sales.

To illustrate this point, assume that a restaurant has a payroll standard of 30 percent and monthly sales of $200,000. Its monthly payroll cost should be $60,000 ($200,000 × .30 = $60,000). If sales increase to $210,000, payroll should increase to $63,000 ($210,000 × .30 = $63,000). As stated earlier, most of this increase would go to adding hours on the schedule to deal with the increased traffic. If the trend continues, then part of the increased available dollars should go into increasing the compensation ranges.

When establishing ranges, keep in mind the total dollars available for payroll. If the range is set too high, the labor cost standard will not be met. If the compensation range is set too low, the restaurant will not attract the necessary caliber of personnel.

Activity

Payroll Costs

Determine the payroll cost for each of these situations.

1. Apple Orchard Restaurant has a payroll standard of 20 percent and monthly sales of $180,000. What should its monthly payroll cost be? _____

2. If sales for Apple Orchard Restaurant increase to $200,000, what could the payroll increase to? _____

3. The Twin Owls Restaurant has a payroll standard of 25 percent, and monthly sales are $350,000. What should its monthly payroll cost be? _____

4. If sales for Twin Owls increase to $400,000, what could the payroll increase to? _____

State and Federal Compensation Laws

Minimum wage laws are important to keep in mind when establishing compensation ranges. The federal minimum wage law falls under the **Fair Labor Standards Act (FLSA)**—a law that requires all employers to pay employees minimum wage plus overtime for any hours worked over forty per week. It currently provides for a minimum wage of $5.15 per hour. It also stipulates that overtime pay of time and a half should be paid for any hours worked more than forty per week. This law applies to any business engaged in interstate commerce with sales in excess of $500,000 per year. It also applies to hospitals, nursing homes, schools, and government agencies. For example, if you manage a pizza restaurant located at the state line and deliver across it, the restaurant falls under the minimum wage law if it also has sales of $500,000 per year. Even if an employer does not meet the coverage test, some of its employees may be covered individually under the law. Individual coverage occurs when a person is engaged directly in, produces goods for, or is closely related to producing goods for interstate commerce.

There are some exceptions to the minimum wage, even if the law applies to the business. These exceptions apply when the worker is not considered an employee under the FLSA. They include disabled workers or others working as trainees, full-time students, youth program and student learners, and independent contractors.

You need to be aware of these exceptions to ensure they are reflected in the company's guidelines and policies as needed. The FLSA also protects child labor; an employee must be at least sixteen years old to work and at least eighteen to work in jobs declared as hazardous. Youth under the age of fourteen typically cannot be employed, but youth between the ages of fourteen and fifteen may work outside school hours in various nonmanufacturing and nonhazardous jobs under these conditions:

- No more than three hours on a school day or eighteen hours in a school week

- No more than eight hours on a nonschool day or forty hours in a nonschool week

Also, work may not begin before 7:00 a.m. or end after 7:00 p.m., except from June 1 through Labor Day, when evening hours are extended to 9:00 p.m.

There are additional qualifications regarding these exceptions, which can be found at *www.dol.gov/esa/regs/compliance.* States also regulate the work of minors. Employers must comply with any state laws that are stricter than federal laws.

Another exception to the FLSA law is tipped employees. They can be paid a minimum wage of $2.13 per hour provided that their tips plus the $2.13 equal a minimum of $5.15. If the tips are insufficient to do this, then the employer must make up the difference to bring the employee's wage up to $5.15.

Furthermore, the Equal Pay Act amended the Fair Labor Standards Act to prohibit gender-based differences in wages and salaries. Although the EPA was implemented in response to a concern about the weaker compensation position of women, men are protected equally under the act. The EPA prohibits discrimination by employers on the basis of sex. It requires equal pay for equal work. The equal work standard does not require that compared jobs be identical, only that they be substantially equal.

Many states have their own minimum wage laws. Some have a higher minimum wage than the federal law, while others are lower or the same. (See *Exhibit 4c.*) When employees are subject to both a state and federal minimum wage law, they are entitled to the law that gives them the greatest benefit.

Think About It...

Many, if not most, foodservice operations now pay over the minimum wage. Do you think that a minimum wage law is necessary? Why or why not?

Exhibit 4c

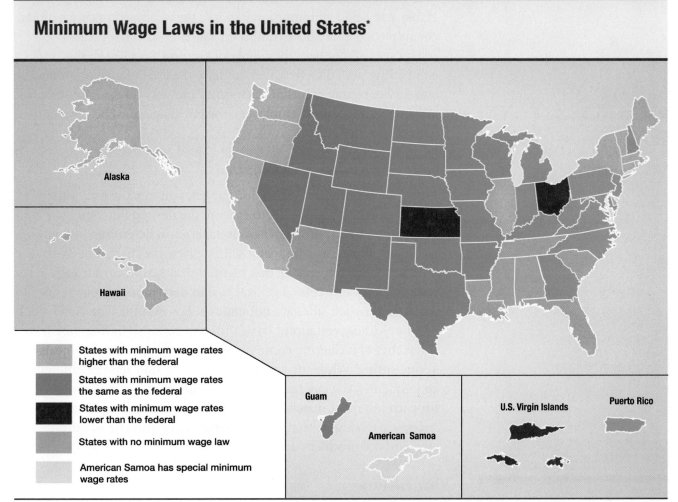

Minimum Wage Laws in the United States*

Alaska

Hawaii

States with minimum wage rates higher than the federal

States with minimum wage rates the same as the federal

States with minimum wage rates lower than the federal

States with no minimum wage law

American Samoa has special minimum wage rates

Guam

American Samoa

U.S. Virgin Islands

Puerto Rico

* as of December 2005, U.S. Department of Labor

Local and Regional Pay Studies

Another factor to consider when establishing pay ranges is what is being paid in the area. Wages for the same job vary widely across the country. Several rules of thumb may be helpful: job wages are normally higher on the two coasts than they are in the Midwest or South. Likewise, they are higher in urban areas than rural areas. Cities that are heavily unionized will have higher wages than cities that are not. The U.S. Department of Labor has regionalized wage studies, and State Restaurant Associations normally have local wage information. These studies should be consulted to establish salary ranges that are in line with what is current in your area.

Competition Compensation

Regional and local wage rates are important to know, but it is imperative to know what the competition is paying. Employees tend to gravitate to the restaurant that pays them the most. While there are many factors that make up employee loyalty, wages are normally a high priority. Consider a small family-owned restaurant that does not fall under the federal or state guidelines for minimum wage. If they pay below minimum wage while their competitors are national chains paying at or above minimum wage, the family-operated restaurant will not have the caliber of employee needed to stay competitive and, therefore, will not have the level of quality product and service to stay in business. Good employees will generate sales. To attract and retain good employees, the pay range must be competitive with the competition.

Type of Service and Skill Required

When establishing compensation ranges, you must consider the quality of employee needed to execute the desired outcome. The menu and the ambiance of the operation determine skill level. Generally, the higher the menu selling price, the higher the skill level necessary to produce that menu. Job descriptions for each restaurant position play a critical role in determining a pay range for each job—job titles are not enough. For example, the chef of a fine-dining restaurant has a different set of skills than one who is the chef of a catering company that serves two thousand meals at one sitting. While the title is the same, the skill sets are different; consequently, the pay range should be different. The pay range for each job must match the caliber of training and experience necessary to execute that job. Pay range must also rise as the standards of production and service rise.

Other Factors

While minimum wage, company standards, area pay scales, competitors' pay, and caliber of personnel are all important when determining pay ranges, there are other factors that can influence the final outcome. One of these factors is fringe benefits. A restaurant that has an extensive fringe program could have a lower pay range than an operation that offers little or no benefits. Many employees will work for less money if, for example, a company-paid health insurance plan is in effect. Another factor can be location. An operation that is not near public transportation may have to pay more than one that is close. In the case of a downtown restaurant, for example, pay considerations for an employee would be affected by whether the employee has to pay for parking or whether parking is free or provided. These, and other factors, will influence compensation ranges.

Think About It...

Unfairness can take many forms in a business. It is one of the most destructive activities in a business. What does a manager need to do to ensure an organization is a fair, pleasant, and successful place to work?

Collective Bargaining Agreements

In some cases, a union will represent employees in a foodservice operation. When this is the case, a team representing management and a team representing labor will negotiate the pay scale for each job. In all likelihood, they will follow the same format or process previously described to come to an agreement. When the negotiators reach a consensus, the union members then vote on the contract. If the contract is agreed to by both management and labor, the pay ranges, along with other working conditions, become a binding contract or a **collective bargaining agreement.**

Putting It All Together

There is no "one size fits all" when it comes to determining pay scale ranges. Even chain operations have different pay scales for varying parts of the country. All of the factors discussed here must be considered before a policy is established. When the pay range is established, it must be fair for all concerned: fair for the employer and the employee.

After pay ranges are developed, most organizations will review its compensation guidelines annually. Inflation, changes in the marketplace, and economic forces can all affect an employee's pay scale. By reviewing these on an annual basis, the restaurant will stay current with competitors and retain satisfied employees.

Think About It...

Some people think that merit pay focuses on politics and patronage rather than performance. Do you think this viewpoint is valid? How would you argue for each side?

Merit Pay Policies and Guidelines

Merit pay plans are widely used by corporations, including those in the restaurant and foodservice industry. Although these plans may have different names, such as incentive or pay-for-performance, the objective is basically the same—to improve performance and increase productivity. The concept of merit pay is derived from a fundamental American ethic that workers should be paid on the basis of their skills and performance. Another underlying premise to this type of pay is that it is the best way to motivate workers.

Merit pay plans need to have guidelines created just like those for general wage and salary. Because merit pay is based on skills and performance, the need for creditable, comprehensive measures of performance are fundamental to any effective merit pay system. Without these, it becomes extremely difficult to relate pay to performance. Once these guidelines have been established, it is essential that you follow them consistently to ensure fairness and continued motivation.

Establishing and Administering Guidelines and Policies for Merit Increases

After pay ranges for each job have been developed, guidelines must be created as to how merit increases will be handled. The policies should provide for equitable compensation for all employees, including management. Factors to include in this policy are (see *Exhibit 4d*):

- Performance
- Current rate
- Accomplishments
- Business goals

Criteria should be developed for each of these factors. An employee, whether salaried or hourly, who meets or exceeds the criteria, should be granted some type of merit increase, as long as the increase is within the compensation range for that particular position.

Exhibit 4d

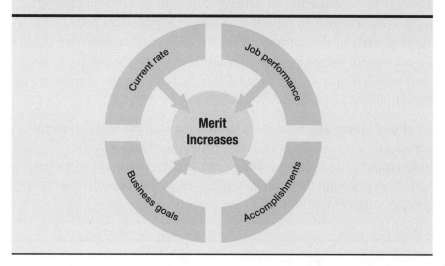

Factors to Consider in Merit Increases

Performance

Performance standards should be developed for each position. A **performance standard** is a criterion set by management that measures the quality and quantity of an employee's work. These standards should be tied into, and be made a part of, the employee's job description. Performance standards should be measurable and not subjective. They should measure the quantity and quality of the employee's work. For example, a server could be evaluated on the number of covers served per hour, along with the server's average sale per customer. This would measure the server's efficiency at turning tables and his or her sales ability. A line cook could also be measured by covers per hour, along with average time to turn out the meal. Rejects or returns could be measured to indicate the quality of work. Dishwashers could be measured by the number of racks completed per hour. Employees that meet or exceed the standard for their position should then be considered for a merit increase.

Other possible performance criteria that could be evaluated in addition to meeting the standards of quantity and quality include:

- Attendance
- Customer service
- Uniform cleanliness
- Attitude
- Being a team player

Think About It...

In a recent study, 46 percent of employees thought there was little connection between pay and performance. What can a manager do to ensure this perception does not occur?

Each criterion that is established can also be weighted in the performance evaluation. The purpose of weighting criteria is to indicate how critical or important that particular standard is to the performance of the organization.

With these established parameters in place, measuring performance can be a factor in merit increases for all employees.

Accomplishments

<table>
<tr><td>

Think About It...

Are you aware of guidelines for merit increases where you work? Do you know how they are administered? What is the attitude toward merit pay in your organization?

</td></tr>
</table>

Sometimes employees go "beyond the call of duty." In addition to meeting company standards, they do more. Some examples of accomplishments include a chef who wins a medal in a culinary competition, a server who organizes a food drive for the homeless, or a counter clerk who aids the police in apprehending a robbery suspect. These endeavors should be recognized. Assuming that the employee has met his or her standards and merits an increase in pay, consideration should be made for additional compensation for the employee's accomplishments. An employee who does his or her job well, and then does even more, is a valuable asset to the organization and should be paid accordingly.

Current Rate

Another factor to take into account is the employee's current rate of pay. Where an employee falls in the established pay range for his or her position should be considered, as well as where the employee stands in comparison with what the competition is paying. While this should not be a problem if the pay range was developed properly in the first place, it should still, however, be investigated.

Business Goals

Performance, accomplishments, and the current rate of pay all look at merit increases from an employee's perspective. Business goals look at merit increases from a company perspective. As previously stated, every restaurant or foodservice operation has, or should have, a payroll standard. This standard tells management how much money can be spent on labor. This number needs to be kept in mind when determining how much can be spent on merit increases. If the restaurant has had a good year and more money is available for payroll, the employees who are meeting or exceeding their job standards should be rewarded for helping the operation become successful. Conversely, if the restaurant has had a poor year, merit increases should be given sparingly to help bring the cost structure back into line.

Establishing Exceptions

As with most policies, there can be exceptions to the rule. In the case of compensation ranges, a common exception could arise when an employee does not receive a merit increase. This can occur for two reasons: the employee is at the top of his or her range, or the employee is not performing up to the company's standards. In the first case, you should consider that the employee might be at the top because he or she is a good employee. The employee could have been hired at the top of the range because of outstanding credentials, or the employee could have been with the organization for several years and received merit increases each year because of outstanding performance. Either way, the person is a valued employee and should be given an exception.

In the case of the employee not performing up to standard, you must decide whether the person should continue to work for the company or be terminated. If the decision is made to retain the employee, a development plan should be created that sets goals and time limits to bring the person up to standard performance. At the same time, if the employee has not had any increases recently, consideration should be given to granting him or her a cost of living increase.

The criteria set for merit increases based upon meeting standards and achieving goals should be administered fairly. The conditions should not be so stringent that no one can achieve them. Remember: the purpose of a merit increase is to retain valuable employees and encourage marginal employees to do better.

Management Compensation

While the emphasis in this section has been on managers evaluating hourly employees, the same factors go into assessing management. Managers should also be held accountable for achieving standards and attaining goals. For management, goals usually include responsibility for maintaining food and labor cost percentages and restaurant sales levels. These goals are either tied into the restaurant's budget or measured against last year's figures, or both. Quite often, additional criteria are established based on events particular to the operation. Some examples of additional criteria include lowering employee turnover, increasing the restaurant's image in the neighborhood, or developing a local marketing strategy. The major difference in merit increases between management and hourly employees is that management is often rewarded with a performance bonus rather than a merit increase.

Exhibit 4e

This manager is providing one of his chefs with an annual review.

Establish Regular Performance Review Cycles

While a few companies conduct performance reviews on a semi-annual or quarterly basis, for the most part, reviews are typically scheduled annually. These **performance review cycles** are meetings that are scheduled on a regular basis between the employee and employer to discuss the employee's job performance and additional pay, if any, for the coming year. (See *Exhibit 4e*.) Some organizations schedule them to coincide with the employee's anniversary date, while others perform this assignment once a year. Both of these methods have merits.

By conducting the performance review on the employee's anniversary date, the task is spread out over the year, with a few each month, resulting in a more thorough review due to less time constraints. When reviews are done all at once, it is usually in conjunction with the preparation of the annual budget. Knowing the dollar amount for increases and, therefore, the labor costs for the next year, is an important part of the budget process.

Regardless of timing, it is important that a schedule is established and followed. An integral part of the performance review should be discussing with the employee any merit increases they will or will not be receiving, along with the reasons for such action.

Maintaining Confidentiality of Payroll Information

It is imperative that payroll information be kept private and confidential. Rumors about pay can be devastating to employee morale and can even set up an "us" (employee) versus "them" (management) mentality.

Think About It...

If you are currently working in the foodservice industry, are you aware of the pay of other workers? If so, do you feel that you are being treated fairly with respect to other employees' pay? Why would it be important to keep this kind of information confidential?

The easiest way to avoid this pitfall is to restrict access to payroll information. The only people in the operation who should have access are management and the person writing the payroll checks. In larger operations, management could include more than one person. For example, a banquet chef in a large hotel could perform the performance review with a cook and recommend to the executive chef that an increase be given based on the cook's job performance. The executive chef would then talk with the food and beverage director, who would then take the recommendation to the general manager. All of these people need to keep payroll information confidential.

If an employee is in a position that requires him or her to know other employees' pay rates, he or she should be counseled to keep the information private. The person writing the payroll checks not only needs to keep this information private, but should also keep payroll records locked up. Because most record-keeping is accomplished using a computer, care needs to be taken that information is not displayed on a screen while anyone is walking by close enough to read it.

Each member of the staff should be counseled about keeping his or her own pay rate confidential. This should be discussed with each employee during orientation. Consequences of violating this policy—be it termination, probation, or some other penalty—should also be explained. Be sure to follow state and local regulations when determining policy-violation consequences. Confidentiality regarding payroll information should be part of the employee manual, and each employee should sign a document indicating acceptance of the policy.

Summary

Pay scales for each position in the foodservice operation should be set according to minimum wage laws, local pay scales, and competition. Three groups of people affect the issues surrounding compensation and pay: the employee, the restaurant owner, and the manager. The potential difficulty of dealing with this issue can be minimized by establishing valid procedures and processes that deal with compensation. Also, the manager needs to be able to examine other factors related to sales, the competition, and union contracts, if applicable, to fairly determine pay scales. Merit increase guidelines should also be set and based on established guidelines for performance. While position pay ranges should be available, specific employee payroll information should always be kept

Review Your Learning

1 A collective bargaining agreement is between

    A. an employee and the manager.

    B. a manager and a contract supplier.

    C. a group of employees and the company.

    D. a customer and a collection agency.

2 Since labor is a semivariable cost, when sales increase

    A. more hours can be added to the schedule.

    B. the pay scale for various positions can increase.

    C. Both A and B

    D. Neither A nor B

3 Which of these statements regarding the federal minimum wage law is *not* true?

    A. A server can be paid $2.13 an hour, providing his or her tips plus the $2.13 equals a minimum of $5.15.

    B. In states that have a minimum wage law that pays more than the federal law, the state law prevails.

    C. Student learners and the disabled are exempt from the minimum wage for a limited time.

    D. A restaurant with sales of $600,000 is exempt.

4 The key to establishing employee compensation policies is to

    A. pay employees the highest amount of money possible.

    B. establish fair pay scales.

    C. pay employees the least amount of money possible.

    D. keep pay scales secret.

5 In a restaurant, who should *not* have access to payroll information?

    A. Owner

    B. General manager

    C. Accountant

    D. All shift supervisors

Notes

_____

_____

_____

_____

_____

_____

_____

_____

_____

_____

_____

_____

_____

_____

_____

_____

_____

_____

_____

_____

_____

_____

_____

_____

_____

_____

Managing Terminations

Inside This Chapter

- Voluntary Termination
- Involuntary Terminations
- Conducting Involuntary Terminations
- Steps for Managing and Conducting Involuntary Terminations
- Defending Involuntary Terminations

After completing this chapter, you should be able to:

- Define voluntary termination, exit interview, unstructured exit interview, structured exit interview, involuntary termination, progressive disciplinary action, terminable acts, and Federal-State Unemployment Compensation Laws.

- Differentiate between voluntary and involuntary termination.

- Defend involuntary terminations.

- Explain the guidelines that apply to unemployment compensation laws.

Test Your Knowledge

1 **True or False:** An employee who consumes alcohol on the job is normally given a one- or two-day suspension. *(See p. 100.)*

2 **True or False:** One of the keys in an involuntary termination is the exit interview that identifies potential rehires. *(See p. 89.)*

3 **True or False:** An employee could be terminated immediately without a written report or probationary period for certain offenses. *(See p. 100.)*

4 **True or False:** The Federal-State Unemployment Insurance Program governs unemployment compensation laws. *(See p. 102.)*

5 **True or False:** Sales volume determines the tax rate for unemployment compensation for restaurants. *(See p. 102.)*

Key Terms

Exit interview

Federal-State Unemployment
   Compensation Laws

Involuntary termination

Progressive disciplinary action

Structured exit interview

Terminable acts

Unstructured exit interview

Voluntary termination

Introduction

Managing terminations is a difficult process that managers must handle. Termination comes in two forms, voluntary and involuntary. Voluntary termination, for the most part, is usually easier to handle and less controversial than involuntary termination, although both forms come with challenges. Policies and procedures must be in place in order to handle terminations effectively.

Voluntary Termination

Voluntary termination occurs when an employee, of his or her own free will, decides to leave an organization. This occurs for one of many reasons, such as a change in career, a better position with more pay in another organization, retirement, starting a family, leaving the area, or returning to school. Voluntary termination is often a bittersweet moment. While management is happy for the employee, at the same time they are losing a valuable member of the team. There are only a few things that management needs to do when an employee leaves voluntarily, but they are nonetheless important. They are:

■ Conduct an exit interview.

■ Identify the candidate for rehire.

■ Retrieve company property.

Exit Interviews

Retaining employees has been a key issue in the restaurant and foodservice industry for many years. When an employee chooses to leave, an exit interview can help the organization learn any concerns the person has, reasons for leaving, and areas in which the company can improve. An **exit interview** is a meeting between the employer and employee when the employee leaves the company. (See *Exhibit 5a*.) It is important to conduct an exit interview for a number of reasons, including:

Exhibit 5a

Every employee choosing to leave the organization should have an exit interview.

■ Determining the real reason an employee is leaving and trying to retain a desirable employee whenever possible

■ Discovering any grievances the employee may have regarding work conditions so that corrective action can be taken

■ Retaining the goodwill of the employee, his or her family, and friends toward the organization

■ Discovering any misunderstandings the employee may have had regarding his or her supervisor

■ Determining whether there is a way to salvage the employment relationship

As you gather information from the interview, the data can be helpful in many ways:

- Reducing turnover

- Developing practices that will improve employees' work experiences

- Identifying any employee-relation or legal concerns

- Assisting a specific manager with developmental needs

- Improving the effectiveness of general management practices

- Identifying and addressing any detrimental patterns in the organization

An exit interview can point out unknown problems and opportunities to management. Consider that employees often are apprehensive to come to a supervisor with complaints, observations, or concerns. Someone who is leaving the company has nothing to lose and is therefore more likely to open up to management. The employee's comments could offer insight into things such as unpopular company procedures, insufficient pay scales, inadequate working conditions, dissatisfaction with other employees, theft, favoritism, etc.

Keep in mind during the interview that if the departing employee does not like a situation or policy, then many of the other employees probably do not like it either. While some observations may or may not be warranted, management needs to listen carefully. You need to ascertain which comments need to be addressed quickly. Properly conducted, an exit interview can be a powerful tool for management that provides insight into the organizational culture they would not otherwise have.

On the other hand, some exit interviews could be just the opposite. The departing employee could have been happy working at the organization and could have few, if any, complaints.

Conducting an Exit Interview

Although there are several methods that can be used to conduct an exit interview, the most effective methods are unstructured interviews or structured interviews. An **unstructured exit interview** is a conversation without prepared questions. Although the interview has a purpose, it is free flowing. The advantage of this type of interview is that it allows for spontaneous responses to questions the interviewer asks. On the other hand, a **structured exit interview** uses a definite format that involves a set of questions to chart the employee's response. The advantage to this type of interview is that it follows a prescribed format while allowing for open-ended questions and answers.

There are four types of questions that can be used in an exit interview. The following list briefly describes them:

Exhibit 5b

Sample Exit Interview Questions

Listed below are samples of the types of exit interview questions that employers commonly ask departing employees

Open-Ended Questions
- What would you improve to make this company's workplace better?
- What could your immediate supervisor do to improve his or her management style?
- Based on your experience with us, what do you think it takes to succeed at this company?
- How do you generally feel about this company?
- What does your new company offer that this one does not?

Close-Ended Questions
- Did you receive sufficient feedback about your performance between merit reviews?
- Were you satisfied with this company's merit review process?
- Can this company do anything to encourage you to stay?
- Before deciding to leave, did you investigate a transfer within the company?
- Did anyone in this company discriminate against you, harass you, or cause hostile working conditions?

Multiple-Choice Questions
U = Unsatisfactory F = Fair S = Satisfactory G = Good E = Excellent
- Pay levels at this company were generally _____
- The amount of training I received when I first came here was _____
- The extent to which I had the opportunity to use or develop my potential was_____
- The level of cooperation among the employees in my department was _____
- Generally speaking, I would rate this company as _____ to work for
- The level of concern for employees here was _____
- As compared to other companies, our benefit package was_____

Written Questions
- What did you like most about working here?
- What did you like least about working here?
- What are your suggestions for improving this company as a place to work?
- Any other additional comments?

- **Open-ended**—Questions that ask for more than a one-word response. These questions are more conversational and allow for free expression of ideas.

- **Close-ended**—Questions in which there are only short answer responses or only two possible answers (yes or no).

- **Multiple-choice**—Questions formatted so the employee chooses the closest answer to his or her feelings or thoughts from a set of responses.

- **Written**—Questions that incorporate several concepts or ideas, or require the employee to describe his or her opinion and suggestions in a concise written form.

In most cases, an organization will establish some mixture of structured and unstructured exit interviews. (See *Exhibit 5b.*)

It is the responsibility of the interviewer to be a genuine listener and honestly encourage the employee to share his or her opinions. The person who is responsible for the exit interview is almost as important as the interview itself. If the employee feels uncomfortable with the person administering the interview, he or she will not be completely honest. It might be a good idea to provide the employee some options as to who will conduct the interview. The interview should also be in a neutral location in which the employee feels safe and able to provide honest responses. The interview should happen shortly after notice of the employee's resignation so that the employee does not feel overlooked and is more willing to provide valuable responses. It is important that, prior to the interview, the employee is aware that the company maintains a policy of exit interviews "for internal use only."

The employee must also be notified that all information obtained from the exit interview will remain private and secure with the interviewer and those in management. At the completion of the interview, always allow the employee to offer any additional input that may not have been covered in the questions. (See *Exhibit 5c.*)

Identifying Candidates for Rehire

Employees who leave, particularly those who leave on a positive note, are excellent candidates to rehire. Keep in mind that they are trained, know company procedures, and can come back ready to go to work. It is very important that management document the exit interview and their opinions as to whether the employee is a candidate for rehire. Conversely, if the employee was marginal, this should be noted as well. Management, like staff, turn over due to promotions or other opportunities. Documented records help the succeeding management team make intelligent decisions.

Retrieving Company Property

An important component of any termination, either voluntary or involuntary, is to retrieve company property. This includes such things as keys, tools, uniforms, or corporate identification. A procedure should be established in any foodservice operation that documents what property is in the possession of an employee. This documentation should be included in the employee's personnel file. Upon termination, all property should be returned. Many companies have a policy of not issuing the final paycheck until all company materials have been returned. (You must confirm that this action is within the guidelines of your state's laws regarding final pay before making such a policy.)

Involuntary Terminations

Involuntary termination is a situation in which management must terminate an employee for one of four reasons, including lack of work for the individual, lack of funding, unsatisfactory performance, or violating a company policy. Management determines that, for the well-being of the organization, an employee must leave. This decision should be made only after thorough consideration of the facts and circumstances. Prior to an employee being terminated, effort should be made to make that person a productive member of the team or to find another position for him or her.

Exhibit 5c

Sample Exit Interview Form

EMPLOYEE EXIT INTERVIEW

1 Why did you initially seek and accept a position with our organization?
- ■ Compensation
- ■ Career change
- ■ Fringe benefits
- ■ Job responsibilities
- ■ Location
- ■ Schedule
- ■ Reputation of the organization
- ■ Other

2 What is your primary reason for leaving?
- ■ Compensation
- ■ Career change
- ■ Fringe benefits
- ■ Job responsibilities
- ■ Location
- ■ Other
- ■ Reputation of the organization

3–8 For each question below, please rate your level of satisfaction by marking the appropriate number
(1 = Very unsatisfied, 2 = unsatisfied, 3 = Somewhat satisfied, 4 = Satisfied, 5 = Highly satisfied)

3 Task completion (the degree to which the job required completion of a whole piece of work vs. small parts) ① ② ③ ④ ⑤

4 Skill variety (the degree to which the job required a variety of activities utilizing a variety of skills and talents) ① ② ③ ④ ⑤

5 Autonomy (job provided enough freedom and independence in doing tasks) ① ② ③ ④ ⑤

6 Task significance (the degree to which the job had a substantial impact on the work of other people or the organization) ① ② ③ ④ ⑤

7 Feedback (individual was given direct and clear information about the effectiveness of their performance) ① ② ③ ④ ⑤

8 What was your level of satisfaction about your experience with the organization? ① ② ③ ④ ⑤

9 What did you find to be least satisfying and enjoyable about your experience with the organization?

_____
_____
_____
_____
_____

10 Do you think you were treated fairly on your performance review? ☐ Yes ☐ No

11 Were there appropriate opportunities for advancement? ☐ Yes ☐ No

12 Is there any other constructive feedback you would like to provide toward improving the effectiveness of the organization as an employer? ☐ Yes ☐ No

A manager should keep in mind the organization made an investment in the employee that would be lost upon termination. Also, there could be significant costs associated with recruiting, hiring, and training a new employee.

Lack of Work or Funding

If an employee is facing a layoff because of lack of work or lack of funding, the organization should attempt to find suitable employment for the person within the organization. If the organization is large enough, the human resources department should assist in finding the employee an opportunity that matches his or her skills.

Unsatisfactory Performance or Violation of Company Policy

Prior to initiating the procedures for termination, the manager and a human resources representative (if applicable), should confer with the employee to identify performance deficiencies and to find ways to improve. Most companies will then provide the employee an opportunity to improve his or her performance. If a skills mismatch has been identified, the employee may be offered to be transferred to a new position. If, however, after repeated warnings and coaching, an employee's performance continues to be unsatisfactory, termination procedures should be initiated.

When an employee violates company policy many times, immediate termination is warranted. Sample policy violations include:

- Possession of drugs (controlled substances)
- Being under the influence of alcohol or drugs during work periods
- Discriminatory or harassing behavior
- Inappropriate conduct toward peers or customers
- Conduct detrimental to the company's image either on or off the job

Conducting Involuntary Terminations

While voluntary terminations are, for the most part, relatively pleasant, involuntary terminations typically are not. In some cases, the employee has violated a company policy, and in other cases, a person has not produced the quality or quantity of work expected.

Quite often, a terminated employee will file for unemployment compensation and, in rare cases, will sue the company. Because of this, every restaurant or foodservice organization should have a written procedure in place regarding terminations. These procedures should support a legal defense in the event a former employee either files for unemployment compensation or sues the company.

These procedures should include:

- Job descriptions and standards
- Management practices for addressing poor performance
- Establishing guidelines for issuing verbal or written warnings
- Time frames
- Training supervisors for consistency in implementing disciplinary action
- Coaching employees

Job Descriptions and Standards

As discussed previously, meeting or exceeding company standards is an integral part of granting employee pay increases. Performance to standards is equally important when disciplining an employee for not producing an adequate quantity or quality of work. There should be a written job description for each position filled by an employee in the restaurant. Among other things, the job description should include standards for that job. The standards should be objective and measurable. All employees should be evaluated on adhering to the requirements of the job description and their output as compared to the standards. Without job descriptions and standards, management does not have any justification when disciplining or terminating employees for poor or substandard performance.

Management Practices for Addressing Poor Performance

When disciplining an employee for inadequate job performance, it should be progressive in nature, which means it should be positive. Every effort should be made to assist that employee in achieving success. **Progressive disciplinary action** is a process that assists the employee in improving his or her performance, and bringing it up to standards to avoid termination procedures. Does the employee need to be retrained? Will coaching by a peer be beneficial? Would an additional tool or piece of equipment help? Does the person have the aptitude to perform the job? Would he or she benefit from a transfer to another department? These are the types of questions a manager should ask before resorting to termination procedures.

The objectives of progressive discipline are:

- Avoid or minimize misunderstandings between the employee and the manager.

- Ensure the employee is provided specific evidence of unacceptable performance, guidelines for improvement, and sufficient time and opportunity to improve.

- Reduce the number of situations that result in involuntary terminations.

- Ensure that documentation is available to support the organization's position in the event the employee later brings a complaint.

When discussing performance with the employee, there should be a dialogue, not a one-way conversation. The outcome of this dialogue should be a program designed to bring the person's performance up to standard. The first step in the process is to discuss the problem informally and directly with the employee. The discussion or dialogue should cover the following:

- Identification of the problem and its apparent causes

- Employee's role in solving the problem

- Specific actions to be taken by the employee and the manager

- Timetable for assessing progress

- Specific disciplinary action that will occur if the employee's performance does not improve

If these steps are initiated by the manager, further action usually is not necessary.

A manager should also keep a record on file of all formal or informal discussions with the employee, by using a form like the one shown in *Exhibit 5d*. The records should include:

- Date the conversation took place and individuals involved

- Nature of the problem in specific detail

- Corrective action agreed to by the employee and manager

- Date for follow-up and progress report completion

When a performance situation becomes more serious, the manager must take more formal action. These actions should include documenting additional meetings with the employee, imposing a probationary period, or proceeding with the process of involuntary termination.

Exhibit 5d

Council and Feedback Form

Counsel and FeedBack Report

Employee ———————————— Position ————
Store/Location ————————————————————
Supervisor ———————————— Date ————

Copies to: General Manager, Personnel File

The following serves as written documentation to the above employee for the incident(s) described below.

CURRENT INCIDENTS
Describe the situation (behavior, performance, policy violation, etc.) that occurred. Include date(s), time(s), location(s), people involved, witness, effects of the incident on the staff member's work or other staff members, and all other relevant circumstances or contributing factors. Please provide specific examples, whenever possible.

PREVIOUS INCIDENT(S) CORRECTIVE ACTIONS
List type of action (verbal warning, written warning, etc.), offense, and date for any previous incident.

GOALS AND TIMEFRAME FOR IMPROVEMENT
What specific actions—within what timeframe—are to be accomplished to improve behavior or performance? Within five (5) working days, supervisor and staff must jointly submit a personal development plan to address each of the crucial areas. This plan may be submitted under separate cover.

CONSEQUENCES
What will happen if the staff member fails to meet the goals set within the designated timeframe?

PLANNED FOLLOW-UP REVIEW DATE(S)
After each follow-up meeting, the supervisor provides a written summary to the employee and HR.

Counsel and FeedBack Report

FOLLOW-UP COMMENTS
The supervisor summarizes the employee's progress and determine if he or she is in good standing, or if further disciplinary action is required.

Date ————————————
Comments ————————————————

STAFF MEMBER'S COMMENTS (Attach additional pages if needed.)
The employee may submit a response within five (5) business days.

————————————————————
————————————————————
————————————————————
————————————————————
————————————————————
————————————————————

Supervisor's signature ———————— Date ————
Division/Department head signature ———— Date ————
*Staff member's signature ———————— Date ————
Human Resources signature ———————— Date ————

*Staff member's signature, with date, indicates the employee met with the supervisor indicated to discuss the incidents cited; it does not necessarily signify that the employee agrees with the Counsel and FeedBack report. In addition, this form does not alter the "at will" employment relationship in any way.

Establishing Guidelines for Issuing Verbal or Written Warnings

When an employee does not measure up to expected standards for behavior or comply with company policy, discipline may be warranted. Based on the severity of the situation, discipline can range from a warning to immediate dismissal. Quite often, a verbal warning is all that is needed to bring the worker up to standard. A discussion could clarify a misunderstanding between the employee and management, or it could result in management giving assistance to the worker to improve the quality or quantity of his or her work.

One example of this type situation might be an employee with an untidy, dirty uniform, or another who chews gum in the front of the house.

Some situations may require the manager to sit down with the employee and present the performance issue in writing. This should be done privately in the manager's office. The written report acts as documentation and should include the date and time of the meeting, a clear definition of the problem, a comparison description of the employee's behavior against the standard or expected behavior, a plan of action to improve the performance or solve the problem, the expected outcome in terms of quantifiable results, and a deadline for achieving those results.

The report should be reviewed with the employee. The employee should have the opportunity to express his or her thoughts in writing regarding the report. The report should then be signed and dated by both the employee and the manager and placed in the employee's personnel file. Examples of behavior that could result in a written warning are excessive absenteeism or failure to follow a manager's instructions.

If the behavior or policy violation makes it necessary to immediately terminate the employee, the termination process should be documented.

There are some employers who use a progressive discipline process to discipline employees for inappropriate behavior or failing to comply with company policies. At these companies, the disciplinary process consists of a series of steps that includes verbal warnings, written warnings, and final warnings prior to termination. For the first violation, an employee is issued a verbal warning. For the second violation, the employee moves to the next step and is issued a written warning. Any additional violation results in a final warning being issued. Once a final warning has been issued, any further violation leads to termination. The manner in which these warnings are issued is the same as described in the previous sections. The difference is that in the process described previously, a manager has the discretion to determine the appropriate type of discipline to administer, rather than being required to follow a progressive step-by-step scenario.

Time Frames

In addition to covering what needs to be done to meet standards with the employee, there needs to be an amount of time given to achieve this. This time frame must be reasonable. It should give adequate time for the employee to overcome the deficiency, but at the same time should not allow the foodservice operation to

Think About It...

How does the knowledge that a job may not be a permanent situation affect an employee—mentally, financially, and socially? How does this fact impact workers as they age? Are employers skeptical of an employee who has been terminated elsewhere?

suffer. Management has to walk a fine line regarding how long they are going to allow a part of the operation to be substandard. For example, the problem of a line cook who continually takes too long to turn out orders would have to be corrected more quickly than one server who is slow in turning tables. The line cook affects the whole operation, while the server affects one station. While both employees bring down the overall performance of the restaurant, one issue is more serious than the other.

Training Supervisors for Consistency in Implementing Disciplinary Action

All workplace rules and standards must be clearly written and comply with legal standards. For example, there cannot be one set of rules for an older worker and a different set for younger workers, nor can there be one set for males and another for females. In addition, management must be consistent in applying those rules. One manager cannot loosely interpret them while another manager enforces them to the letter. Achievable and measurable goals, rules, and standards are easier to enforce consistently than are ones that are not quantifiable. Training a manager regarding the expected outcome of company standards makes the job of consistent applications easier.

Coaching Employees

Think About It...

In today's business world, being unemployed at some point is not as uncommon as it used to be. Have you either experienced it yourself or known someone who has filed for unemployment compensation? What was the process? How were you or the person treated? Could the process be improved in some way?

When an employee fails to meet company standards and has been notified by his or her manager in writing on exactly what needs to be done to meet the standards, the job of coaching has begun. As a manager and coach, you need to work with that employee. You should find out why the employee does not meet the standards, and then assist the employee in finding a solution. You should also be available as the employee tries to implement the solution.

For example, a salad prep person working in a large employee cafeteria kitchen fails to deliver the salads to the cafeteria line on time. In working with this person, the manager notices that he or she is chopping large quantities of celery, onions, and green peppers by hand. The manager inquires as to why the employee does not use the cutter-mixer. The manager finds out that the employee does not know how to use it, and is fearful of the sharp blades. The manager instructs the employee in the safe use and cleaning of the machine, and eases the employee's fear of operating it. The time saved by using this equipment solves the problem of late-arriving salads and the unsatisfactory performance has been eliminated.

Punishable and Terminable Acts

Terminable acts are actions by an employee that typically cause immediate termination. These behaviors usually justify discharge without going through any progressive disciplinary process. They include:

- Disruptive or destructive behavior
- Insubordination
- Theft of organizational property or funds
- Harassment
- Alcohol or drug abuse

Some foodservice operations may have other violations to add to the list. All terminable acts, however, should be explained in writing and be part of the employee handbook. Employees should agree to abide by the conditions and be required to sign a document showing agreement. As with any worker dispute, violations of company policy should be documented in writing and kept on file in case of legal proceedings later.

Steps for Managing and Conducting Involuntary Terminations

The procedure to follow for involuntary termination is:

1. In the case of lack of work or funding, every effort should be made to find suitable work within the organization for the employee. If work cannot be identified, the employee should be given notice.

2. In the case of unsatisfactory performance or behavior, positive disciplinary action should include the following steps:

   - Conduct an informal discussion with the employee identifying the performance problem.
   - Identify ways to improve performance.
   - Coach the employee on performance.
   - Continue with additional meetings and discussions as needed.
   - If no improvement occurs after efforts and time have been exhausted, involuntary termination procedures should be implemented.

3. Document the performance issues. If you have a human resources department, work with them to handle terminations properly. Check with either your manager or human resources on established guidelines for documenting the process.

4. Conduct a meeting to formally terminate the person.

5. Arrange for someone to supervise the person as he or she removes personal items from the operation.

6. Have the person turn over any company property.

7. Escort the person out of the building.

Notification Guidelines

In some instances, it is inevitable that an organization has to let an employee go due to lack of work or funding to support their continued work. In these instances, employees appreciate the opportunity to plan for their unemployment. Knowing how long they have before their current employment will expire gives them an opportunity to find employment, and hopefully reduces the risk of having a period where they are without income. An organization should have guidelines and/or policies that cover the factors affecting employees who are involuntarily terminated, as well as a notification process to be followed in these situations.

Notification process guidelines are intended to assist managers in preparing for job terminations and in communicating these preparations to the affected employees. In cases of involuntary termination, managers should monitor and review their staffing and work needs on a regular basis so affected employees can be given adequate notice. This process is outlined in *Exhibit 5e*.

Guidelines for the notice period typically relate to an employee's length of service with the organization. Some general guidelines are:

- Ten to twelve weeks of notice for eight or more years

- Four weeks of notice for less than eight years but more than one year

- Two weeks of notice for more than six months but less than one year

- No notice period for employees with less than six months

Exhibit 5e

Notification Process for Involuntary Terminations

1. Monitor and review staffing needs.

2. Examine skills and length of service of possible terminated employees.

3. Attempt to locate other employment or provide additional training for the worker.

4. Make termination decisions.

5. Communicate termination decision in writing.

6. Identify amount of notice being provided.

7. Set expectation for remainder of employee's performance.

Defending Involuntary Terminations

There are unemployment compensation laws to follow and actions to take to help defend the operation when involuntary terminations go awry. This section, however, is not intended as legal advice. When confronted with legal action, managers should always seek an attorney's legal counsel.

Unemployment Compensation Laws

Unemployment compensation provides benefits and money to workers who become unemployed through no fault of their own. The **Federal–State Unemployment Compensation Laws** govern unemployment compensation. This joint federal and state program is administered at the state level, following federal guidelines. While there are many similarities between the states, there are differences as well. The guidelines given below apply to most, but not all, states. Exact requirements for your location can be obtained from your state government.

- Benefits to recipients are based on a percentage of an individual's earnings over a fifty-two-week period, up to a maximum amount determined by the state.

- Benefits can be paid for a maximum of twenty-six weeks in most states.

- Recipients must be unemployed through no fault of their own as determined by state law and must meet the eligibility requirement as determined by state law.

- Recipients have the right to appeal if they are denied benefits.

- Employers have an assigned tax rate based on their average annual taxable payroll, unemployment claims against their account, and taxes previously paid.

- If an employer has been at the maximum rate for two consecutive years, a surcharge can be added to the rate.

While these guidelines are by no means a complete summation of the law, there are two items that every manager should know: the definition of eligibility and the assigned tax rate.

As part of the definition of eligibility, potential recipients must be unemployed through no fault of their own. In many states, this is a grey area. What constitutes "no fault of their own" can be open to interpretation. When an employee files for unemployment compensation, the state agency gathers information from the

Activity

The Case of the Drinking Cook

You are the owner and manager of a restaurant and lounge in a small midwestern town. Your place is known for good food and service. You credit your staff for much of the restaurant's success. One of your line cooks is particularly good and he consistently turns out meals quickly and accurately. He has a quick wit and gets along well with the waitstaff. His only fault is that he is sometimes late and has missed work on occasion because of a drinking problem. You have talked to him about his lateness and he has promised to do better.

After work one evening, he stops by a pub and stays too long. On the way home, he broadsides a parked, unoccupied police car. Thankfully, no one is injured; however, the incident makes the local paper. The name of your restaurant is mentioned prominently in the article. The day he returns to work, you terminate him.

1 Was termination the correct response? Why or why not?

_____

_____

_____

_____

2 How much control should a restaurant have over its employees' off-duty activities?

_____

_____

_____

_____

3 What is an employee's responsibility to his or her employer?

_____

_____

_____

_____

4 Could this situation have been prevented? If so, how?

_____

_____

_____

_____

employee and the employer and determines whether the employee is entitled to compensation. As stated previously, every action taken by management regarding an employee who does not meet the company's standard should be put in writing and signed by both the employee and management. When presenting or appealing its case, management can use the written documents to reinforce its position. Either side can appeal the decision.

Documentation is also important for assigning a tax rate because, in most states, the rate is based on the number of claims a business has against its account. The more claims, the higher the rate. By working with employees and coaching them, there will be fewer terminations. By documenting everything in writing, there will be fewer claims against the business.

Summary

Of the two types of terminations, involuntary and voluntary, voluntary termination is the easiest to administer. Involuntary termination should be used as a last resort. Establishing guidelines for managers to follow when handling involuntary terminations is essential. Documenting the process that was used to bring the employee up to expected standards is a necessary precaution in case legal action is taken by the employee. Part of the process includes counseling and retraining the employee so that his or her performance can meet the company standard. All meetings regarding an employee's performance should be documented.

Activity

Role-Playing in a College Foodservice Department

You will be participating in two role-play situations. In one, you will play the role of a manager of a college foodservice operation, and in the other you will be the employee. Choose a partner to role-play with you. As the manager, select one of the scenarios below and plan how you will conduct the meeting between you and the employee. Consider how the employee might react and what your response would be to that reaction. Each scenario should take from three to five minutes. After each role play, share your thoughts, feeling, and insights with either the class or your partner.

Scenario 1:	Scenario 2:	Scenario 3:	Scenario 4:
The employee is being put on probation because he or she is slow at busing tables.	The manager must terminate an employee, who was seen stealing on camera.	A student has complained that the employee swore at him because he did not have money ready and the line got backed up.	The manager must inform the employee that he or she has to stop breaking dishes or be terminated.

1 Employee: How did you feel when the manager informed you of the situation?

_____
_____
_____
_____
_____

2 Employee: How could the manager have improved the initial communication of the situation?

_____
_____
_____
_____
_____

3 Manager: What might you have done differently to get a better reaction to the situation?

_____
_____
_____
_____
_____

4 Manager: Did you feel the employee was justified in his or her reaction to your message?

_____
_____
_____
_____

Review Your Learning

1 A sufficient time to give an employee to correct a deficiency is

A. a week.

B. three weeks.

C. a month.

D. None of the above

2 Unemployment compensation is based on

A. state law and federal guidelines.

B. state guidelines and federal law.

C. state law.

D. federal law.

3 An exit interview is conducted between a

A. manager and a disgruntled customer.

B. manager and an employee who is leaving the company.

C. host/hostess and a disgruntled customer.

D. chef and a cook who are leaving for the day.

4 Regarding termination,

A. voluntary is more difficult to handle.

B. involuntary is more difficult to handle.

C. both voluntary and involuntary are difficult to handle.

D. either voluntary or involuntary are difficult to handle.

5 Retrieving company property is a key component of (an)

A. voluntary termination.

B. involuntary termination.

C. Both A and B

D. Neither A nor B

Motivation and Employee Development

6

Inside This Chapter

- Motivating Employees
- Building a Positive Work Climate
- Mutually Respectful Workplaces
- Interpersonal Communication
- Conflict Resolution
- Employee Performance Appraisals
- Delegation

After completing this chapter, you should be able to:

- Define motivation, satisfiers, motivators, favoritism, nepotism, interpersonal communication, performance appraisal process, delegation, empathy, conflict resolution, mediation, arbitration, affection, control, inclusion, motivation, self-disclosure, work styles, respectful workplace, sexual harassment, and standard.

- Explain methods of motivating employees.

- Identify common expectations that employees have about managers.

- Explain challenges in motivating employees.

- Identify ways to create a positive work environment.

- Explain the importance of setting a positive example for employees' motivation.

- Identify and demonstrate relationship building skills.

- Describe guidelines and processes for a harassment-free work environment.

- Identify steps in handling conflict resolution with employees.

- Explain and conduct an employee performance appraisal.

- Explain how to delegate responsibilities to an employee.

- Determine appropriate tasks to delegate.

Test Your Knowledge

1. **True or False:** Employees' main concern is their paycheck. *(See p. 110.)*

2. **True or False:** Motivation is the characteristics and personality traits of employees. *(See p. 109.)*

3. **True or False:** Making job tasks interesting is a motivating factor. *(See pp. 110–111.)*

4. **True or False:** Empowering employees to make decisions serves as a motivator. *(See pp. 110–111.)*

5. **True or False:** Time does not affect a manager's ability to build relationships. *(See p. 115.)*

6. **True or False:** One criterion for delegating tasks to employees is to select specific tasks based on skills. *(See p. 140.)*

7. **True or False:** Collaboration in resolving conflicts creates a win-win situation. *(See p. 130.)*

8. **True or False:** Performance appraisals are the builders of performance improvement. *(See p. 135.)*

9. **True or False:** Identifying employee satisfiers will motivate employees in the long term. *(See pp. 110–111.)*

Key Terms

Affection	Inclusion	Personal treatment
Arbitration	Interpersonal communication	Professionalism
Conflict resolution	Mediation	Satisfiers
Control	Motivation	Self-disclosure
Delegation	Motivators	Sexual harassment
Empathy	Negotiation	Standard
Favoritism	Nepotism	Work styles

Introduction

One of the greatest challenges a manager faces today is how to motivate employees. The challenge becomes more severe when an industry tends to have high turnover and an extremely fast-paced environment that caters to high customer satisfaction. Most effective foodservice managers know that the success their organization has achieved would not have been possible if not for the efforts of their staff. What do these managers know that many do not? How do these managers get higher levels of performance from their employees than others can?

Exhibit 6a

Motivational Spectrum

Although operational competence is important for today's foodservice manager, ultimately, understanding the people side of management is critical to higher organizational results.

In this chapter, you will learn about the relationship between employee expectations of managers and motivational techniques. Occasionally, even the most effective manager will have to deal with trying situations that will test the application of accepted motivational theories. This chapter examines some of the challenges to applying motivational theory to the restaurant and foodservice industry. Numerous methods that can be used to create a positive, motivating work environment will be examined. The role that interpersonal communication plays in building and supporting a high-performance work environment will also be reviewed. In today's business world, no workplace is free from conflict. Extending the concept of respectful workplaces, this chapter investigates how to handle conflict resolution situations.

Finally, employee performance appraisals and employee development will be examined. Factors that influence an employee's interest in his or her own development as well as the advantages of an employee being involved in goal setting are explored. The appraisal can lead to identifying tasks that can be delegated to employees. Delegation is the number one tool a manager can use to accomplish all of the many organizational goals that are planned. In fact, the inability to delegate to staff is a leading cause of manager failure. This chapter will examine the delegation process and ways to determine if an employee is ready for delegated tasks.

Motivating Employees

The traditional definition of **motivation** is "those factors that cause a person to behave or act in either a goal-seeking or satisfying manner and may be influenced by physiological drives or by external stimuli." Motivation is basically the incentive to get people in motion or get them moving in the right direction.

High motivation usually occurs when there is either a great chance for advancement for the employee or the possibility of punishment. (See *Exhibit 6a.*) Most job-related activities occur in the middle area between these edges of the spectrum. This area tends to provide little motivation, and the perception of the work situation is also considered neutral at best for most employees. In other words, the employee does not perceive his or her work as favorable or unfavorable. In some cases, the employee simply does not care about the work opportunity. In addition, an element that drives

Think About It...

The manager acts somewhat as the employee's mother or father, as he or she "encourages and threatens."

How can you apply this to management situations you will encounter?

employee motivation is how employees perceive the manager's communication. Motivating employees provides an interesting challenge to managers because different things motivate different employees.

Employees are motivated basically by two categories of factors. These factors are classified as hygiene factors and satisfiers. Hygiene factors are often referred to as maintenance factors because employees must perform a job only at a minimal level. Factors that can be classified as hygiene factors are:

- Money

- Benefits

- Work conditions

Exhibit 6b

Motivational Methods Chart

Create a sense of engagement in the employee.	■ Find out what is important to each employee. ■ Find out the type of working style each employee has. ■ Explain the role each employee plays in achieving goals. ■ Make job tasks more interesting by giving more responsibility for multiple tasks.
Model appropriate professional behavior.	■ Take time to meet and listen to your staff. ■ Use proper operational procedures. ■ Demonstrate collaboration and teamwork with staff. ■ Be enthusiastic. ■ Get all the facts and remain nonjudgmental when employee conflict occurs. ■ Do not intimidate staff in meetings.
Keep a positive attitude.	■ When a customer is difficult, maintain a pleasant demeanor during and after the encounter. ■ When your sales goals are not being met, get staff input and think of creative ways to increase sales. ■ Be energetic and passionate about work and the business.
Treat employees with respect.	■ Use please and thank you. ■ Ask them what they think. ■ "Do unto others as you would have them do unto you."
Treat employees fairly and equitably.	■ Nothing is as unfair as the equal treatment of unequal performers, and there is nothing fair about the unequal treatment of equal performers. ■ Give employees opportunities to grow and learn new skills. ■ Apply organizational policy consistently; that is, if pay is docked for lateness, then it applies to everyone.
Get to know your staff.	■ Ask employees about their backgrounds. ■ Learn about their families.

However, simply providing employees with more hygiene factors does not usually motivate them to work harder. To motivate an employee, a manager needs to target satisfiers, or motivators, which are factors that incite an employee to put out more effort and enthusiasm for his or her job. Employees want to carve out a role for themselves and use all of their creative resources to work in unison with others. Learning to motivate others to the point in which they can feel this same kind of exhilaration for a job well done is part of being an effective manager. Although the best motivation is self motivation, a manager needs to discover ways that will provide a work environment that encourages self motivation and freedom to perform well.

Exhibit 6b provides several examples of ways that managers can encourage employees to excel at their jobs. The ultimate consequence

Encourage open feedback.	■ Keep an open door policy.
	■ Ask for feedback.
	■ Do not react negatively if someone does not agree with you.
	■ Encourage new ideas and suggestions.
	■ Learn from mistakes instead of punishing staff for them.
Encourage employee involvement and inclusion.	■ Create team challenges.
	■ Include employees in their own goal setting.
	■ Involve employees in decisions that affect them.
	■ Provide staff with a sense of ownership of their work and workspace.
Communicate regularly.	■ Give timely updates.
	■ If a learning opportunity is present, communicate it immediately to the employee.
	■ Provide information on how the organization makes and loses money.
	■ Explain the employee's role in overall plans for upcoming products and services.
	■ Give employees praise for exceptional performance.
Share operations and industry knowledge.	■ Share information from conferences and courses you have attended.
	■ Leave industry magazines in the staff room.
Empower employees.	■ Do not micromanage.
	■ Identify staff who are eager to accept responsibility and delegate various tasks to them.
	■ Allow your staff to do great work by applying their personal creativity to solving problems.
Identify factors that motivate each employee.	■ What is a reward and incentive for one person is not for another—ask the employees what they would like in the way of rewards and recognition.
	■ Create a rewards and recognition list.
Recognize high performance and achievement.	■ Celebrate individual and team success by acknowledging it to the entire staff.
	■ Send thank-you notes for a job well done.
	■ Place a note in the employee's personnel file for a job well done.

of orchestrating the appropriate motivating factors for each employee is a win-win for both the manager and employee.

Truly motivated employees are moved more from within rather than from external factors such as compensation and benefits or reward programs. These employees behave differently when engaged in stimulating work activities than just "doing what was assigned." Work becomes its own reward if an employee feels an attachment to the goal and is allowed to focus on getting the job done. Although the motivational spectrum would position too many employees in low levels of performance and job satisfaction, it is human nature to want to find satisfaction with worthwhile activities. Managers would profit from learning and applying techniques that will transport their employees to a more positive state on the motivational spectrum.

Activity

What Do People Want from Their Jobs?

Everyone has his or her own set of motivators. Employees, teams, and bosses all have their own view of what motivates them and others. Divide into groups. Individually, review the list of factors below that can be motivators to employees. Then decide which of the ten items listed would be the most important in contributing to employee motivation. Weight the items, assigning 10 to the most important item, 9 for the next important item, and so on in a reverse order so that all ten numbers are used. Put your ranking in the column marked "Individual." Now, as a group, total the individual weights for each factor for each person in your group. Rank them again under the column marked "Group."

What Do People Want From Their Jobs?		
Factors	**Individual**	**Group**
High wages		
Job security		
Promotion in the company		
Help on personal problems		
Stimulating work		
Personal loyalty of supervisor		
Tactful discipline		
Full appreciation of work done well		
Good working environment		
Feeling of being involved in things		

Exhibit 6c

Expectations of Employees

Professionalism

- Demonstrate knowledge
- Demonstrate leadership
- Practice honesty
- Practice confidentiality
- Practice respect
- Practice moral behavior
- Practice ethics

Personal Treatment

- Practice fairness
- Practice consistency
- Provide support
- Practice compassion
- Provide feedback
- Avoid embarrassing employees

Work and Task Support

- Provide clear directions
- Provide tools and resources
- Encourage professional growth and development
- Include employees in decision-making that affects them
- Provide a safe environment
- Practice reasonable and rational behavior

Expectations of Employees

Employees respond and are more easily motivated by managers who they respect and trust. Employees come to the workplace with expectations and hopes of working with managers that have these qualities. Their expectations fall into three groups: professionalism, personal treatment, and work and task support. (See *Exhibit 6c.*)

Professionalism refers not only to a person demonstrating exceptional industry skills and knowledge but also consistently conducting themselves with high standards. The foodservice industry as a profession demands the highest level of competence with regard to knowledge, skills, attitudes, and behavior in the delivery of products and services and in all interactions with peers, staff, and customers. The essence of professionalism requires managers to serve the interests of the customer and their employees and to adhere to the concepts of leadership, excellence, honesty, integrity, and respect for others.

Personal treatment refers to the way in which managers interact with staff and the value system that governs their daily conduct. Employees expect their managers to practice ethical behavior.

The last category of expectations deals with work resources, work life, and environment. Employees expect the necessary tools and resources needed to perform duties adequately, and to meet standards that will be provided to them. Employees also expect that a manager will provide coherent directions on what is required. An extension of these resources includes providing a safe and harassment-free work environment. Hazards and risks in the immediate workplace are always present in the foodservice establishment, and a manager needs to ensure that they are minimized for employee safety. Finally, employees need and want support for their own personal and professional development. Creating a work environment that takes care of and meets these expectations is a critical task that managers face.

Effective managers discover ways to meet these expectations by devoting time to examining work conditions and developing strong relationships with their employees. The results that managers get from meeting these expectations are usually in direct proportion to the amount of time they allocate to them. If you devote time to developing yourself and others and provide an encouraging work environment, motivational challenges are more likely to be minimized.

Challenges to Motivation

Managers must be able to understand and deal with the many factors that challenge employees' motivation. The more managers learn

---

Think About It...

Managers demonstrate concern for their employees by spending time with them. Do you think you need to plan your schedule so that you have time for your staff? How does time management help with this?

---

about addressing these factors, the more effective they become in developing a high-performance staff. Understanding some common motivational theories is a good place to start. These theories attempt to explain why and how people are motivated.

Theory X and Theory Y

A long-standing and accepted theory describes two ways of viewing an employee's attitude toward work: Theory X and Theory Y.[1]

Theory X states that people do not really like to work, and so the motivational strategy to apply is to control, direct, and threaten employees with punishment to get them to perform on the job. Theory X assumes that the manager is the ultimate authoritarian—dishing out rules, supervising, and coercing people to perform. On the other hand, Theory Y suggests that people are internally driven. Therefore, a manager needs to identify and provide the appropriate conditions for workers, who will accept and seek work activities to achieve self-fulfillment and gratification. Theory Y assumes workers' underlying achievement-oriented motives are for self-satisfying situations, meaning they will work toward specific goals to achieve success for themselves and for the organization.

Process Theories

Another set of motivational theories, referred to as process theories, include the expectancy theory, equity theory, and reinforcement theory. Each of these theories focuses on the processes and systems that surround a worker, examining techniques to maintain positive behavior in the workplace.

- **Expectancy theory** suggests that motivation is a measure of how much people want something.[2] If the employee perceives a reward to be meaningful, then the behavior to receive that reward is displayed. On the other hand, if the employee perceives that the performance is beyond his or her ability, then the challenge will not be taken.

- **Equity theory** proposes that employees compare the inputs to the outputs of the job. The required efforts—or inputs—include hard work, loyalty, commitment, skills, abilities, and other factors. The outputs include financial rewards, benefits, perks, and tangibles such as recognition, praise, and thanks. If the employee perceives a fair balance between what is required and what is rewarded, then the employee is happy and motivated to continue the desired effort. However, if the employee feels that the inputs outweigh the outputs, he or she will not perform up to standard.

- **Reinforcement theory** suggests that behavior is influenced by positive reinforcers, which will sustain behavior and motivation.

---

[1] *The Human Side of Enterprise.* Douglas MacGregor. 1960
[2] *Work and Motivations.* VH Vroom. 1964

If an employee's actions are rewarded, then the behavior that produced the reward will increase. In contrast, if an employee's actions are punished, then the behavior will decrease. Lastly, if an employee's actions produce no consequence at all, then the behavior will stop altogether.

Addressing Multiple Work Styles

While understanding the basic premises of motivational theories is important, a manager nevertheless will find other factors challenging the consistent application of these theories. Today's restaurant and foodservice workers are hugely diverse. With that diversity comes different work styles. **Work styles** are personal characteristics that are work-related. Style attributes include:

- Achievement orientation
- Conscientiousness
- Social influence
- Independence
- Interpersonal orientation
- Practical intelligence
- Adjustment

Everyone has a different set of strengths and weaknesses related to these characteristics. (*Exhibit 6d* on the next page provides more detail on the components of each attribute.) Understanding how to leverage these qualities can make managing and motivating workers less challenging. You might also consider asking your employees to rate themselves on these dimensions, to help you get a better picture of what is important to them.

The Effect of Time and Turnover on Relationships

Another factor that can impact the ability of a manager to motivate employees and build strong relationships with them is time constraints. The foodservice industry is a fast-paced and stressful environment. The many responsibilities a manager has to perform daily can interfere with developing strong bonds with employees. However, using time management techniques, creatively scheduling duties, and delegating tasks to others can free up time to focus on those important employee relationships. It is not uncommon for an effective manager to schedule time specifically for learning more about his or her employees. You can also multitask, combining floor observations or other duties with small talk with your staff.

Finally, the high turnover rates in the foodservice industry can also affect individual and team motivation. Like the effective manager who has strong relationships with workers, employees also develop bonds and relationships with their coworkers. Not knowing how long a coworker may stay often stunts or disrupts this relationship development.

Exhibit 6d

Work Style Attributes Worksheet

For each attribute below, rate how important it is to you by selecting 1 through 5—
1 being least important, and 5 being very important.

Achievement Orientation

Achievement/effort; establishing and maintaining personally challenging achievement goals, and exerting effort toward task mastery. ① ② ③ ④ ⑤

Persistence; in the face of obstacles on the job. ① ② ③ ④ ⑤

Initiative; being willing to take on responsibilities. ① ② ③ ④ ⑤

Social Influence

Energy and stamina; to accomplish work tasks. ① ② ③ ④ ⑤

Leadership orientation; willingness to lead, take charge, and offer opinions and directions. ① ② ③ ④ ⑤

Interpersonal Orientation

Cooperation; pleasant with others on the job and displaying a good-natured, cooperative attitude. ① ② ③ ④ ⑤

Concern for others; sensitive to others' needs and feelings, and understanding and helpful to others on the job. ① ② ③ ④ ⑤

Social orientation; preferring to work with others rather than alone and being personally connected with others on the job. ① ② ③ ④ ⑤

Adjustment

Self-control; maintaining composure, keeping emotions in check, controlling anger, and avoiding aggressive behavior even in very difficult situations. ① ② ③ ④ ⑤

Stress tolerance; accepting criticism and dealing calmly and effectively with high-stress situations. ① ② ③ ④ ⑤

Adaptability/flexibility; open to change (positive or negative) and to considerable variety in the workplace. ① ② ③ ④ ⑤

Conscientiousness

Dependability; reliable, responsible, and dependable, and fulfilling obligations. ① ② ③ ④ ⑤

Attention to detail; careful about detail and thorough in completing work tasks. ① ② ③ ④ ⑤

Integrity; honest and avoiding unethical behavior. ① ② ③ ④ ⑤

Independence

Developing one's own ways of doing things; guiding oneself with little or no supervision, and depending on oneself to get things done. ① ② ③ ④ ⑤

Practical Intelligence

Innovation; creativity and alternative thinking to come up with new ideas for and answers to work-related problems. ① ② ③ ④ ⑤

Analytical thinking; analyzing information, and using logic to address work or job issues and problems. ① ② ③ ④ ⑤

Building a Positive Work Climate

Motivation and strong professional relationships contribute to a successful work environment. If employees feel valued and involved in achieving the organization's goals, they will more than likely feel better about their workplace. Furthermore, when these contributions are recognized and rewarded, employees become more motivated and involved. This dual reinforcing cycle of involvement and motivation results in sustained, effective work performance as well as increased profits and sales. (See *Exhibit 6e.*) Creating a positive workplace environment that supports employees and provides engaging work activities also contributes to excellent individual and organizational performance.

Exhibit 6e

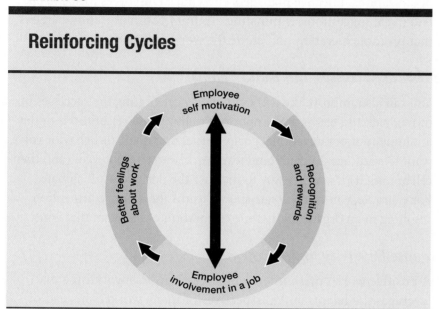

Reinforcing Cycles

Employee self motivation

Recognition and rewards

Better feelings about work

Employee involvement in a job

Ways to Build a Positive Environment

Managers can build a positive work climate in many ways. As stated above, focusing on employees is a critical component.

Focus on Employees

You can build a supportive climate by spending some time with each of your employees. Conduct one-on-one sessions for either training or performance reviews, and make an honest effort to meet each employee's needs. Nothing can affect an employee's feelings about the work environment more than a manager who does not keep his or her promises. Additionally, be honest and upfront about what you can do to satisfy employees' needs. This will always prove beneficial to your relationship with your staff. Ultimately, a worker appreciates the attention and interest a manager provides. They take pride in their work environment when they feel valued and respected. This personal focus will eventually result in an improved work climate.

On the other hand, be aware that individual focus should avoid favoritism and nepotism. **Favoritism** is being unfairly partial to one or more employees. **Nepotism** is a hybrid of favoritism in which a manager favors a relative for special assignments or promotions. These issues can rapidly destroy a positive work climate.

Think About It...

Employees should be given the opportunity to feel comfortable opening up to others in the workplace. It is a leader's responsibility to set the stage for this type of personal interaction. The team really functions as a family and managers can help create this environment for their staff.

Open Communication Channels

Open and honest communication between managers and employees is critical for creating a positive workplace. Opening communication channels by soliciting feedback makes employees feel more involved with operations and improves their attitude about the workplace. Lack of openness creates "departmental silos" that run rampant in many organizations. Effective managers encourage employees to speak up and make suggestions, eliminating arbitrary communication barriers that promote hierarchy and erode the work environment.

Celebrate Successes and Build Teams

You can also improve the work climate by celebrating the successes of individuals and teams. It is important to link these celebrations to the attainment of organizational goals, special initiatives, or behavior you want to reinforce. Encouraging teamwork among employees (and then celebrating it) is another way to increase the positive work climate. For example, you could create special teams for a store competition, resulting in an organization-wide celebration of the team that wins.

Promote Diversity and Fairness

A positive work environment embraces a diverse workforce that leverages the talents and perspectives of many workers instead of just a few. Hiring practices should also reflect the value of diversity in the workplace. When employees see that an organization values a spectrum of workers, they feel appreciated for their own qualities as well as what they can do for the organization. As part of human resource policies, you should follow through in an efficient manner on any harassment or discrimination claims that may occur. Employees who observe unfair practices such as these occurring in the workplace do not enjoy their work experience, subtracting from any effort a manager makes to improve the work environment.

The Manager's Role

You may have noticed that the common element in all these methods for building a positive work environment is the manager. As a manager, you are ultimately responsible for your establishment's work climate. The power of the position, however, will only take your efforts so far. At the core of your strategy for creating a positive, supportive environment, you must demand of yourself the following three ingredients:

1. **Patience.** Any sustainable environment takes times to nurture and thrive. Effective managers know that a positive environment will not happen overnight. They persevere because they value their workers.

2 **Dedicated effort.** People management is a full-time job. Without a focused effort, the work climate can easily deteriorate from factors that were not monitored.

3 **Genuine concern.** Employees value a manager who values them. Effective managers know that being concerned about individuals as well as work performance produces long-term benefits, such as meeting goals and increased organizational performance.

Additionally, one of the most important things managers can do is to set a positive example in their organization. Ask yourself: how do I help or impede my staff when they are trying to do their jobs? By analyzing your own behavior and motives, and ensuring that you present the best image for the organization, you can contribute to the improvement of the work climate.

Activity

Improving the Work Climate Begins with Me

Effective leaders are enthusiastic about the workplace. They also spread their enthusiasm to their staff. The manager must keep going, even under adverse conditions, and avoid appearing down or angry. One way to create a positive work climate is to think of yourself as a positive person. If you act and behave with many of the characteristics that employees value and expect in a manager, then your staff will begin to exhibit these behaviors as well. This exercise looks at the role that enthusiasm plays in creating a positive work climate. In groups, brainstorm each of the questions below.

1 Identify ways to improve enthusiasm during daily work activities.

_____

_____

_____

2 Write as many words you can think of that imply enthusiasm.

_____

_____

_____

3 In what way can you use this exercise in the future?

_____

_____

_____

_____

Thorough self-analysis and good intentions, however, are not enough if you cannot energize your staff. Effective managers are organizational catalysts who use their energy to inspire staff to reach organizational goals. By conveying your own excitement about the work the team must accomplish, your staff will, as time goes by, display similar energy and excitement about working for the organization.

In the end, you must employ a variety of strategies to build and sustain a positive work environment, focusing on both your employees' needs and your own contributions to the climate. With dedication, your efforts will produce not only engaging and motivated workers, but also a profitable organization for which people want to work.

Mutually Respectful Workplaces

Two critical aspects of a positive work environment are respectfulness and equal treatment for all employees. Over the past several decades, the number of complaints involving on-the-job problems related to sexual harassment and discriminatory treatment of minorities and women has steadily increased. As a manager, you must understand what a harassment-free environment means so you can handle complaints appropriately and foster and support a mutually respectful workplace on an ongoing basis. Harassment covers five categories: sexual, ethnic, age, religion, and physical limitations. In some cases, local statutes also prevent discrimination based on sexual preference. As you will see in this section, preventing harassment and discrimination is just as important as responding to it, for the welfare of your employees, your organization, and yourself.

Sexual Harassment

The most commonly known type of harassment is sexual harassment. The Equal Employment Opportunity Commission (EEOC) defines **sexual harassment** as any unwelcome sexual advance (see *Exhibit 6f*), request for sexual favors, or any conduct of a sexual nature, when compliance is:

- A condition of initial or continued employment

- A basis of working conditions, including promotions, salary increases, work assignments, or termination

- Interfering with and creating an intimidating, hostile or offensive work environment

Sexual harassment has been illegal since 1965. Millions of dollars in court settlements have since been awarded to male and female employees from companies whose managers were accused of sexual misconduct or mistreatment. Settlements have also covered work environments defined as hostile and offensive to the discriminated parties.

To be classified as a hostile work environment, the behaviors in question must be frequent, severe, and pervasive. Situations that have been ruled to constitute a hostile environment include:

- Posting of sexually suggestive pictures in employee work areas

- Consistently telling dirty jokes or stories in which all employees in the area can hear

- Tolerating employees who make sexually suggestive remarks within earshot of coworkers

- Allowing peer employees, customers, suppliers, or any other person to persist in unwanted attention, such as asking for dates

- Allowing the use of derogative terms with a sexual connotation to be used to describe coworkers

- Allowing frequent physical contact even when it is not sexual

Exhibit 6f

Unwelcome contact can be considered sexual harassment.

Other Forms of Harassment and Discrimination

Although sexual harassment has had the most written about it, other areas of harassment are also covered by civil rights laws in the United States. Ethnic or racial slurs and other verbal or physical conduct related to a person's race, color, religion, or medical condition constitutes harassment when it unreasonably interferes with the person's work performance or creates an unhealthy work environment.

Addressing Harassment

Most companies have implemented some type of harassment-free workplace policy that provides guidelines and procedures regarding conduct in the workplace. Many of these policies are limited to a reactive response; however, courts have recently indicated that a passive complaint-based approach is no longer adequate to remedy

Exhibit 6g

As the manager, it is your responsibility to emphasize mutual respect among all employees in the establishment.

these situations. Company policies need to adopt a prevention approach that acknowledges mutual respect as the goal for all who work in the environment.

The purpose of these policies is to provide a productive and pleasant work environment that protects all employees from harassment. Although the focus is on employee-related harassment, the policies should also cover harassment by non-employees, since these situations—once reported to a supervisor—also must be remedied.

Each organization will have its own statement regarding harassment, but in general, these statements should include some or all of the following aspects:

- Emphasizes mutual respect for all (see *Exhibit 6g*)
- States the values of respect held by the organization
- States that all staff are expected to adhere to the policy
- Defines the areas covered by the Civil Rights code
- Addresses the covered situations as defined by its respective jurisdictions, but also considers expanding the areas based on other types of abuse not covered by civil rights laws
- Alerts managers to their responsibility for maintaining a harassment-free environment
- Gives employees options for help with dealing with harassment
- Allows for informal resolution if the affected parties choose it
- Indicates the process for handling a complaint
- Indicates that the organization has no tolerance for disrespectful behavior and misconduct, any of which may result in disciplinary action—including termination

Policies must also ensure that any employee who feels that he or she has been harassed is encouraged to voice his or her objection to the offending person and bring the subject to the attention of a manager. The following guidelines can be used in a complaint resolution or management process:

- An open-door policy should be put into place that prevents fear of reprisal against the complainant.
- Complaints should be reported initially to the complainant's direct supervisor or manager, unless that supervisor or manager is the subject of the complaint. In that event, the next level of management or a human resources representative should receive the complaint.

Think About It…

Sexual harassment costs companies millions of dollars each year in absenteeism, employee turnover, low morale, and low productivity.

How does an open-door policy on harassment help minimize or eliminate these things from effecting employees and the organization?

■ The complaint should be processed in accordance with any local or state law, and then following company policy.

■ Complaints should be investigated thoroughly by the complainant's direct supervisor or manager, unless that supervisor or manager is the subject of the complaint. In that event, the next management level or human resources representative should conduct the investigation. In all cases, investigations must be done in confidence.

■ Employees should be prohibited from discussing the situation with other employees.

■ Managers should communicate the information with only the appropriate parties.

■ Managers need to document the complaint and collect statements from all involved parties.

■ If the investigation reveals that an employee has harassed another, the offender must be subject to appropriate disciplinary procedures, including termination.

As seen above, managers have significant responsibility for addressing harassment in the workplace. They are legally liable for maintaining a harassment-free environment. In fact, managers at all levels, including company presidents, have been cited and fined for not dealing with harassment effectively. It is therefore crucial that you acknowledge and respond to complaints immediately, as well as act upon any type of harassment you see or become aware of. The best approach is a proactive one that upholds applicable laws and follows and promotes company guidelines and policies.

Creating a Preventive Atmosphere

A proactive approach for preventing occurrences of harassment relies on company-wide recognition of the organization's harassment policies, including frequent communication between managers and employees. Managers at all levels must relate the regulations, guidelines, and zero-tolerance policies to employees. Remind employees that sexual harassment is against the law, and that harassment of any kind is not tolerated and will result in disciplinary action. Post in a common area the company policies and local, state, and federal posters that explain applicable laws (See *Exhibit 6h.*) Also, be sure that employees recognize their right to raise the issue of harassment, as well as how to file a complaint.

New employees should be introduced to the guidelines as part of new-hire orientation programs. Various cultural diversity, sexual harassment, and valuing programs should be offered and conducted

Exhibit 6h

Post company policy where everyone can see it.

on an ongoing basis with all employees. Once employees have completed these types of training programs, have them sign a policy statement indicating their understanding of the policy, willingness to support it, and intention to behave accordingly.

Training should also include sessions for managers so they can ensure that their staff follow and uphold the guidelines. As part of the program, managers must learn how to conduct a harassment investigation based on company policy and regulatory laws. Additionally, as amendments or modifications to existing laws or policies occur, managers need to participate in ongoing refresher courses to learn about the latest developments in these areas.

Other methods for promoting a mutually respectful workplace include:

■ **Modeling positive behavior.** Staff will take cues from their managers regarding acceptable and unacceptable behavior. Managers need to understand this responsibility, and senior management must hold their staff accountable for engaging in disrespectful behavior, if necessary. Senior management and company policy should also discourage managers from dating employees and fraternizing with them beyond all-inclusive events.

■ **Emphasizing its value in the organization's goals.** Management could add statements to its documented vision or mission that reflect the importance of a zero-tolerance environment.

A respectful workplace is worth attaining, and managers are key to its development and sustainability. Organizational policies set the stage for a work environment that respects and appreciates its employees. Employees who know that their fears and concerns regarding harassment will be dealt with effectively will help maintain a lasting, mutually respectful workplace.

Exhibit 6i

Your interpersonal communication is critical to creating a positive and respectful workplace.

Interpersonal Communication

Since the primary responsibilities of a manager include creating both a positive work climate and a respectful one, the role of interpersonal communication cannot be underestimated. But what is interpersonal communication exactly? **Interpersonal communication** differs from other forms of communication in that there are usually only a few participants involved (often just two people), the individuals are in close proximity to each other as shown in *Exhibit 6i*, and the feedback is immediate. Interpersonal communication occurs in all types of relationships; however, it can vary depending on the relationship type. For example, the short interaction you have with a salesperson is different than the relationship you have with friends and family.

Reasons for Using Interpersonal Communication

Interpersonal communication is important because of the functions it performs. Its main function for the sender is to seek information while attempting to improve interactions with the receiver. At the same time, since the communication is two-way, the sender is also giving information through a variety of verbal and nonverbal cues.

The way in which a person gains information in interpersonal communication is usually through self-disclosure. **Self-disclosure** is a strategy to share information that the receiver would not normally know. By sharing information, the people involved become closer, and the interpersonal relationship is strengthened. Self-disclosure usually involves vulnerability on the part of the sender because it can reveal or disclose "unknowns or secrets," which some people feel opens them up to attacks or extreme scrutiny.

Other reasons for engaging in interpersonal communication include:

- **To better understand what someone says in a given context.** For example, the words a manager uses can mean different things depending on how they are said or in what context.

- **To establish an identity with a person.** In the workplace, people play different roles, and interpersonal communication helps establish a person's identity. For example, a manager has the role of evaluator, coach, scheduler, and cheerleader, while workers have various other roles.

- **To fulfill interpersonal needs.** Interpersonal communication helps people fulfill some relationship needs, including inclusion, control, and affection. **Inclusion** refers to the need to feel a part of a group. **Control** refers to the need to exercise leadership and apply authority over others. **Affection** refers to the need to develop relationships with people as individuals or in groups.

Factors That Affect Interpersonal Communication

How effective managers are at interpersonal communication depends on how well they exhibit appropriate people skills. The ability to connect with people is dependent upon skills in two categories: visible actions and verbal messages.

The Impact of a Manager's Actions

Effective managers understand that actions often speak louder than words. Actions such as showing tolerance for cultural differences, conducting oneself in an ethical and professional manner, creating a

125

safe and fun environment, and remaining humble, disclose much about who you are as a manager. Often, an employee will make judgments about your effectiveness and personal integrity based on how well you model positive attitudes and behavior in the organization. Employees who observe positive behavior are also more likely to set equally high standards for their own behavior.

Managers' actions also allow employees to better predict how they will react. For example, making the work environment a fun place by telling a funny story or having fun, friendly activities can lead employees to view you as more approachable. Additionally, showing humility has a significant impact on employee-manager relationships. No employee likes to work with a manager who feels solely responsible for why the organization is performing well and achieving its goals. Effective managers remain humble and give credit where credit is due, looking for every opportunity to build trust and respect among the staff.

Once managers engage in these types of behavioral actions, as well as in self-disclosure, employees will usually model the actions and also disclose personal information about themselves. This interaction is known as the norm of reciprocity. Mutual disclosure further deepens trust in the employee-manager relationship and helps both people understand each other better.

The Impact of a Manager's Verbal Messages

Verbal messages also have a significant impact on interpersonal communication, and thus on the relationships you have with your employees. Whatever the intention of their message, managers must remember that how a person receives the message also affects the outcome of the interpersonal communication. For example, showing empathy to employees who are having personal challenges creates a stronger bond with them. **Empathy** is the act of identifying with the feelings, thoughts, or attitudes of another person. Often it is referred to as "standing in someone else's shoes." By using empathic statements in your communications with staff, they will feel you are genuinely concerned about them and understand their situation.

Along with being empathic, respecting your employees' views and opinions is another way of building stronger interpersonal communications with them. Displaying this type of acceptance conveys the message that you value their ideas and believe in collaboration. Additionally, employees perceive managers' feedback as interest in their development and performance. Similarly, by receiving their feedback, you convey to employees the message that you are open to improving yourself. In both situations, the message creates a long-lasting impression on the receiver, which improves the relationship.

Forms of Interpersonal Communication

Managers need to utilize all the available and appropriate channels of communication to interact positively with their staff. Additionally, a key part of interpersonal communication is a manager's opportunity to convey to employees the organization's values. The most common channel to communicate these concepts is through various types of verbal messages.

Exhibit 6j

Employees prefer continuous feedback about their performance.

■ **Chatting or having casual conversations with your staff can set the ideal tone.** You want to build a friendly environment, which can increase your employees' trust. The nonverbal cues that accompany these types of chats, such as a pat on the back, a smile of thanks, or a "thumbs up," can also create an appreciation of positive values, resulting in a stronger bond with your staff.

■ **Finding opportunities to coach, counsel, and provide feedback to an employee supports both the employee and the organization.** The easiest and most immediate way to convey positive values and support by the organization is through feedback. Most manager feedback—whether positive or constructive—is related to an employee's performance. Employees prefer continuous feedback about how they are doing on the job, rather than once a year at a performance review, and it is the manager who can provide them with this information. (See *Exhibit 6j.*) Likewise, the more feedback employees get, the more they will feel comfortable with it and look forward to the experience. Some initial ways to approach feedback with employees include:

☐ Offer to provide clarification or help with tasks.

☐ Invite them to join you for coffee to put them more at ease.

☐ Point out positive things they are doing along with your constructive feedback.

☐ Thank them for their efforts even when there is room for improvement.

Understanding the appropriate demeanor in conducting one of these conversations is also essential for ensuring an employee views the feedback as constructive, and is willing to listen to it and then act upon it. *Exhibit 6k* on the next page identifies characteristics that will help a manager set the appropriate tone of the conversation as well as the openness to feedback that both parties need to demonstrate.

■ **Using verbal counseling is a strong daily approach for communicating with employees.** Verbal counseling can occur many times during the day and with a variety of employees. It ranges from simple spur-of-the-moment corrections to more formal meetings with in-depth conversations about the

Exhibit 6k

Approach to Handling Constructive Feedback

Follow these guidelines:	To ensure the following:
Do not be quick to judge.	All of the facts need to be gathered first.
Keep an open mind.	Decisions are based on facts, not emotions.
Maintain a positive demeanor.	The employee is open to receiving feedback, welcomes it, and does not feel like he or she is being punished.
Do not be condescending.	The employee does not feel patronized or feel you convey a superior attitude.
Be straightforward.	The employee values the directness of your communication.
Be positive.	The communication is viewed as a learning opportunity and the employee feels that you believe he or she can change.
Be patient.	The employee understands that you will support him or her over the time it takes to adopt the change.

importance of performing well and the steps needed to improve behavior. Whichever form it takes, it is an opportunity for the manager to display a positive and upbeat attitude.

■ **Coaching helps reinforce and improve performance on the job.** Coaching can be used when an employee needs more direction during on-the-job training, or when an employee needs support and encouragement to stick with a task. As a manager, an important role you play is that of the team coach. Coaches provide additional guidance, clear directions, and more training (if necessary), yet they also understand the delicate balance between coaching and doing. Employees need to develop on their own; coaches should never act as a substitute for a worker.

The Role of Written Communication

Although various forms of verbal communication are the most common types of interpersonal communication, written and electronic communication can also be used to develop employee-manager relationships. The situations in which you might use this communication channel include thank-you notes, short positive messages for encouragement, and letters that are copied to higher-level bosses.

Still another form of written communication that an effective manager uses are employee surveys that measure whether positive values are being communicated to employees. Surveys can measure whether the message was received, how well it was received, and whether it was a valued message by the employees.

Activity

Animal Analogy Exercise

The way a manager communicates is integral to building strong relationships with employees. The interactions that employees experience shed light on your ability to lead and relate to your staff. Find a partner in class and think about a time that you had a meeting with one of your bosses. If you do not have a boss that comes to mind, think of a professor or teacher you have had. Instead of verbally describing your impression of the boss during that meeting and how he or she handled it, sketch out a picture of whatever animal you think depicts the manner in which the manager related to you. Then answer the questions below and share the sketch with your partner, and briefly explain the situation and why this animal depicts the person.

1. How might you tactfully tell your boss your impressions and feelings about the meeting and how he or she handled it?

_____

_____

2. What might be considered the "ideal" animal when communicating and interacting with employees?

_____

_____

Conflict Resolution

Every manager has to deal with conflicts that arise among employees. Just as knowing how to deliver feedback to an employee is an important skill to develop, understanding how to approach and deal with conflict resolution in the work environment is equally essential. **Conflict resolution** refers to a wide range of processes that encourages solutions to problems that do not require formal grievance steps within an organization. Typically, conflicts can occur because of two reasons:

1. Disagreement about a work-related situation

2. Disagreement due to personal incompatibilities between workers

The process of conflict resolution fosters understanding and cooperation, as well as an agreement that works for both individuals. The process should be confidential, allowing employees to avoid embarrassment or other work-related situations that might interfere with getting the problem solved. Some common forms of conflict resolution that a manager can use include:

- **Negotiation**—discussion between involved people with the goal of reaching an agreement that both can accept.

- **Mediation**—process in which a neutral third party facilitates a discussion of difficult issues and negotiates an agreement.

- **Arbitration**—process in which a third party listens and reviews facts and makes a decision to settle the conflict.

All three forms of conflict resolution follow similar basic steps, which are outlined in *Exhibit 6I*. Ultimately, the process you use should result in a solution that both individuals can accept and feel good about. Additionally, allowing the employees involved to resolve their conflict through one of these means gives them greater control over their own work and lives, as well as the ability to make their own decisions on how to solve the problem.

Mediation is the most preferred method for conflict resolution. It usually works well because it results in a win-win compromise for all parties. The only downside is that it can be time-consuming. At the onset, you must explain the process to the people involved— they need to understand the method for it to be successful. A unique feature of mediation is that, as part of the three-way meeting you have with the employees, each person must state his or her understanding of the other person's perspective. This forces people to listen, and it can also uncover and clarify any misunderstandings. Conflicts are often caused by these misunderstandings; therefore, this step can resolve issues quickly.

Exhibit 6I

Handling Conflict Resolution

---

1 **Acknowledge** the issue causing the conflict between the employees as well as any feelings that either person may have related to the situation or the other individual.

2 **Evaluate** the situation.

    A. Define the conflict and impact of the problem.

    B. Determine the severity of the problem.

    C. Review and enforce company policy.

    D. Follow any company policy regarding how to handle conflict on the job.

    E. Determine other resources needed to handle the situation such as human resources, legal counsel, or family members.

3 **Interview** each person separately. Explain the purpose of a three-way meeting to follow. Gain agreement from both to attend.

4 **Create** an agenda for the three-way meeting.

5 **Conduct** the meeting.

6 **Use collaboration techniques** to make sure that both parties needs are being met.

    A. Identify critical factors for each.

    B. Verify that each party is comfortable with the solution/resolution.

7 **Document** the agreement reached by each party.

8 **Discuss** next steps for everyone to ensure the conflict does not arise again.

9 **Follow up** on the agreement.

As the mediator, you should take notes to help with the issue's resolution. You must also ensure both parties agree to live with the proposed solution. Be sure to follow up on the decision to verify the problem has been resolved for good.

If the individuals cannot come to an agreement through negotiating or mediation, then arbitration is an option. The difference between these two processes and arbitration is that the manager makes the final decision about the conflict's resolution. To arbitrate appropriately, gather all the facts, listen to both sides, evaluate the information, and determine some alternative solutions. Once you have completed these steps, you must make the decision and then inform the parties involved. It is important that you ensure both employees understand the decision fully, agree to it, and are committed to its implementation.

Activity

Mediating a Misunderstanding

You will be divided into groups of three. Decide who will play the role of the mediator and who will play the employees involved in the conflict. Take about five minutes to become familiar with the facts regarding your role. Then follow the process below.

1	The mediator will explain the process.
2	Employee 1 will state his or her view of the situation described on the fact sheet.
3	Employee 2 will then listen and provide feedback on what he or she heard Employee 1 say.
4	Employee 2 will describe the situation from his or her perspective.
5	Employee 1 will then listen and provide feedback on what he or she heard Employee 1 say.
6	The mediator should take notes throughout these descriptions.
7	Once both employees have taken their turns, the mediator should take a few minutes to review his or her notes.
8	The mediator will then describe any commonalities each employee has regarding the situation, as well as identifying the real conflict.
9	The mediator will propose a solution. The employees need to indicate their agreement or disagreement with the solution.

Role-Play Facts

Employee 1

You are one of three team leaders for a sales campaign to increase the number of desserts sold in the restaurant. The team with the highest increase in sales will win a pizza party. You have the following characteristics:

- Very confident

- Talks with a disapproving tone to everyone

- Has an attitude of "Accept me for who I am and if you don't, it's your problem"

- Wants to get promoted soon

- Uses nonverbal signs to emphasize you think you are better than other people

The conflict arose when you said to a team member, "Hey, I noticed you weren't offering desserts at the register this morning. Don't you want to win the contest?" This happened a week ago, and the team member is now avoiding you on shifts and letting it interfere with other aspects of the job. You are getting irritated because the team is in last place.

Your boss has asked you to enter into mediation, to which you have agreed.

Employee 2

You are a team member for a sales campaign to increase the number of desserts sold in the restaurant. The team with the highest increase in sales will win a pizza party. You have the following characteristics:

- Very polite
- Shy
- Wants to get along
- Does not like people who are arrogant
- Does not have high self-esteem
- Tries hard

The conflict arose when your team leader said to you, "Hey, I noticed you weren't offering desserts at the register this morning. Don't you want to win the contest?" This happened a week ago, and now you are avoiding the leader on shifts and letting it interfere with other aspects of your job. The team leader is getting irritated because the team is in last place.

Your boss has asked you to enter into mediation, to which you have agreed.

Mediator

The conflict arose when a team leader said to a team member, "Hey, I noticed you weren't offering desserts at the register this morning. Don't you want to win the contest?" This happened a week ago, and now the team member is avoiding the leader on shifts and letting it interfere with other aspects of the job. The team leader is getting irritated because the team is in last place.

You have noticed the situation and have asked them to resolve this conflict on their own, but it is not working. Now you ask them to enter into mediation, to which they have agreed.

Use the following space to take notes on the mediation process and answer the following questions during the role-play.

1 What are the issues for Employee 1?

_____

_____

2 What are the issues for Employee 2?

_____

_____

3 How do you see the situation?

_____

_____

continued on next page

Mediating a Misunderstanding *continued from previous page*

4 What solution are you going to suggest?

_____

_____

_____

5 Did you get resolution?

_____

_____

_____

Role-Play Questions

Once the group has role-played the situation, individually answer the following questions.

1 Did you think that each person involved in the conflict was able to listen and communicate the other person's view of the situation clearly? Explain.

_____

_____

2 What was the conflict really about?

_____

_____

_____

3 How was it resolved?

_____

_____

4 How did the process help make for a win-win solution?

_____

_____

5 How might you apply this process in other activities?

_____

_____

_____

Employee Performance Appraisals

Employee performance appraisals are an integral part of developing staff. They are part of an overall system of goal setting, judging performance outcomes, motivating, coaching, and ongoing feedback. Employee appraisals offer several advantages, including:

- Communicating past performance feedback
- Establishing new performance goals
- Discussing job-related issues
- Talking about career development opportunities
- Documenting performance officially

Performance appraisals typically focus on three areas:

- Performance (not personalities)
- Relevant issues and facts (instead of subjective feelings)
- Consensus and agreement on performance opportunities and goals

The appraisal process is cyclical, as seen in *Exhibit 6m*. It should cover an entire year of job performance by the employee (although some operations evaluate hourly employees on a six-month basis). Too many managers approach the appraisal process in a hurried manner and only focus on the most recent examples of an employee's performance. Coupling this approach with a lack of continuous feedback, many employees have a negative feeling about their appraisal meeting.

Engaging in a full performance discussion and talking about future personal development for the employee benefits the relationship you have together. Effective managers understand the importance of this process to the development of their staff and the organization, so understanding how to conduct a proper performance evaluation is essential. The performance appraisal checklist (see *Exhibit 6n* on the next page) outlines several tasks involved in preparing for and conducting employee performance appraisals.

Exhibit 6m

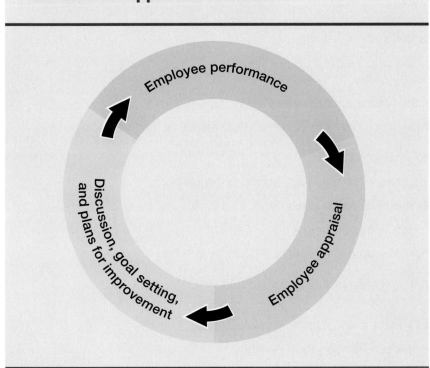

The General Appraisal Process

Employee performance

Employee appraisal

Discussion, goal setting, and plans for improvement

Exhibit 6n

Performance Appraisal Checklist

Preparation	☐ Review expectations of job duties, job descriptions, goals, standards, projects, and any performance facts related to the employee.
	☐ Consult your personnel file on the employee instead of relying on memory.
	☐ Focus on performance measures and not personality traits.
	☐ Review employee's background including skills, training, and attendance records.
	☐ Identify the employee's performance strengths and areas in need of improvement.
	☐ Gather specific documentation on performance from all managers.
	☐ Identify areas you feel the employee needs to concentrate on for the next period.
	☐ Provide the employee with a self-evaluation form, which you want them to complete and bring to the meeting.
	☐ Set up a time and place for the meeting with the employee and communicate this information.
Conducting the Appraisal Meeting	☐ Create an open and friendly atmosphere for the meeting.
	☐ Explain the purpose of the meeting.
	☐ Clarify that this is a joint discussion.
	☐ Try to put the employee at ease.
	☐ Discuss job requirements, strengths and opportunities, and results of performance against goals set.
	☐ Be prepared to provide information on each point discussed.
	☐ Use open and reflective questions to engage the employee.
	☐ Take notes during the meeting.
	☐ Encourage the employee to outline a plan for self-development and then offer your own suggestions.
	☐ Set dates and times for targets identified.
	☐ Reach agreement on goals, timetable, and any resources that would be needed.
Closing the Meeting	☐ Summarize what was discussed.
	☐ Ask the employee if they have any additional suggestions.
	☐ Show enthusiasm for future plans.
	☐ End on a positive, friendly note.
	☐ Identify any follow-up dates to meet.
Post-Appraisal Follow Up	☐ Document the meeting including plans made, points covered, and commitments made.
	☐ Make a copy and provide it to the employee.
	☐ Reflect on how you handled the meeting.

Within the general appraisal process, a number of steps should be followed to ensure the appraisal meeting is a productive one for you and the employee. They will help you and your employees optimize the benefits of a performance appraisal.

Step 1: Schedule the Meeting

Set a time and place for the employee appraisal meeting and notify the employee in advance. Employees need to know when the meeting is scheduled so they can prepare for it just like you do.

Step 2: Prepare the Appraisal

During the time preparing for the meeting, you should gather facts that support your review and evaluation of the person's performance. Review your personnel file, and ask for information from the team leaders who work with the employee. At the same time, the employee should complete a self-evaluation, which will be discussed during the meeting. This self-evaluation should focus on the employee's strengths, opportunities, highlights of accomplishments, and future developmental areas.

Step 3: Conduct the Meeting

The performance evaluation meeting is an opportunity for the two of you to have a meaningful, open exchange of how the employee performed since the last appraisal meeting. You should start with the employee's view of his or her performance. The employee should also discuss any constraints on his or her performance or attainment of goals. You must first listen to what the employee has to say, structuring the meeting so questions are welcome. (Beware, however, that sidebar issues should be handled in other meetings. These issues only distract from the main purpose of the appraisal.) After the employee has provided perspective, share your feedback on the individual's strengths and opportunities.

Step 4: Gain Agreement

Once both of you have discussed the employee's performance, you need to gain agreement from the employee on his or her past performance, as well as how the employee will move forward for improvement. Discuss ways the employee can improve, and be sure to ask how you might be able to help the employee in the future.

Step 5: Develop a Plan

A development plan should be discussed with the employee. Several goals should initially be identified, and then the employee should have the opportunity to refine them further. Include timelines, resources needed, and specific objectives. There are numerous reasons to involve the employee in the goal-setting process during performance discussions, as follows:

- Besides leveraging the meeting as a means to create consensus and support, involvement creates ownership for the employee in his or her own development.

- The goal-setting process can be a motivation tool that helps develop leadership skills in the employee.

- The employee will have a better understanding of how he or she is assisting the organization in reaching its goals.

- The process helps foster employee retention, pride in his or her work, and team spirit.

- The manager gains important viewpoints by learning the line perspective of the business.

When discussing performance or setting goals for the employee, you need to frame the discussion around standards that are used to measure the performance. A **standard** is simply stated criteria used to determine whether a goal has been met. Applying the SMART criteria (as discussed in Chapter 2) to individual goals aids in the discussion. As an assigned task, the employee can complete a more detailed plan. Schedule a follow-up meeting to finalize the plan with the employee. Completing all the steps in the process brings you and the employee back to the first step—where you start the process again in a continuous improvement effort.

Addressing Negative Performance

When part of the appraisal discussion turns to missed opportunities or performance problems, the attitude underlying this discussion should be that you and the employee are partners in a problem-solving dialogue focusing on individual performance. The format that a manager should use in talking with the employee about performance problems is:

1. Eliminate any misunderstandings.

2. Quantify what is expected of the employee.

3. Describe exactly when it is expected.

For example, if a manager has documented that an employee routinely arrives late to work, the manager should address the tardiness in the appraisal discussion, giving the employee an opportunity to respond. The employee might not have realized he or she was late so often, or might have thought there was a grace period for arrival time. Whatever the case, the manager should then clarify the company's tardiness policy. ("You are expected to arrive by 8:30 a.m. every day.")

The manager should also be clear about the ramifications of continuing to be tardy. ("If you are late two more times within the next six weeks, you will be placed on probation.") The manager should also make sure the employee acknowledges in writing the need for improvement and the potential consequences for continuing to be late.

Delegation

Once you have conducted a performance appraisal with an employee, you may find that one way to help the person develop is to delegate either a specific task or several tasks to them. **Delegation** is a process of working with and through others to get a significant task or project completed. It shares authority and entrusts the employee with responsibility to accomplish the task assigned to them. Delegation offers many advantages to the organization, including involving the employees more meaningfully in organizational goals, improving morale in the work environment, and helping realize the full potential of all employees.

Two critical questions a manager needs to ask is, "What needs to be delegated or is appropriate for delegating?" and "To whom should I delegate the task?" To answer the question about what needs to be delegated, a manager should look at what categories of activities are appropriate for others to complete. Certain tasks seem to be more conducive to delegation than others including:

- **Fact-finding tasks.** The more important element of problem solving is analyzing the problem. But before you can do that, you need to gather the facts. This task can be assigned to a team member so that you focus on devising solutions to problems.

- **Detail work.** This type of work can be time-consuming and you need to focus your efforts on larger tasks that have the greatest impact and which allow you to leverage your team.

- **Repetitive tasks.** There are many routine tasks that could be delegated to an employee such as weekly production reports, waste counting and reporting, and sales monitoring. Examine these tasks and determine their suitability to be assigned to employees and how much training would be required.

- **Standing in for you tasks.** Although there are many meetings that you need to attend such as budget meetings and strategic planning meetings, there are some meetings that you could delegate to an employee. Not only does this delegation free up some of your time but it also gives the employee exposure and new perspective on job growth potential.

■ **Future job opportunities.** One of your key responsibilities is to develop staff and no better way to do that is through delegation. Using the performance appraisal process as a stepping stone, you and the employee can determine what possible tasks could be assigned to give them a taste of more responsibility or as a stepping stone into management positions.

If you determine that a task or project can be delegated, then you need to determine which employee will receive the assignment. Factors to consider include:

■ Does the employee have the qualifications or possess the talent to accomplish the task?

■ What is the employee's availability?

■ How much training does the employee need?

■ Who would benefit most in his or her development by completing this task?

■ Who will contribute most to departmental productivity if assigned this task?

Delegation Process

There are several steps to effectively delegating responsibilities to your staff: preparation, planning, execution, assessment, and appreciation.

Step 1: Preparation

In the preparation phase, you must first select the task to be delegated and then clearly define it. Initially, tasks should be fairly simple and straightforward. As an employee develops confidence and skills, tasks can become more complex. You should also create a checklist for each task so it can be monitored easily. Additionally, outline the results anticipated, resources needed, relevant information to consider, and the time frame for completion. Finally, identify who will do the task.

Step 2: Planning

The next phase is planning. You should meet with the chosen employee and describe the assignment in detail, outlining all the facts and required results. In the meeting, discuss resources needed, including other people, equipment, budget, and additional materials. Any constraints should be identified, as well as how to overcome them.

An important part of this phase is determining the level of involvement that the chosen employee is able to handle. Delegation levels for employees begin at no delegation responsibility, increasing at various levels until an employee has a high degree of freedom and decision-making authority. (See *Exhibit 6o*.) Share and discuss the degree of authority or level of delegated responsibility the employee will have while completing the assignment. You should also explain why the task is being delegated to the person. Additionally, all involved employees who may be affected by this assignment should be notified.

Step 3: Execution

In the execution phase, the manager turns the project or task over to the employee. As the task progresses, you must monitor the situation and discuss any requested adjustments to the original plan. Discussions should include problems or issues and plans to resolve them.

Exhibit 6o

Levels of Delegation

Takes action without direct supervision
Highest level of confidence

Takes action and follows up with manager
Confidence in abilities, follows up to ensure
that any potential risks are resolved quickly

Decides and proceeds, yielding to manager's advice
Controls more actions but requires checks and
measures to flag any potential risks

Decides course of action, waits for approval
Trusted to judge options correctly but
needs approval before taking action

Gives recommendation with options
Manager checks thinking before
a decision is made

Finds information, manager decides
Investigates, analyzes, but
makes no recommendations

Waits to be told
No delegated
responsibility

During this phase, your feedback and encouragement to the employee is vital. This style of managing is called coaching—the employee still requires some direction but also needs increasing support and backing from you. As a coach, you need to find the balance between telling the employee exactly what to do and offering no support whatsoever.

Step 4: Assessment and Appreciation

The final phase of delegation occurs once the task has been completed. A meeting to discuss the results, process, and lessons learned is key to effective delegation. You must acknowledge the employee's efforts. Recognizing the employee's efforts also provides motivation for future assignments and acknowledges the employee's contribution.

Activity

Dealing with Jana

Jana Byrd was one of the emerging stars at Appleton's Restaurant. She knew the operation of the restaurant, especially the purchasing function. She developed a sound system of purchasing that reduced the time by one-half. She always had excellent ideas for improvement. Unfortunately, upper-level management decided to outsource the purchasing function and assign Jana to production. Since the change, Jana has changed noticeably. She is capable of handling the new duties, but she has decided that she does not wish to perform them. She is very unhappy. She says that the work assigned is irrelevant and she is no longer needed. As a result, she comes to work later and leaves earlier. Upper management has noticed the change. As Jana's manager you have been instructed by your immediate supervisor to fire Jana, unless she can turn things around.

1 What is the problem with Jana?

_____

_____

_____

2 What would you do as her immediate supervisor?

_____

_____

_____

3 What behavior is Jana displaying?

_____

_____

_____

4 What steps might you take to motivate Jana to pursue the new job with her "usual" vigor?

_____

_____

_____

5 How might you leverage a delegated task to Jana to improve her behavior?

_____

_____

_____

Summary

One of the greatest challenges managers face today is motivating and developing their employees. This chapter provided numerous reasons for why it is advantageous to assist your staff in their development. There can be a discrepancy between what a manager perceives as important to the employee and what in reality the employee really wants from his or her job. An array of motivational concepts and techniques help a manager create a positive work climate in which the employee is self-motivated to achieve goals of the organization. However, challenges can impede motivational strategies used in the workplace. The positive role the manager plays is a vital component in motivating employees to excel. Not only is the manager as a positive role model essential to creating a motivating work atmosphere, he or she must also have the ability to develop strong, trusting relationships.

An integral part of a motivating workplace is the establishment of a harassment-free work environment. Guidelines for enforcing and supporting legal and company policies regarding any type of harassment must be in place.

At times, individuals will find themselves at odds with each other in the workplace. These conflicts can be related to either specific work duties and projects or reflect personality issues. Procedures for handling conflict resolution can minimize these situations in the workplace.

Finally, an important part of motivating an employee is the role that the performance appraisal process provides. The process, includes scheduling the meeting, preparing the facts for the meeting, conducting the meeting with the employee, gaining an agreement, and developing a plan for the future. An outgrowth of an appraisal meeting is the identification of opportunities to delegate various tasks to employees for developmental purposes. There are many questions to ask when determining what tasks to delegate and to whom. Once you can answer those questions, monitor and provide positive, timely feedback to motivate the employee for future tasks.

Review Your Learning

1 One aspect of developing employees is to

   A. monitor workload closely.

   B. keep the lines of communications closed.

   C. start with the mission and goals.

   D. show favoritism.

2 When tasks are delegated to employees,

   A. a delegation process and criteria must be developed.

   B. skills and knowledge tests taken by the employee must be considered.

   C. the employee must request it during his or her appraisal.

   D. the lowest level of delegation must be used initially.

3 One critical aspect of resolving conflicts is to

   A. have upper management intervene.

   B. identify what is critical to each side of the conflict.

   C. have the employees involved attend a counseling session.

   D. use peer pressure to resolve it.

4 When delegating tasks, mangers take on the role of

   A. mentor.

   B. coach.

   C. director.

   D. facilitator.

5 A satisfier for an employee is

   A. intrinsic motives.

   B. challenging assignments.

   C. money.

   D. work flexibility.

6 Theory Y suggests that people in the workplace

   A. really do not like to work.

   B. compare the amount of inputs to their outputs.

   C. measure their productivity by how much they want something.

   D. are internally driven and seek gratification.

7 An organizational catalyst

   A. channels energy of the organization to reach goals.

   B. leverages motivational strategies to build relationships.

   C. directs teams or employees through conflicts.

   D. conducts continuous feedback and employee appraisals.

8 Sexual harassment does *not* require which of these compliance issue?

   A. A condition of initial or continued employment

   B. A basis of working conditions including promotions and salary increases

   C. An intimidating and hostile work climate

   D. A terminated employee to support claims

9 Harassment in the workplace does *not* fall into which of these categories?

   A. Ethnic   C. Nepotism

   B. Age   D. Physical limitations

10 Self-disclosure is an information-sharing strategy that

   A. involves vulnerability.

   B. exercises leadership qualities.

   C. includes nonverbal messages.

   D. empathizes with the communicators.

Win-Win Scheduling Practices

7

Inside This Chapter

- Master Schedules
- Additional Scheduling Considerations
- Creating the Actual Crew Schedule
- Backup Strategies for Crew Scheduling
- Developing and Preparing the Management Schedule

After completing this chapter, you should be able to:

- Define the following terms: scheduling, master schedule, historical sales information, sales projections, covers, budget, pro forma income statement, deployment chart, crew schedule, time-off request policy, Family Medical Leave Act (FMLA), employee absence policy, Fair Labor Standards Act (FLSA), contingency plan, cross-training, shift leader, management schedule, standard and floaters.

- Describe the components of a master schedule and the importance of each.

- Determine if payroll standards are met on a master schedule.

- Explain the use of a deployment chart.

- Describe the importance of backup strategies in developing schedules.

- Prepare a management schedule.

- Explain factors to consider in the development of employee schedules.

- Develop a crew schedule.

- Describe how FLSA and FMLA affect scheduling in a restaurant.

- Describe the importance of cross-training staff and the use of floaters.

Test Your Knowledge

1 **True or False:** A deployment chart tells management how many servers to schedule on any given shift. *(See p. 155.)*

2 **True or False:** Communication between management and employees is paramount when scheduling. *(See p. 157.)*

3 **True or False:** The Family and Medical Leave Act provides for paid time off for medical and family emergencies. *(See p. 159.)*

4 **True or False:** An employee who is fifteen years old can operate a slicer if a supervisor is present. *(See p. 164.)*

5 **True or False:** Overtime should never be scheduled or planned. *(See p. 164.)*

6 **True or False:** The needs of the business as well as the employee should be taken into account when writing a crew schedule. *(See p. 156.)*

7 **True or False:** A master schedule is static and should not be changed when writing a crew schedule. *(See p. 163.)*

8 **True or False:** External events could affect the crew schedule so that it has more hours than are indicated on the master schedule. *(See pp. 161–162.)*

9 **True or False:** Management schedules, for the most part, follow the same criteria as crew schedules. *(See p. 170.)*

Key Terms

Budget

Contingency plan

Covers

Crew schedule

Cross-training

Deployment chart

Employee absence policy

Fair Labor Standards Act
  (FLSA)

Family and Medical Leave Act
  (FMLA)

Floaters

Historical sales information

Management schedule

Master schedule

Sales projections

Scheduling

Shift leaders

Standard

Time-off request policy

Introduction

In general, the restaurant and foodservice industry is a people business. To operate, restaurants need friendly, outgoing, and energetic employees. Having the right people as well as the correct number of people at any given time requires a work schedule. This chapter introduces the mechanics of scheduling. **Scheduling**— to plan or appoint employees to work at a certain time and date—

is not creating a haphazard list of names and times, but carefully developing a thought-out plan that takes into account many factors. In this chapter, you will learn about the three most important factors that affect scheduling: the business itself, its employees, and its profits.

Although schedules are prepared for the business, you must remember that people are the ones being scheduled. They have lives outside of work: family, activities, and events that they want to attend, and sometimes emergencies that need to be handled. You will learn how to balance the needs of an operation with the needs of its employees.

Finally, no matter how carefully a schedule is crafted, changes can occur at any time. Therefore, it is imperative for a savvy manager to have a backup plan. When an unforeseen event takes place and an employee cannot come in, there should always be a contingency plan in place. This chapter will assist you in creating backup strategies to cover emergencies that may occur.

Master Schedules

A **master schedule** is a template used for creating weekly employee schedules. This plan shows which hourly positions need to be filled and at what times, in order for a foodservice establishment to serve its customers. It does not include names because those will change.

The master schedule must be created carefully, since other schedules are derived from it. If the master schedule is done properly, it will provide for the right number of people at the right time to handle sales volume. It also helps a manager achieve the operation's labor cost standard which includes all payroll costs—both for hourly employees and management staff.

There is a lot of work and research that must be done prior to developing a master schedule. Sales history, sales projections, budgets, cost standards, which positions must be filled at all times, and who will cover secondary positions, must all be taken into consideration before a master schedule can be created.

Two primary purposes of a master schedule are:

- To assure that the correct number of hourly staff is on hand so customers will receive prompt, efficient service and properly prepared food

- To assure that the dollars spent on payroll meet the company standard

Exhibit 7a

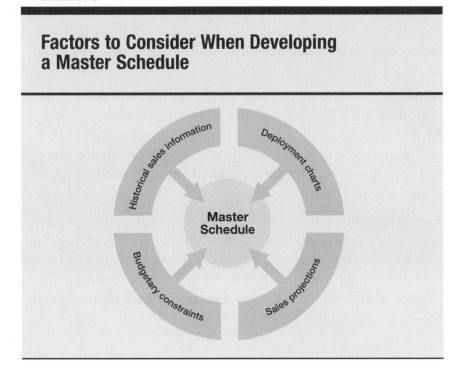

Factors to Consider When Developing a Master Schedule

Developing an effective master schedule involves taking the following into consideration:

- Historical sales information
- Sales projections
- Budgetary constraints
- Deployment charts

All of this information is gathered and used when creating a master schedule. (See *Exhibit 7a.*)

Historical Sales Information

Gathering sales history is important because what has occurred in the past is likely to occur in the future. This is particularly true for the foodservice industry. Most operations fall into a pattern of business volume. **Historical sales information** is simply an account of past sales volumes in a foodservice operation. This historical pattern is valuable in developing sales projections that are used to make up the master schedule.

Sales are tracked for different periods: yearly, monthly, weekly, daily, meal period, and hourly. Yearly and monthly data are used for budgeting and income statement purposes. Weekly sales information is used for purchasing and scheduling. Daily, meal period, and hourly data are also used for scheduling, in addition to being used for production planning.

Sales information can come from several sources. Yearly and monthly sales information come from the income statement. Hourly, daily, and weekly figures come from point-of-sale (POS) system printouts. In operations that do not have POS systems, this information comes from tabulating guest checks or periodic cash register readings.

Accurate historical sales information for all these time periods is vitally important. Inaccurate information can cause too many people to be scheduled, which would increase labor costs and reduce profit. Conversely, inaccurate information may result in fewer employees being scheduled than needed, resulting in poor service, and ultimately, a loss of sales.

Sales Projections

Precise sales projections are paramount to developing a sound master schedule. **Sales projections** are an estimate of future sales based on historical sales records and other information viewed as relevant by management. In developing sales projections, past sales records are used as a baseline. This baseline is either increased or decreased, based on current, local, and national trends. (See *Exhibit 7b*.)

As projected sales increase, the number of employees will increase, and as projected sales decrease, the number of employees will decrease. Therefore, a master schedule is based on a norm. It is created with the idea that a certain sales level is most likely to be reached. As sales change from that norm, either up or down, the master schedule should be adjusted accordingly. In some operations, more than one master schedule will be needed.

For example, if a new office park is slated to open across the street from a restaurant, then lunch sales would be projected to show an increase over last year. Conversely, if a manufacturing plant in town is expected to shut down, a restaurant would probably lower its projections, as some residents would have little or no disposable income to spend on eating out.

Adjusting Projections According to Trends

Managers need to examine more than just the previous year's sales information when calculating future sales projections. To make the best estimates for a reasonable master schedule, they also need to consider current trends. While local trends are more important than national ones, the latter should not be overlooked. The economy, unemployment, and other national and international events will all affect a person's desire or ability to eat out. (See *Exhibit 7c* on the next page.)

Exhibit 7b

Both local trends, such as increased tourism or convention business, and national trends, such as the economy or unemployment rate, affect sales projections.

Exhibit 7c

An Example of Projecting Sales

Audrey and Miguel are managers working on the sales projections for next year's budget at Elton's Grill, an upscale chain restaurant featuring Mexican cuisine. The restaurant is part of a very popular year-round resort area located on the outskirts of a small coastal city in Florida. The restaurant gets most of its business from the town's residents, but some tourists dine there too.

Creating the sales projections for the upcoming calendar year presents some challenges for Audrey and Miguel. Here are some of the factors that affect their planning:

■ A major hurricane recently damaged many of the area's vacation homes and resorts. Rebuilding has been slow, and as a result, tourism is projected to be down next year.

■ A national retailer is opening a store immediately adjacent to the restaurant next September. Audrey and Miguel expect sales to increase because of the new store, but they have also heard that the city is considering widening the street in front of the restaurant.

The pair decides to split up and do some research on the potential impacts of the hurricane and the new store. Here are their findings:

■ After talking with an old college friend who is also a manager at one of the chain's other restaurants, Miguel learns that his friend's restaurant experienced an 8 percent sales increase after a large store opened in the neighborhood.

■ Audrey finds out at a Chamber of Commerce meeting that the community expects a 20 to 30 percent decline in tourism through May, but then expects it to rebound and quickly return to normal.

■ Audrey also discovers at the meeting that a countywide fair is going to be held in July, at a location close to the restaurant, featuring fireworks and a major country music star.

■ Miguel calls the mayor's office to find out about the road widening and learns that the mayor believes that the city council will approve it. Construction will most likely start in January and last for four months.

Starting with last year's figures, Audrey and Miguel create these sales projections for the year. Note how their research affects each month's numbers.

Month	Sales Projection	Reason
January	Down 10%	8% due to beginning street construction, and 2% due to tourism drop
February	Down 15%	13% due to construction, which is now in high gear, and 2% due to tourism drop
March	Down 15%	Same reasoning as February
April	Down 15%	Same reasoning as February
May	Down 2%	Construction should be done; 2% due to tourism drop
June	Up 5%	Major promotion to celebrate the end of construction will increase sales 7%, minus 2% due to tourism drop
July	Up 10%	Fairgrounds celebration, tourism back to normal
August	Same as last year	
September	Up 10%	Retail store opens, and its grand opening will create traffic
October	Up 8%	Business spike expected from the retail store
November	Up 8%	Same reasoning as October
December	Up 10%	Retail store 8%, plus 2% due to new promotion

Creating a Master Schedule Based on Covers

After your projection baseline is adjusted according to current trends, the sales figures are then broken down into monthly and weekly figures, and then broken down further still into daily, meal period or shift, and hourly figures. From this information, you can determine how many employees are needed for each position.

Having the correct number of staff on hand is normally planned according to the anticipated number of **covers,** or meals to be served. Management should determine the standard for covers per hour, which is affected by the style of the operation, type of service, and complexity of production, among other factors. This standard is then measured against the sales forecast to determine the number of servers to be scheduled. Here are the formulas:

$$\frac{\text{Forecasted covers}}{\text{for the period}} \div \frac{\text{Number of hours}}{\text{in the period}} = \frac{\text{Anticipated covers}}{\text{per hour}}$$

$$\frac{\text{Anticipated covers}}{\text{per hour}} \div \frac{\text{Covers per hour}}{\text{standard}} = \frac{\text{Number of servers}}{\text{needed for the period}}$$

For example, if the standard in an operation is 20 covers per server per hour, and the forecast for lunch this week is 300 covers (assuming a 4-hour period), then 3.75 servers need to be scheduled.

300 ÷ 4 hours = 75 covers per hour

75 ÷ 20 covers = 3.75 servers needed

The figure in this example, however, needs to be further refined, since the guests will not arrive in an orderly fashion of seventy-five per hour. Additionally, when the calculation produces a decimal figure, the question then becomes: do you round up or down? There is no set answer for this, since it depends on the caliber of the personnel involved. If the staff is relatively new and not yet fully trained, then it would probably be wise to add another person. If the staff is more experienced, you could probably drop a person.

Consequently, the schedule may call for one server to open and more waitstaff to be added as the customer count increases over the meal period. The schedule could end up looking like the example in *Exhibit 7d* on p. 153. Note that this schedule does not list names; it focuses on positions and the number of employees in those positions.

Servers, cashiers, hosts, bussers, and line cooks can be scheduled according to covers per hour, though not all restaurants use the covers method. Some operations, such as quick-service restaurants, create a master schedule based on the anticipated number of customers per hour (which focuses more on customer traffic than meals served), while some restaurants use sales per hour.

Creating a Master Schedule Based on Productivity

Some positions are more productive than others. Servers, who have to travel from the kitchen to a guest table and engage in conversation with the guests, are less productive from a covers per hour standpoint than dishwashers are, who only travel a few feet and do not converse regularly with guests. A spike in sales of forty covers per hour might result in adding two servers to the schedule, but not any additional dishwashers. Prep cook, pantry, and bakeshop positions typically are also scheduled based on production needs rather than covers.

Budgetary Constraints

In an ideal world, managers could put as many employees on the schedule as they desire, and then add a few extra to cover any emergencies that might come up. The reality, however, is that labor costs are also usually one of the highest costs an operation has and management has several scheduling constraints. One of these is the **budget,** a projection of sales, costs, and profit that is used to guide day-to-day operational decisions. Budgets are created based on historical figures and educated forecasts of what will happen in a specific period.

The sales projections that managers use to help create the master schedule are also crucial to the budget. In order for an operation to achieve its budgeted profit, the sales projections listed in its budget must be met. Additionally, the operation's costs must be held to their **standards,** which is the budgeted dollar amount for each type of cost.

Managers need to create the master schedule to reflect budgeted labor costs, keeping both sales projections and the payroll standard— which includes hourly wages and managers' salaries—in mind. *Exhibit 7d* shows a master schedule with the required number of hourly employees performing the required number of tasks for an operation's lunch shift, but the schedule must also be tested to see whether it meets the operation's payroll standard. (Note that this schedule may look different for weekdays and the weekend.)

The operation in *Exhibit 7d* has a payroll standard of 26 percent. Its total hourly payroll for one day, as seen in the schedule, is $276.95. Therefore, the total hourly payroll for the week, based on a six-day week, is $1,661.70.

Daily hourly payroll $\times$ Number of work days $=$ Total hourly payroll

$276.95 $\times$ 6 $=$ $1,661.70

Now the cost of management must be added to find the total payroll amount for the operation that week. In this operation, the management crew makes $1,460.00 each week. So the total payroll is $3,121.70.

Total hourly payroll + **Total salary payroll** = **Total labor payroll**

$1,661.70 + **$1,460.00** = **$3,121.70**

Finally, you must compare the total labor payroll to the sales for the week to see if the operation's payroll standard has been met. This week, the operation posts $12,000.00 in sales, which results in 26%, meaning the operation has met its payroll standard.

Total labor payroll ÷ **Total sales** = **Payroll standard**

$3,121.70 ÷ **$12,000.00** = **.26 or 26%**

Exhibit 7d

Example of a Master Schedule for Lunch Day Part

Time	8:00	9:00	10:00	11:00	12:00	1:00	2:00	Total Hours	Rate	Total Payroll
Covers			15	75	80	90	40			
Position										
Server A			X	X	X	X	X	5	2.13	10.65
Server B				X	X	X	X	4	2.13	8.52
Server C				X	X	X		3	2.13	6.39
Server D				X	X	X		3	2.13	6.39
Host/Cashier			X	X	X	X	X	5	7.50	37.50
Busser				X	X	X	X	4	6.00	24.00
Dishwasher				X	X	X	X	4	6.50	26.00
Line cook 1	X	X	X	X	X	X		6	10.00	60.00
Line cook 2		X	X	X	X	X	X	6	8.00	48.00
Pantry	X	X	X	X	X	X		6	8.25	49.50
										$276.95

Activity

Meeting Payroll Standards with the Master Schedule

Apple Orchard Restaurant has a total payroll of $286.19 per day, and the cost of management is $1,420 per week. The payroll standard is 25%. The sales for the week are $13,650.00.

1 What is the total hourly payroll for the week
if the restaurant is open seven days a week?   _____

2 What is the total payroll?   _____

3 Is the payroll standard met?   _____

Apple Orchard Restaurant										
Time	5:00	6:00	7:00	8:00	9:00	10:00	11:00	Total Hours	Rate	Total Payroll
Covers			35	45	65	70	30			
Position										
Server A			✗	✗	✗	✗	✗	5	2.13	10.65
Server B			✗	✗	✗	✗	✗	5	2.13	10.65
Server C				✗	✗	✗		3	2.13	6.39
Host/cashier			✗	✗	✗	✗	✗	5	7.50	37.50
Busser			✗	✗	✗	✗	✗	5	6.00	30.00
Dishwasher				✗	✗	✗	✗	4	6.50	26.00
Line cook 1	✗	✗	✗	✗	✗	✗		6	11.00	66.00
Line cook 2		✗	✗	✗	✗	✗	✗	6	8.50	51.00
Pantry	✗	✗	✗	✗	✗	✗		6	8.00	48.00
										$286.19

Other Factors to Consider When Creating a Master Schedule

A master schedule can get quite complicated depending on the volume and number of shifts involved. Many restaurants create the master schedule electronically with spreadsheet software. No matter how it is created, keep in mind that a master schedule is not a static instrument, and it will need to change often.

Deployment Charts

For a restaurant to function, certain tasks must be performed, which are assigned to individuals who hold various positions. The tasks are not performed all the time, and not all of the positions have to be filled by separate individuals all the time. Some positions are critical and must be filled any time the restaurant is open, while other positions are secondary and have tasks that can be added to another position. For example, a restaurant that has a hostess and a cashier can combine the tasks of these positions into one position during a slow period. Many restaurants have no cashier position, as each server is responsible for collecting either cash or a credit card for their guest checks.

A **deployment chart** shows which job classifications are essential or primary to staff and which are secondary. *Exhibit 7e* illustrates how a restaurant might divide these tasks among various positions. Knowing which positions are primary, which are secondary, and who will handle the secondary staff job tasks when people are not specifically scheduled to do them, is important when it comes to creating the master schedule. A deployment chart is not "one size fits all," since each foodservice operation is different.

Exhibit 7e

Example of a Deployment Chart

Job Task	Staff Position	Primary/ Secondary	Other Positions That Can Cover Task
Taking cash	Cashier	P	
Seating guests	Host	S	Cashier, waitstaff
Service	Waitstaff	P	
Busing tables	Busser	S	Waitstaff
Receiving deliveries	Receiving clerk	S	Chef
Prep soups, sauces, entrées	Prep cook	P	
Grill, fry	Line cook 1	P	
Dish up short orders	Line cook 2	S	Line cook 1
Prep salads, cold food	Pantry cook	P	
Bake breads and desserts	Baker	P	
Dish up salads, desserts	Pantry line	S	Pantry cook/Line cook 1
Coordinate line	Expeditor	S	Line cook 1
Wash dishes	Dishwasher 1	P	
Wash dishes	Dishwasher 2	S	Dishwasher 1
Wash pots and pans	Pot and pan washer	S	Dishwasher 1
General sanitation duties	Janitor	P	

Additional Scheduling Considerations

The master schedule is used as the foundation for preparing both the management and crew schedules. Although the target employees are different, there are common considerations for both groups. These include:

- Using all the elements that go into the creation of the master schedule as a source of information for the management and crew schedules

- Communicating well in advance and considering various events and business needs when developing the schedules

- Using established guidelines regarding time-off requests

- Keeping the schedule as balanced and equitable as possible for all employees

- Building flexibility into the schedules

- Using sales projections

- Leveraging deployment charts for key positions

Knowing these common scheduling factors can make the entire scheduling process less cumbersome.

When developing schedules, there should be a balance between the needs of the restaurant and the needs of its employees. A **crew schedule** is a chart that shows employees what days and hours they are expected to work. It is created by using the master schedule as a template. (See *Exhibit 7f.*) The crew schedule needs to be developed with flexibility in mind. Nothing will upset employees more than finding out they have to work when there is an important event going on in their lives. Nothing will upset a manager more than finding out that an employee cannot, or will not, work a shift when he or she is desperately needed. While not all of these situations can be avoided, most of them can be alleviated by having clear policies and open, two-way communication.

The next sections describe in more detail the factors that a manager needs to consider when planning for effective utilization of staff and creating a flexible crew schedule.

Exhibit 7f

Example of a Crew Schedule Developed from the Master Schedule

Name	Position	Monday	Tuesday	Wednesday	Thursday	Friday	Saturday
Jennifer	Server	10–3	10–3	10–3	10–3	10–3	10–3
LaTonia	Server	11–3	11–3	11–3	11–3	11–3	11–3
Bill	Server	11–2	11–2	11–2	11–2	11–2	11–2
Tony	Server	11–2	11–2	11–2	11–2	11–2	11–2
Candace	Host/Cashier	10–3	10–3	10–3	10–3	10–3	10–3
Mike	Busser	11–3	11–3	11–3	11–3	11–3	11–3
Sung Lee	Dishwasher	11–3	11–3	11–3	11–3	11–3	11–3
Carlos	Line cook 1	8–2	8–2	8–2	8–2	8–2	8–2
Judy	Line cook 2	9–3	9–3	9–3	9–3	8–2	8–2
Charisse	Pantry	8–2	8–2	8–2	8–2	8–2	8–2

Communicating Long- and Short-Range Business Needs

Communication plays an important role in scheduling employees effectively. Most employees want to see the restaurant do well. They realize it is a team effort to ensure success—if the operation is successful, they will continue to have jobs. Therefore, it is important to keep employees informed as to what is going on.

Company plans, such as a change in menu or hours of operation, or an upcoming advertising promotion, all need to be communicated to the staff. Employees should also be made aware of community events that can potentially affect sales. This includes both a spike upward or a significant decreases. For example, if the street in front of the restaurant is closed for a week for repaving, and the only way into the restaurant is through a back alley, one could assume that sales will be down that week. By telling employees well in advance, the line cook may decide to go on vacation that week. This would be a win-win situation for both the employee and management: you could schedule one less lead person during a slow week, and that person could have a well-deserved break. Conversely, by informing the employees of an art festival next month that could draw ten thousand people into the neighborhood, your waitstaff would probably not request time off because of the potential for increased tips.

While open communication will not solve all scheduling problems, it will help solve some of them. Employees who know what is going on in a restaurant or the surrounding community will be more inclined to schedule their personal time around the events affecting their workplace.

Establishing Guidelines for Requesting Time Off

When establishing either a crew or a management schedule, there are three issues to consider: time off for vacations, time off for other days, and the Family and Medical Leave Act (FMLA).

Assuming that a foodservice operation has vacation benefits, a **time-off request policy** should be established, which is the procedure and guidelines for employees to follow when they want time off from work. It informs the employee of the steps they need to follow in making such a request.

Vacations

To determine when vacation time is available for your employees, you must look at the annual sales budget, as well as an events calendar, to determine which weeks during the year could have particularly heavy sales volume. If so, those weeks need to be "blocked off" on the vacation calendar and request form. As part of the policy, a stipulation should be made that not more than one person from each area or department can be off at the same time.

Vacation requests are normally assigned according to seniority. So the person who has been working in the restaurant the longest has first choice, the person working the second longest gets second choice, and so on. Vacation request forms should be submitted in advance, so management has adequate time to prepare for those absences. They should also be in writing. Occasionally, another employee will have to be trained to take the place of a person going on vacation.

Day-Off Requests

The procedure to request a day off should have guidelines. First, a time frame needs to be established. Since day-off requests are usually short-term, one week prior to the posting of a schedule should be sufficient. A policy should be in place regarding how many persons in an area can be off at one time. In the case of servers, it could be several, but in the kitchen, possibly only one person could be allowed off at a time. Should a conflict occur, a guideline should be established as to whether requests will be honored on a seniority or first come, first served basis. Holidays, which will be covered later, are normally off-limits for requesting time off; religious holidays are an exception. Day-off requests are normally not an issue unless there is also a major event taking place, such as a prom, athletic event, or concert. Then it can quickly become a major issue, which is best diffused by having a policy in effect and agreed to by all concerned.

Family and Medical Leave Act (FMLA)

The **Family and Medical Leave Act (FMLA)** is a federal law that allows eligible employees to take an extended amount of time off for medical and other personal reasons. The FMLA applies to businesses employing fifty or more persons. An employer who is covered by the act must grant an eligible employee up to a total of twelve weeks of unpaid leave during a twelve-month period for the following reasons:

- Birth and care of a newborn child

- Placement of a son or daughter for adoption or foster care

- Caring for an immediate family member (spouse, child, or parent) with a serious health condition

- Taking medical leave because of a serious health condition

The act provides that an employee must, upon returning to work, be given the same position at the same rate of pay as when he or she left. For a complete discussion of the FMLA, consult the U.S. Department of Labor's Web site at *http://www.dol.gov/esa/whd/fmla.*

Employee Absence Policy

While the previous discussion has been about employees requesting time off in advance, occasionally they will need time off without warning. This can be due to sickness, a family emergency, or some other unforeseen event. **Employee absence policies** are guidelines and procedures that explain how employees must notify management if they are unable to work. These policies often require employees to contact management as soon as they know they will not be at work, as well as how long they anticipate being off.

Many organizations have a policy that if employees are ill, they must secure a doctor's release prior to returning to work. This is particularly important in the foodservice industry, since contagious diseases and infections can easily spread.

Posting Schedules in Advance

To help avoid conflict with an employee's personal life, the schedule should be posted well in advance. Giving employees a week or ten days to make their plans will go a long way in eliminating any conflicts that could arise.

Activity

Time-Off Policy Dilemma

You own and manage a family restaurant located in a mountain resort town. The employees who work for you seem happy, and over the years you have seen no need for written employee rules. But now there is Benjamin, a seventeen-year-old dishwasher—and a marginal one at best. He barely keeps up with the dishes on an average night, and when the restaurant is busy, he falls behind. He sometimes fails to show up for work, always blaming it on his mother, who is quite ill. Dishwashers are hard to find in your town, so you have put up with him. But last weekend, he did not show up at all, and he did not even call. When he came in on Monday, you fired him. Benjamin has threatened to sue the restaurant, claiming you fired him because of his age.

In small groups, discuss the following questions. Then as a class, share your answers.

1 What do you think your chances of success would be in court?

_____

_____

_____

2 How would you prepare your case?

_____

_____

_____

3 What might Benjamin say?

_____

_____

_____

4 What should you do to prevent this from happening in the future?

_____

_____

_____

_____

Creating the Actual Crew Schedule

Now that the master schedule has been written and the employees' needs and wants have been addressed, it is time to put the crew schedule together. You have established fair policies and have communicated information to your employees about scheduling needs. Although you should make every effort to accommodate employees, you also have to consider the needs of the business. When assigning staff to shifts on the schedule, there are several things to keep in mind. These include:

- External events and sales volume projections

- Effective staff utilization

- Building flexibility into the schedule

- Scheduling minors and other legal constraints

- Overtime

- Overloading expertise on one shift

- Scheduling holidays and weekends in a fair and equitable manner

External Events and Sales Volume

As previously discussed, the master schedule is a plan to be followed under a normal operating pattern. The truth of the matter is that "normal" is not an everyday occurrence in the restaurant industry. Exceptions can occur at any given time. The schedule needs to reflect expected sales variations as close as possible. Remember that labor is a semivariable cost that goes up or down as sales go up or down. If managers are to meet the budget and show a profit, they must react to these fluctuations through scheduling. Some factors that would cause an exception to the master schedule include:

- **Holidays.** Some holidays cause sales to explode, while on other holidays, the restaurant closes due to lack of business. For most commercial operations, Mother's Day is the highest-volume day of the year; conversely, many operations close on Christmas Day. Thanksgiving is a good holiday for some, but not for others. Knowing the past sales history for each holiday and adjusting the master schedule accordingly will allow the restaurant to achieve its maximum potential for a particular day.

- **Seasonal adjustments.** The weather often plays a critical role in seasonally adjusting a schedule. Extreme heat or cold will normally cause sales to drop. Typically, advanced adjustments cannot be made, due to the suddenness of weather-related events. Hurricanes, tornadoes, and snowstorms all affect sales, but the master schedule is posted long before these conditions develop. However, some employees will not make it in, and thus the problem will often solve itself. In severe cases, the foodservice operation might have to close. Other seasonal adjustments include the holiday shopping season, which will spur sales, and income tax time, when sales historically drop.

- **Advertising and promotions.** These factors are known well enough in advance for making adjustments to the master schedule. A well-planned promotional event should have a dramatic effect on sales. Management should take full advantage of this by having the proper number of staff on hand to handle the additional traffic. Conversely, if the competition runs a well-planned promotion, it would have an adverse effect on sales, and scheduling must be adjusted accordingly. Being aware of the competition is an extremely important function of management.

- **Community activities.** Fairs, ethnic festivals, and athletic events will all get people out of their homes and into the community. Depending on the location of the event and its proximity to the restaurant, these activities can have a large impact on sales. The astute manager will know what is going on in the community and its potential effect on the operation.

- **Economy.** Restaurants are affected differently by the economy. In some instances, fine-dining operations are influenced negatively, while more casual restaurants are affected positively. At other times, the opposite is true, and in other cases, all foodservice operations are affected. If economic conditions are temporary, the crew and management schedules should be adjusted to reflect these conditions. If they are long-range situations, then the master schedule should be adjusted accordingly.

Effective Staff Utilization

In any restaurant or foodservice operation, there are great employees, good employees, and those whose skill levels need to be improved. When deciding which employee to schedule on which shift, each employee's capabilities need to be taken into account. Workers whose skill levels need improvement should be placed, if possible, with an employee who can mentor them, coach them, and help them improve.

In most operations, there are days in which the sales volume is heavier than others, as well as meal periods with heavier volume. During these periods, emphasis should be placed on putting the more experienced and productive employees on the schedule. Sales need to be made when the opportunity presents itself.

Think About It...

Efficient crew planning and scheduling are essential for restaurant operators who want to improve service quality, particularly when cost is a primary factor. How might a scheduling software program help a manager ensure that the right people are in the right place at the right time?

However, be careful not to overload all the expertise onto one shift and leave the other shifts with a weak crew. Training should be relegated to the slower days and meal periods.

Building Flexibility into the Crew Schedule

While the master schedule is rather rigid in showing how many employees are needed to achieve projected sales, some flexibility needs to be written into the crew schedule. Every employee will not be available every day for every shift. Sometimes arrangements are made when an employee is hired; for example, a server could request Tuesday and Thursday evenings off to attend class.

There are internal factors to consider when writing the crew schedule that are often not considered on the master schedule. For example, receiving deliveries should be taken into account. Who is going to receive them? How much time will it take? Is there sufficient time for someone to do this and still get his or her regular work completed, or do additional hours need to be scheduled? Is there a piece of equipment that has broken down or is out for maintenance, which will cause a delay in employee productivity? These are just a few of the issues that could necessitate an adjustment to the crew schedule.

Exhibit 7g

Managers must consider the effect that training has on productivity, which in turn affects the schedule.

Employee training also must be considered when a schedule is created. (See *Exhibit 7g.*) A worker who wants to improve his or her productivity, or a new employee who needs training, will affect scheduling. A lead employee who is mentoring this person may be taken away from regular tasks, and perhaps another person would need to be scheduled to maintain efficiency.

Another activity that sometimes is not listed on the master schedule is employee meetings. If management wants to hold such a meeting, then the time should be set aside on the crew schedule.

Scheduling Minors and Other Legal Constraints

For those operations that hire persons under the age of eighteen, there are some legal constaints regarding scheduling that management should know. The **Fair Labor Standards Act (FLSA)** is a federal law that sets minimum wage, overtime pay, equal pay, record-keeping, and child-labor standards for covered employees. Additionally, the act prohibits persons younger than eighteen years old from operating power equipment.

According to the FLSA, fourteen- and fifteen-year-olds may work the following:

■ Three hours on a school day

■ Eighteen hours in a school week

■ Eight hours on a nonschool day

■ Forty hours in a nonschool week

■ Work may not begin before 7:00 a.m. or end after 7:00 p.m., except from June 1 through Labor Day, when nighttime work hours are extended to 9:00 p.m.

The FLSA has major implications for restaurants that hire minors, and the person responsible for preparing the crew schedule should be familiar with the law's content. Some state laws may supersede this federal law. For more information and a complete breakdown of the FLSA, consult the U.S. Department of Labor's Web site at *http://www.dol.gov/*.

Overtime

Overtime should never be scheduled. It is a waste of precious payroll dollars. While it is sometimes necessary to have an employee work overtime due to another employee not showing up at the last minute, it should never be planned into a schedule.

Scheduling in a Fair and Equitable Manner

It was stated earlier that a scheduled shift should have a mix of highly experienced, productive employees and those whose productivity is not up to standard. It was also stated that during periods when the sales level is at its highest, this mix should favor the more productive worker. However, care should be taken not to overextend one employee or group of employees because they are exceptional at their positions. For example, if the restaurant is busiest on the weekends, the outstanding employees should not be scheduled every weekend; in other words, they should not be penalized for being good at their jobs. Likewise, holidays should be scheduled in a fair and equitable manner. *Exhibit 7h* is an example of an establishment's holiday schedule, showing which holidays each employee has worked or plans to work. This type of schedule is useful for distributing holiday work hours equally among the staff.

Exhibit 7h

Sample Holiday Schedule

Jerry's Bar & Grill
HOLIDAY SHIFTS 2006

Name	Position	New Year's Day	Valentine's Day	Easter	Memorial Day	Fourth of July	Labor Day	Thanksgiving	Christmas Eve	Christmas Day	New Year's Eve
Jennifer	Server			X		X		X	X	X	
LaTonia	Server	X	X		X		X				X
Bill	Server	X	X	X	X		X				
Tony	Server					X	X		X	X	X
Candace	Host/Cashier	X		X			X		X	X	
Patti	Host/Cashier		X		X			X		X	X
Mike	Buser/Dishwasher		X	X	X				X	X	X
Sung Lee	Buser	X				X	X				X
Carlos	Line cook 1	X	X	X				X			X
Judy	Line cook 2					X	X		X	X	X
Charisse	Pantry	X				X	X	X		X	X
Betty	Pantry		X		X	X			X	X	

165

Activity

Developing a Crew Schedule

On the next page is a master schedule for the Blue Diamond Café. The restaurant is open from 8:00 a.m. to 2:00 p.m., Monday through Saturday. Based on this schedule, create a crew schedule from the chart on the next page. Here are some employee requests, as well as additional information about their availability:

- Brad cannot work on Wednesdays because of classes.

- Amanda cannot work on Thursdays.

- Christine cannot work on Mondays or Tuesdays.

- Rosaline can only work afternoons on Mondays.

- Sally can only work mornings on Tuesdays.

- Denise is seventeen years old.

- Amanda will be late this Friday because of a dentist's appointment.

Compare your schedule with others in the class and discuss the following questions:

1 What factors did you consider as you planned the schedule?

_____

_____

_____

_____

2 What difficulties did you have, if any?

_____

_____

_____

_____

3 Do you think the employees will be satisfied with their schedule? Why or why not?

_____

_____

_____

_____

_____

Time	6:00	7:00	8:00	9:00	10:00	11:00	12:00	1:00	2:00	Total Hours	Rate	Total Payroll
Master Schedule for Blue Diamond Café												
Covers			20	30	30	65	75	70	25			
Position												
Server A			✗	✗	✗	✗	✗			5	2.13	10.65
Server B					✗	✗	✗	✗	✗	5	2.13	10.65
Server C						✗	✗	✗		3	2.13	6.39
Server D						✗	✗	✗		3	2.13	6.39
Host/Cashier			✗	✗	✗	✗	✗	✗	✗	7	7.50	52.50
Busser				✗	✗	✗	✗	✗	✗	6	6.00	36.00
Dishwasher					✗	✗	✗	✗	✗	5	6.50	32.50
Line cook 1	✗	✗	✗	✗	✗	✗				6	11.00	66.00
Line cook 2				✗	✗	✗	✗	✗	✗	6	8.00	48.00
Pantry	✗	✗	✗	✗	✗	✗				6	8.20	49.20
												$318.28

Name	Position	Monday	Tuesday	Wednesday	Thursday	Friday	Saturday
Crew Schedule for This Week							
Rosaline	Server						
Sally	Server						
Paul	Server						
Brad	Server						
Chad	Server						
Denise	Server						
Kendra	Host/Cashier						
Mike	Busser						
Juan	Dishwasher						
Jim	Line cook						
Terry	Line cook						
Amanda	Pantry						
Christine	Pantry						

Backup Strategies for Crew Scheduling

While policies, procedures, and guidelines for proper scheduling will go a long way in assuring a smooth-running operation, problems can and will occur. Employees can get sick, have illnesses in their family, or have to deal with any number of problems. To prevent a crisis if one or more employees do not show up for work, a contingency plan should be developed. A **contingency plan** is a document outlining specific actions to take in the event of an emergency, crisis, or unexpected event. This plan should include:

- Cross-training employees
- Identifying shift leaders
- Identifying floaters

These strategies should cover unplanned employee needs and ensure that the business is still able to perform at optimal levels.

Cross-Training Employees

All staff positions in a foodservice operation should have several employees trained to perform that job. **Cross-training** is a process for developing employees' abilities to do tasks other than the ones they are regularly assigned to do. While they may not do a job on a day-to-day basis, they would be able to perform that function if a need should arise. For example, cashiers could be trained as servers and hosts; servers could be trained as cashiers and hosts. A baker might be trained for pantry and line-cook functions, and a line cook for pantry and baker duties. The more staff who are cross-trained for more positions, the more flexibility management has in reassigning positions when someone does not show up to work or is scheduled for time off.

Exhibit 7i provides an example of a typical restaurant employee roster showing which employees are trained for which positions.

Identifying Shift Leaders

Shift leaders are used in many foodservice operations. **Shift leaders** are employees who, in addition to their regularly assigned tasks, train new hires and perform other functions assigned by management. They are hourly employees who have some management responsibilities, and—because of their additional duties—are usually paid at a higher rate. Their primary duties as shift leaders are to occasionally train a new employee, work with an employee who is not up to standard, or answer work-related questions that others in their position may have.

Exhibit 7i

Employee Cross-Trained Chart

Name	Position	Trained For
Wendi	Cashier	Host/Server
Carlos	Host	Server
Boomer	Floater	Host/Server/Cashier
Hunter	Server	Host
Judy	Server	Host/Cashier
Bill	Server	Host/Cashier
Juan	Server	Host
Heather	Server	Cashier
Mohammad	Server	
Mike	Server	Host
Mokie	Server	
Carol	Server	Cashier
Theresa	Server	Host/Cashier
Conner	Busser	Dishwasher
Gunter	Busser	Dishwasher
Alphonso	Busser	
Charles	Busser	Dishwasher/Pot-pan
Shawna	Busser	Dishwasher
Jerry	Dishwasher	Pot-pan
Felix	Dishwasher	Pot-pan
Corrine	Dishwasher	Pot-pan
Ona	Dishwasher	Pot-pan
Susan	Pot-pan	Dishwasher/Busser
DeJesus	Floater	Dishwasher/Pot-pan/Busser
Jaunetta	Prep cook	Line cook 1/2
Yvette	Line cook 1	Prep cook/Line cook 2
Candace	Line cook 2	Line cook 1/Pantry
Jack	Pantry	Baker/Line cook 1/2
Anthony	Baker	Pantry
Latreese	Floater	Line cook 1/2 /Baker/Pantry

For example, an exceptional server could be designated as a server shift leader. He or she would normally work as a server, but occasionally would train new hires or answer questions from other servers.

Shift leaders are more common in the quick-service segment of the industry. Shift leaders are chosen because they are good at what they do, follow company policy, meet or exceed company standards, and show some leadership ability. Quite often, a shift leader position is a stepping stone into management.

Identifying Floaters

Floaters are employees who have the ability to perform more than one job on a regular basis within a foodservice operation. They are used to fill in for employees taking time off or vacation days. For example, a floater in a kitchen might work the line-cook position two days, pantry two days, and baker one day, covering those positions for the regular employees. Floaters are different from employees who have been cross-trained. Floaters do different tasks on a daily basis, while cross-trained employees do their regularly assigned task on a daily basis and only occasionally do a different task. Floaters are invaluable to management because of the flexibility they provide if another employee cannot work a shift.

Developing and Preparing the Management Schedule

In addition to a crew schedule, management also needs a schedule. A **management schedule** is a chart that shows which days and times the management staff is expected to work. It is derived from the master schedule.

The development of the management schedule should follow the same process and consider the same factors as the crew schedule:

- Develop a master schedule for management first.

- Consider special events, promotions, etc.

- Follow the policy for requesting time off.

- Schedule in a fair and equitable manner.

While the criteria for a management schedule are basically the same as for the crew schedule, there are some exceptions that should be noted.

1. Typically, management staff members, are salaried and are not held to a specific number of hours worked. Management employees are paid for that position and work as many hours as necessary to get the job done. Unlike the staff employees who work on an hourly basis and leave at the end of their shift, managers stay until their responsibilities are fulfilled. This is not to imply that managers should not have scheduled hours; although they may work longer hours than the staff, there should not be an unreasonable demand placed upon them.

2. Management schedules can include an "on call" designation. All too often, managers are contacted several times on their days off to solve problems occurring in the operation. This negates the benefit of downtime away from the restaurant and leads to burnout. To prevent this from happening, a member of the management team should be scheduled to be on-call, in case any problems come up. The on-call list should be rotated so that all members of the management team can enjoy a day off from work. For example: the chef is off, and the dining room manager is the manager on duty when a problem occurs in the kitchen. Not being familiar with that area, the dining room manager calls the general manager, who is on-call, for a solution to the problem.

3. At least one member of the management team should be on duty whenever there are employees working in the restaurant. In the event of any emergency that might occur, a manager can take action. A manager is also available to answer any questions that the staff might have or settle any disputes that might occur.

Additionally, many states require that at least one person on the premises be trained and certified in food safety and sanitation principles.

Exhibit 7j illustrates how a management team might be assigned throughout the operations of a restaurant to ensure coverage on a daily basis.

Exhibit 7j

Example of a Management Schedule

Position	Monday	Tuesday	Wednesday	Thursday	Friday	Saturday	Sunday
General manager	Off	11–7	11–7	11–7	11–7	11–7	Off
Asst. gen. mgr.	11–7	Off	Off	4–close	4–close	4–close	11–7
Executive chef	10–8	Off	Off	Off	1–8	10–8	10–8
Culinary shift leader	Off	10–8	10–8	10–8	Off	Off	Reg. shift
Dining room mgr.	4–close	4–close	4–close	Off	Off	4–close	4–close
Bar manager	4–close	Off	Off	4–close	4–close	4–close	4–close
Service shift leader	Off	4–close	4–close	Reg. shift	Reg. shift	Reg. shift	Off

Summary

For any foodservice establishment to be successful, it must have well-trained, friendly, and enthusiastic employees at the right time, in the right number, with the right mix. To do this, management needs to develop a master schedule that will assure the restaurant is properly staffed and that the labor cost stays in line with the budget, which will result in profitability for the business. Payroll is a high-expense item in the foodservice industry, and the schedule is the foremost tool in controlling this cost. There is a fine line that must be drawn in having an adequate staff on hand while also achieving profits.

It is important to create a master schedule on which crew and management schedules are based. When developing a crew schedule, two-way communication is key. Management needs to communicate the needs of the business to the staff, while the staff needs to communicate to management what their personal needs are in terms of time off. With this open communication, the most effective and flexible schedules can be created.

Even in the best scenario, things can go wrong, and occasionally one or more employees will not make it into work. A well thought-out backup or contingency plan will help alleviate these problems. Cross-training and the use of shift leaders and floaters can give management flexibility in covering the staffing needs of foodservice operations.

Review Your Learning

1 Employee names, along with the days and times they are expected to work, are listed on the

   A. master schedule.

   B. management schedule.

   C. crew schedule.

   D. All of the above

   E. B and C only

2 A master schedule takes into account

   A. historical sales information.

   B. sales projections.

   C. budgetary constraints.

   D. All of the above

   E. A and C only

3 When writing a schedule, which periods provide the most helpful sales information?

   A. Yearly and semi-annually

   B. Quarterly and monthly

   C. Daily and hourly

   D. All of the above

   E. A and B only

4 Budgetary constraints are taken into consideration when writing a

   A. deployment schedule.

   B. management schedule.

   C. crew schedule.

   D. master schedule.

   E. cross-training schedule.

5 A deployment chart is used to

   A. create a master schedule.

   B. show which tasks in the restaurant are primary and which are secondary.

   C. station the crew when unexpected absenteeism occurs.

   D. None of the above

   E. A and B only

6 A master schedule shows

   A. an employee's name, day, and time to work.

   B. an employee's name, total hours worked per week, and pay rate per hour.

   C. a position, day and time to work, and rate per hour of that position.

   D. a position and which employee is qualified to work it.

   E. an employee's name, position, and total wages earned for the week.

7 A crew schedule is developed from a

   A. master schedule.

   B. deployment schedule.

   C. management schedule.

   D. cross-training schedule.

   E. floater schedule.

8 The federal law regarding the use of a slicer by a minor is covered by

   A. the Family and Medical Leave Act (FMLA).

   B. the Fair Labor Standards Act (FLSA).

   C. Both acts

   D. Neither act

9 **Crew schedules should be posted**

A. one to three days in advance.

B. seven to ten days in advance.

C. twenty to thirty days in advance.

D. over one month in advance.

10 **Management can develop an effective backup strategy by**

A. cross-training employees.

B. employing floaters.

C. identifying shift leaders.

D. B and C only

E. A, B, and C

11 **A person who works at different positions on a regularly scheduled basis is known as a**

A. shift leader.

B. cross-trained employee.

C. manager.

D. floater.

E. None of the above

Notes

Teamwork in the Foodservice and Hospitality Workplace

8

Inside This Chapter

- The Importance of Teamwork in Foodservice
- Stages of Team Growth
- Goal Setting with a Team
- Managing Team-Based Projects

After completing this chapter, you should be able to:

- Define teamwork, interfunctional team, problem-solving team, cross-functional team, self-directed team, and debrief meeting.
- Identify the advantages and disadvantages of teams.
- Describe stages in team growth.
- Identify management behaviors that support or hinder team development and growth.
- Identify factors that support or hinder team goal setting.
- Describe an effective way to manage team-based projects.
- Explain the roles of lessons learned and a debrief meeting.

Test Your Knowledge

1 **True or False:** The manager is the person who evaluates the goals of a team project. *(See p. 194.)*

2 **True or False:** The manager overseeing the team is responsible for identifying the root causes of the assigned problem. *(See p. 179.)*

3 **True or False:** It is important to have a team member who is an expert in interpersonal skills. *(See p. 179.)*

4 **True or False:** Teamwork benefits should connect to the mission statement or values. *(See p. 192.)*

5 **True or False:** Most teams go through four stages of developing, including modeling. *(See p. 183.)*

6 **True or False:** The manager should not use a leadership style of directing with teams. *(See p. 183.)*

7 **True or False:** Teams should have information goals. *(See p. 190.)*

Key Terms

Brainstorming	Performing
Cross-functional team	Problem-solving team
Debrief meeting	Self-directed team
Directing	Storming
Forming	Supporting
Interfunctional team	Team
Norming	Teamwork

Introduction

Leaders in foodservice organizations, both large and small, are looking to the power of teams to help accomplish tasks. Competitive pressures are driving leaders to rely on collaborative work teams to react rapidly to customer demands and the business climate.

In today's competitive foodservice and hospitality industry, managers must learn how to direct and coordinate effective team behavior and team results to have a successful and enduring organization.

To carry out activities in an establishment, a manager can utilize a variety of team types. This chapter will look at those different types and discuss the advantages and disadvantages of working with teams. Leveraging teams means getting people to work together as a unit. As teams make progress on their assigned tasks, they move through various stages of growth. This growth pattern will be presented along with factors that support or hinder the building and sustaining of a team.

Finally, advantages will be described for including teams in goal setting for projects. As part of setting goals, effective managers and their teams use a systematic process to complete projects, which will be reviewed as well.

The Importance of Teamwork in Foodservice

Given today's organizational climate and pace, the use of teams has become an inevitable solution to tackling some of the pressing challenges a foodservice manager must face. From finding ways to reduce costs to increasing customer sales, these issues usually impact more than one area or department and can benefit from a multi-perspective team approach.

The organizations that leverage teamwork and team-based activities will be better positioned to make the necessary adjustments to supply and meet customers' demands. The rationale for using teams versus a single individual is that, although individual employees can make a difference to an organization, no one person has enough knowledge, creativity, or experience to tackle some of today's complex problems.

Many organizations look to managers to leverage teams whenever possible. A **team** is simply a group of individuals who operate as a unit for an assigned task or goal. Teams differ from other work groups or committees because teams typically have performance goals to achieve. Team members usually feel some type of accountability for working together to achieve these goals. Consequently, **teamwork** is the state of acting in a collaborative and cooperative effort to create positive results for the achievement of a common goal.

Activity

Puzzle Pieces

Look at the puzzle picture. Think about the ways that puzzle pieces are similar to the composition and operation of a highly effective work team. Make a list of these similarities.

1 How is this puzzle similar to a highly effective work team?

_____

_____

_____

2 Does the number of similarities surprise you?

_____

_____

_____

3 In what ways could you use this metaphor within a team?

_____

_____

_____

4 What could you do when assigned to a team to help it become a highly effective team?

_____

_____

_____

Complementary Skills Needed for Teams

One factor that a manager needs to understand is how to select members for a team based on complementary skills that will increase the performance power and effectiveness of the team. Effective teams have the right blend of skills. These skills fall into three categories: technical expertise, problem solving, and interpersonal. Putting together a team with all three types of skills will use the individual strengths of each member and increase the probability of team success and organizational achievement. Part of your responsibilities as a manager is selecting team members whose skills complement each other.

1. **Technical expertise** is a core competency that each team needs. The type of problem that will be assigned to a team dictates to a certain extent what expertise you will need to bring together. Proficiency in several areas may be needed, depending on the scope of the problem. For example, if your organization is investigating new menu items to offer to its customers, a team composed of nutritionists, food prep specialists, servers, operations personnel, and marketing specialists would supply the necessary blend of expertise to ensure a thorough analysis of what customers want, rather than just a team made up of one of these groups. Utilizing the knowledge and skills of a cross section of an organization will strengthen the likelihood of a team achieving its goal.

2. **Problem-solving skills** are also needed by teams to identify the root cause of a situation or challenge, as well as to identify potential solutions and trade-offs. Initially, a team needs to have at least one member with this capability. As the team makes progress, more team members should develop these skills.

3. **Interpersonal skills** are the third category of skills a team needs. Members who communicate effectively and facilitate group processes are critical to the success of a team. Team members who possess these skills help create an environment of openness and trust, which allows the team to flourish and make progress towards its goal.

The balancing of these elements is essential for a manager to consider when putting a team together.

Team Types

Besides selecting the right mix of these critical skills in a team, a manager needs to determine the type of employee involvement required for a project or task. There are essentially four types of teams that can be used to solve organizational problems.

Exhibit 8a lists the different types, with a description and example of each. **Interfunctional teams** expand the responsibilities of a particular group of employees, while **problem-solving teams** are created for the specific purpose of solving an immediate problem. **Cross-functional teams** are composed of employees from different areas who focus on solving problems that impact their particular areas as well as the organization. They are widely used in larger organizations because of the complexity and interrelatedness of the problems they face. **Self-directed teams** are intact work units of a small group of employees who manage many daily operational issues with little supervision. They are used by some organizations if team members have acquired the experience and competency to complete their work with little supervision. Being in a self-directed team does not mean that it is not a managed team; it simply means that it is managed in a different way.

Exhibit 8a

Team Types

Type	Description	Example
Interfunctional team	Team composed of employees from the same area or department who are given more responsibility for solving a problem or making an improvement in their immediate area	A restaurant manager works with the assistant managers on a flexible crew scheduling process, which will allow the assistant managers to assume more responsibility for scheduling.
Problem-solving team	Temporary team composed of employees selected to solve a specific problem	An event manager in a hotel is given a large association conference to plan. To meet the association's needs, the manager puts together a team to study the conference requirements for breakout sessions and special keynote sessions.
Cross-functional team	Team composed of employees from different areas who focus on solving problems that impact their particular areas as well as the organization in general	A major restaurant corporation has determined that customers want healthier meals—specifically, a wider selection of salads. A team of nutritionists, restaurant managers, and staff from the marketing department will come up with new salad menu items that could increase sales.
Self-directed team	Intact work unit of a small group of employees who manage many daily operational issues with little supervision	The training director for a quick-service restaurant chain decides her training managers are ready to handle more responsibility. After being trained on how to function as a self-directed team, the team takes over planning, scheduling resources, and monitoring progress on projects, using weekly update meetings and intermittent discussions to keep the director current.

Advantages of Working in Teams

Teamwork offers many benefits. Some of the clear advantages to using teams are greater productivity and better quality products and services. In fact, some of the benefits to using teams can be linked directly to an organization's values or mission statement. Other benefits include more effective use of limited resources, increased creativity and innovation in products and services, and better problem solving. An effective manager knows that teamwork can ultimately have a direct impact on the customer experience and the service provided.

Using teams also creates internal benefits. These include:

- **Positive work environment.** Employees on teams feel a closer connection to their coworkers, the organization, and organizational goals. This promotes a sense of common purpose and focuses teams' efforts more effectively. Teamwork also reinforces the contributions each member makes to the establishment.

- **Open communication channels.** Teams help break down barriers that may exist between departments or groups. For example, communication can flow more seamlessly when cross-functional teams are used.

- **Support systems.** Teams often help employees feel less stress from individual failure. Team support can make it easier for a novice employee to tackle an assignment without fear. The employee does not have to worry that the entire project might suffer or be sacrificed because other members are there to help. This support creates greater opportunities for more than one individual to succeed. More employees can receive recognition or rewards for their contribution to team tasks.

- **Workplace diversity.** Opportunities to blend a diverse workforce together to complete tasks or solve organizational problems can help everyone value the talents and differences that each member brings to a project.

Finally, the combination of these advantages can help suppress turnover, which is one of the most pressing issues in the foodservice and hospitality industry.

Disadvantages of Working in Teams

There are also some clear disadvantages to working in teams. Here are some of the common pitfalls to teamwork, as well as some suggestions for combating them:

- **Taking too long to make a decision**—One of the major challenges to using teams is controlling the amount of time the group deliberates over issues. Understanding ways to conduct meetings, or making assignments within the team, can minimize the length of time it takes to achieve results.

- **Mishandling team disagreements**—While most people have participated in group processes, working in teams can be a source of conflict for some individuals. Although team disagreement might make some members uncomfortable, conflict can actually lead to a broader understanding of a project's problems. If a conflict arises, team members should be careful to stay focused on project issues, not on people or personalities. If a conflict turns personal, a manager must intervene to ensure that the team remains effective in reaching its goal.

- **Working inefficiently**—Putting a team together to tackle a task better suited for an individual can result in a negative reaction by team members, who will question the need for all of them to work on the task. The resulting situation will cause inefficiencies in achieving the goal, as well as ineffective team interactions. It is a manager's responsibility to know when a team is an appropriate strategy to use in meeting a goal.

- **Avoiding responsibility**—Employees can be hesitant to participate in a team if they fear the project will fail, meaning they will fail. Team projects can actually be a source of group failure. Managers must encourage trust and communication within the team to ensure the team's success.

In the final analysis, the benefits or drawbacks to using teams depend on the manager's ability to determine the best way to achieve a particular goal.

Stages of Team Growth

Dr. Bruce W. Tuckman, an educational psychologist, published his theory of the four stages of group development in 1965.[1] He called these stages Forming, Storming, Norming, and Performing. (See *Exhibit 8b* on p. 184.) Dr. Tuckman developed this well-known model after careful observation of the different phases in the development and maturity of a group or team.

[1]"Developmental Sequence in Small Groups," *Psychological Bulletin.*

Think About It...

When a team focuses less on individual performance and more on working collaboratively, its members build more team confidence, resulting in better products and services for the organization. How does team confidence contribute to increased performance and productivity in the workplace?

In stage one, **forming,** teams are getting to know each other, in addition to learning what will be required of them in order to achieve their assigned goal. This stage is defined by the way team members approach each other and investigate the limitations of group behavior. The team is also assessing the manager's role and leadership. During this stage, the manager takes a large role in directing the progress of the team. **Directing** involves telling the group what specifically needs to be accomplished, establishing guidelines, and providing specifics on the five Ws (Who, What, Where, When, Why) and How. At this stage, the team members are focusing on being part of a team.

In stage two, **storming,** the reality of the project sets in for the team and various interpersonal conflicts begin to surface. Typically, this is the most difficult stage for any team to maneuver through, since power clashes and competition between team members are common. Besides this realization, team members become impatient with their lack of progress and rely more on individual approaches instead of collaboration. At this time, the manager needs to utilize a coaching style to clarify and explain tasks repeatedly. The manager will need to persuade team members often to work together and refocus their efforts.

Stage three, **norming,** sees team members settling their differences and developing more cohesive and trusting work relationships. The team realizes that they can work together and help each other achieve success. The members understand the team's needs and accept the team ground rules and the roles that each person plays in achieving the project goals. Conflict decreases as these realizations occur and team members develop more confidence in their ability to work together and accomplish the task. At this time, the manager transitions into a leadership style of **supporting** the team by providing encouragement, listening more than telling, and promoting team discussions.

Finally, in stage four, **performing,** team interdependence is recognized. Team members can analyze and solve problems effectively together. They have accepted each member's strengths and weaknesses and can adapt to meet the needs of each member. The team becomes very productive and truly adds value to the organization. At this point, the manager can use a delegating style, which follows the delegation principles outlined in Chapter 1. The manager no longer needs to provide much direction and can periodically monitor the team's progress with update meetings.

Exhibit 8b

Stages of Team Development

Stage	Forming	Storming	Norming	Performing
Team feeling	■ Excitement ■ Optimism ■ Pride in being selected ■ Wondering what role and influence they will have ■ Anxiety ■ Questioning why they and other team members were selected	■ Resistance to approaches different from what the team is comfortable with ■ Swings in attitudes about the team and project ■ Questioning many aspects of the task	■ Expressing constructive criticism ■ Membership acceptance ■ Relief that things are finally going smoothly ■ Understanding own contribution ■ Acceptance of membership	■ Insights into group processes ■ Understanding of each member's strengths and weaknesses ■ Satisfaction with progress ■ Trusting ■ Friendly ■ Having fun
Team behavior	■ Friendly ■ Agreeable ■ Deciding how to accomplish the task ■ Determining acceptable team behavior ■ Information gathering ■ Handling complaints about the organization ■ Discussing barriers to the task	■ Arguing ■ Choosing sides ■ Perceived "pecking order" ■ Increased tension ■ Jealousy ■ Power struggles ■ Lack of progress ■ Loss of interest	■ Attempts for harmony ■ Avoiding conflict ■ Discussing team dynamics ■ Sense of common purpose ■ Establishing and monitoring team rules ■ Expressing ideas	■ Individual behavior modification ■ Working through team problems ■ Close attachment to members ■ Flexibility ■ Humor ■ Ownership of results
Leadership style	■ Directing	■ Coaching	■ Supporting	■ Delegating

The Manager's Role in Team Development

The amount of time a team takes to move through the four stages will vary, and the manager will play a key role. The manager will interact with teams in varying degrees during these stages. This contact will assist in changing the individual focus of each member to a more collaborative team effort. As the manager, you must understand each stage to minimize overreacting to situations that are normal for a particular stage. Some factors that you can use to support team building and development are:

- **Communicate effectively and clearly with the team.** Good communication supports smooth team functions.

- **Select the appropriate leadership style for each stage.** Good management is vital to a team's consistent performance.

- **Conduct team-building exercises so team members understand the development process.** The activities a manager selects should be integral to the team's process in achieving its goal and should not be perceived as "just-for-fun" events.

- **Understand and explain the role of the team in accomplishing its goal.** This factor goes hand in hand with effective communication because a team that does not know the extent of the role it plays in a project will not perform as effectively as one that does.

- **Apply effective management skills to support the team.** Knowing that every team will navigate these phases—some more successfully than others—means that strong leadership by the manager is essential to an effective team.

Challenges to Team Development

No matter how effectively a manager engages and monitors a team in its development, some factors can contribute to a team's ineffectiveness. Factors that can inhibit or diminish a team's effectiveness include:

- **Poor management style.** Although managers must be present throughout the team's development, using only one management style over all the stages of team development is not conducive for sustaining a high-performing team.

- **High turnover.** A harsh reality of the foodservice industry is that employee retention rates are low. This factor can also contribute to the team's ineffectiveness. If team membership turns over too frequently, teams can lose the cohesiveness and camaraderie that have developed.

- **Not understanding what to emphasize in team development.** Another factor that can hinder a team is overemphasizing personal team relationships instead of focusing on achieving the project goal. For example, a manager might engage in too many fun activities or team-building exercises to get the team started. This approach might cause team members to think that interpersonal relationships should be the focus of the team effort.

Activity

Analyzing Team Dynamics

The team in the following case works in the western region of U.S. operations for the global Haincus Hotel chain. A regional initiative has just been planned and the team will be working together for an extended period. During this time, the team will have responsibility for certain decisions and recommendations, and must report to its stakeholders as requested.

The team consists of the following individuals:

Perry

■ Thirty-eight-year-old male

■ Four years of experience with the hotel in the western region; managed a small restaurant business for eight years

■ Likes the "big picture" and looking at connections between various organizational systems

■ Has made company-wide presentations on leadership and interpersonal issues

■ Does not like dealing with details

■ Thinks team should meet after working hours

■ Works best under pressure with impending deadlines

Olivia

■ Twenty-nine-year-old female

■ Six years of experience with the hotel: two in San Francisco and four in Boston, before accepting a recent promotion to the western region

■ Feels anxious about the pressure associated with her new position

■ Enjoys handling the details of a project; likes to plan and organize things

■ Prefers completing work comfortably ahead of a deadline

■ Prefers to meet often, during work hours, to make sure that things are getting done

■ Cannot stay after hours without prior planning

Deirdre

■ Forty-year-old female

■ Ten years of experience with the hotel: five in the front line—two in the southern region, and three in the western region; ten years with a major competitor in a similar function

■ Often takes over work of others to make sure that it meets her standards

■ Not particularly concerned with "people issues"

■ Impatient with people who cannot make decisions quickly

■ Excellent project management skills

■ Prefers to have lengthy meetings once a week, after working hours, because it is more efficient

Hal

- Twenty-six-year-old male
- Three years of experience with the hotel
- Feels honored to be a part of this team with his limited work experience
- Will do anything to help the team, especially behind-the-scenes tasks
- Very quiet in team meetings; reluctant to speak in front of large groups
- Uncomfortable with conflict; likes harmony

Calvin

- Fifty-year-old male
- Twenty-five years of experience with the hotel: seven years in the front line; remaining years in positions of increased responsibility throughout the hotel chain
- Hopes that being on this team will help him get the promotion he deserves
- Wants to be involved in the roles that provide the greatest visibility in the organization
- Overlooks his responsibilities to the team if something else would benefit him more
- Work experience gives him valuable information that will help the team succeed
- Reluctant to set a regular schedule for meetings; likes to call impromptu meetings when needed

Answer the following questions:

1 What are the positive elements about this team that could help it be successful?

_____

_____

2 What type of team has been formed?

_____

_____

3 What issues are likely to limit the team's success?

_____

_____

4 What can the team do to get off to a strong start?

_____

_____

continued on next page

Analyzing Team Dynamics *continued from previous page*

A month has passed since the team formed, and the first big milestone is coming due soon. Deirdre has been acting as the informal leader of the team, and Olivia has been scheduling the meetings and keeping minutes. When Hal offered to take a turn with the minutes, Deirdre quickly told him that Olivia has been doing it very well and will continue throughout the project.

Whenever the team seems close to a decision on an item, Perry offers several other options, which throws the team back to the beginning. Both Perry and Calvin have expressed that they think the team spends too much time on details and not enough on strategic issues. Over the past month, Hal has been very quiet in meetings, rarely speaking. The one time he offered a suggestion, Deirdre told him that the decision had already been made.

Calvin has missed several meetings. Hal contacted him to see if he was planning to come to the next meeting and to ask about the progress on his portion of the project. After talking to Calvin, Hal started doing behind-the-scenes work for Calvin and speaking on his behalf at meetings.

As the deadline for the first milestone approaches, Perry has not completed his part of the project, but assures the team that he will have it finished by the deadline. Hal is working on both his part and Calvin's. Deirdre volunteers to pull the whole project together, with the help of Olivia. The team agrees to meet again one hour before their deadline to make sure that everything will be ready for presentation to the key stakeholders.

Answer the following questions:

5 What issues have surfaced with this team?

_____

_____

_____

_____

6 How would you describe the situation from the perspective of each team member?

_____

_____

_____

_____

7 What suggestions do you have for this team to improve its effectiveness?

_____

_____

_____

_____

The project is now more than half-completed. The feedback from the key stakeholders has generally been positive, especially for Calvin's part. Perry's portion, completed at the last minute without feedback from the others, was not consistent with the other parts of the project, which upset the other team members.

There is a significant amount of work yet to be completed by the team. Although they have had successes and continue to receive support and encouragement from the stakeholders, the team has lost momentum. Deirdre has been focusing her energy on another big project, and she has missed the last two meetings. Olivia has tried to take over the team leadership, but her attempts to run the meetings do not seem to have the backing of Calvin and Perry. Hal is becoming more confident in his role with the team because of Calvin's support.

Olivia is very worried that the team does not have the energy and commitment to meet the upcoming milestones and is frustrated because her attempts to make things happen have not succeeded. She leaves messages with each of the members expressing her concerns.

Answer the following questions:

8 What has happened to this team?

_____

_____

_____

_____

_____

9 How have the roles changed?

_____

_____

_____

_____

_____

10 What can be done to salvage the team?

_____

_____

_____

_____

_____

_____

_____

Goal Setting with a Team

No matter what stage of development teams may be in, they are most effective when they understand and accept the goals of their assignment. One way to gain consensus with the team is to allow members to provide feedback on defining and refining project goals. Managers should also provide feedback on establishing and refining goals. Synergy between team members and managers in establishing project statements will result in achieving goals. This discussion should typically occur at the initial project meeting, which should also describe team-building goals and information goals.

Effective teams contribute to the achievement of three types of goals throughout the life of a project.

1. *Team-building goals* focus on:

   - [ ] **Getting to know each team member.** Teams are most effective when they take time to discover each member's background, skills, work style, and so on.

   - [ ] **Learning to work together.** Teams need to identify the strengths of each member and set processes in place to work efficiently together.

   - [ ] **Setting ground rules.** Members need a common understanding of how the team will conduct itself, and what is acceptable and unacceptable behavior. Some of the topics for discussion are meeting attendance, promptness, conversational courtesy, assignments, and breaks.

   - [ ] **Figuring out decision-making processes.** A characteristic of ineffective teams is that decisions just seem to happen. Teams need to discuss how decisions will be made to avoid conflicts in the future.

2. *Information goals* include:

   - [ ] **Getting updates from team members on progress.**

   - [ ] **Learning about the tools used to support the team's various tasks.**

   - [ ] **Communicating with stakeholders.**

3. *Project goals* focus on:

   - [ ] **Understanding the project and each member's assignment.** Teams should be able to ask questions about their tasks and the stakeholders' expectations.

☐ **Identifying the business needs supported by the goals.** If a manager cannot define the relationship between project goals and business needs, team members will have greater difficulty striving to achieve these goals because they will not see the purpose of their assignment.

☐ **Understanding the process that will be used.** Not only do team members need to understand the overall process, but they also need to understand which steps are their responsibility.

☐ **Identifying resources needed.** Team members need to discuss resources that might be needed sooner rather than later in the process. This discussion ensures that necessary resources will be available at their designated times.

☐ **Developing a project plan or outline of how the team will accomplish their goals.** Without a roadmap, teams can flounder. The team leader should discuss the logistics of the project with team members. Breaking the process into smaller steps and assigning duties will help build team collaboration. Teams should continue to review and revise these plans as they move toward reaching their goals.

Think About It...

The term "groupthink" was coined in the 1970s to describe what sometimes happens to the decision-making process of teams— everyone shapes their opinions to what they think the consensus of the group might be. Have you ever experienced groupthink? How do you think it could be avoided?

Benefits and Challenges of Team Goal Setting

Teams that participate in crafting goals function better. Members are more likely to support goals if they feel they have helped define them. Assisting with goal setting also increases a member's opportunity for success, which helps build confidence in the ability to accomplish goals. However, it is essential that managers provide effective leadership and communication with the team during this period. Without these two elements, the team can misinterpret its value and contribution to the organization. Rewarding the team, for example, with personal thank-you notes, for its contribution to goal setting supports feelings of accomplishment and should be part of a continuous improvement process.

Conversely, several factors can hinder the effectiveness of a team when setting goals. These factors can be categorized within the three types of goals described previously:

■ For example, in team-building goals, a trusting environment is essential in order for teams to flourish. Teams can fail in goal setting if personal agendas conflict with project goals or corporate mission statements. Identifying ways to eliminate these impediments through various team-building activities can help.

■ Poor communication can negatively affect goal setting. In fact, lack of communication can result in teams not being on the same page once the project gets started.

■ Another factor that can hinder a team's contribution to goal setting is the lack of a strong connection between their project goals and a business need. Managers need to examine each project goal to ensure that it links back to the larger needs and mission of the organization.

Activity

Who Should Solve the Problem?

Determine whether a team of employees or the manager should solve each of the following challenges. For each challenge you would assign to a team, create a draft of that team's goals.

1 A customer complains that the food on the buffet is cold.

_____

_____

_____

_____

2 Customers are concerned about the amount of time they have to wait to be seated.

_____

_____

_____

_____

3 Shortages have occurred in weekly orders. Vendors have assured the manager that they are not responsible.

_____

_____

_____

_____

4 In recent weeks, customer complaints have been on the rise, and sales have also declined.

_____

_____

_____

_____

Managing Team-Based Projects

Whether a project has been assigned to an individual or a team, it is essential to apply the appropriate methodology for managing all your projects. Using a systematic process offers many advantages and ensures that your employees will function optimally. Too often, however, the "Ready, Fire, Aim" method is applied to many team-based projects. This approach encourages teams to take action even if it may not be the appropriate thing to do.

In Chapter 2, you learned about a process for achieving organizational goals that involves planning, incorporating, executing, and evaluating. This process can also be effectively applied to managing teams and their projects. A major reason for teams to learn about and then use this process is to have them anticipate and think through the steps or potential problems they may encounter. Although the process may take time up front, its thorough execution will increase the likelihood of achieving success in the long run.

Planning

The start of any worthwhile project begins with planning. Of the many activities involved in initial planning efforts, one essential task is verifying that project goals are linked to an identified business need. Providing input on goals helps the team create a solid footing from which the project plan can be developed. Teams should ensure that SMART criteria (specific, measurable, achievable, relevant, time-bound) have been applied to their creation. Team members can also assist in developing assumptions about the desired results, determining resources that are needed, suggesting methods for improvement, and ensuring the plan is feasible.

Additionally, since team members must determine resources, they can also consider how to utilize those resources. Brainstorming suggestions for resource utilization is key to team efficiency. **Brainstorming** is a method of collecting ideas from all participants without criticism or judgment. While in team meetings, the manager can leverage a number of tools to assist in brainstorming. Electronic whiteboards can help capture ideas easily, and the information can be printed for team members to review. Flip charts can also be used. The important thing to keep in mind is that a brainstorming session should encourage everyone to provide ideas, and the more ideas suggested, the better. Whatever resources are used to capture these ideas, they should be visible and invite participation and creativity.

During the planning stage, managers also need to consider whether the team needs any special training to be successful. If the team does need training—in process, decision making, team building, etc.—then the manager needs to schedule this before the team starts implementing its plan. The final step before moving to the next phase is for the team to communicate its approach and plan to the manager and key stakeholders.

Execution

Once the team has scoped out its approach, roles and responsibilities, and resource allocations, it will begin executing its plan. During this phase of the team project, the manager must monitor the progress of the team, as well as of each member. It is during this phase that teams can become victims of the storming and norming stages of team development. If this occurs, the manager should be proactive and ask the team to evaluate how it can become more effective in implementing its plan and achieving its goals. The manager can also redirect some of the team's efforts to minimize any conflicts between members or inabilities to perform.

Communicating status to stakeholders is essential in this phase. Input and updates from the team can be sources of ongoing revisions and improvements to the plan. Managers should also conduct meetings periodically with team members. These meetings provide support and feedback, as well as an opportunity to discuss priorities and any other possible redirection of efforts.

Evaluation

In the evaluation phase, the manager's efforts are concentrated on determining whether goals have been achieved. Using established measures that were identified in the initial stages helps make this determination. Team input can also help determine how successful the team was in goal achievement. Feedback from key stakeholders about the results is another source of information.

Besides knowing how well a team achieved its objectives, you must also evaluate how well the team functioned together. A **debrief meeting** should be conducted, in which all aspects of the project are evaluated. Ask the team to evaluate how effective or ineffective they were in performing tasks. Questions about team interaction are also important. Since most employees will periodically work in teams, it is vital for them to explore how they functioned in their relationship with other team members. Lessons learned should be recorded for both task- and team-oriented conclusions. This information should be distributed to team members and to other relevant employees, so the entire organization can benefit.

Finally, as part of project closure, the manager needs to recognize and celebrate the accomplishments of the team and its individual members. This celebration can be conducted during the debrief meeting or at an alternative, more suitable time.

Summary

Teams are critical to the new competitive foodservice and hospitality marketplace. It is important to understand how teams function if they are to be used effectively. Two important elements in teamwork are collaboration and cooperation when working toward common goals. Teams can bring a wider range of skills and experience to solve problems in the workplace than individuals. Often teams provide better quality decisions than one person might. The right blend of skills among team members, however, is important to ensure the team's effectiveness. Three types of teams are interfunctional, problem-solving, and cross-functional. Teams typically go through a series of stages before becoming high-performing groups: forming, storming, norming, and performing.

Applying a systematic process to goal setting and the general team assignment offers numerous benefits. Once the team completes a task, it is important to conduct a debrief meeting, along with discussing lessons learned. In evaluating the effectiveness of a team, the main criteria to consider is whether the end result met or exceeded the expectations of the manager and key stakeholders.

Activity

Why Are We Here?

June at the Bella Luna restaurant in the Towns-Benedict Resort is one of the busiest months of the year. Located in the heart of Napa Valley, the resort is a featured wedding destination for hundreds of couples and their families. This year is no different. At the weekly status meeting, my manager, Rob, and the rest of the banquet planning team were planning wedding events for each weekend, including six weddings spread throughout the next four weeks. But though the schedule was hectic, it was working out to be a well-planned and organized month. The meeting was quickly becoming an endurable experience—even agreeable. That is, until Rob suddenly said, "I think it might be a good idea to go to the Southwest Regional Restaurant Management Conference in Phoenix."

I could not believe it. The conference was four days long, in the middle of our busiest month of the year. It was also being held in one of the hottest cities in the United States. Why would anyone possibly want to go to this conference?

But my coworker, Jen, spoke up, saying, "I think that's a great idea. The conference will be a good learning experience for all of us. What do you think, Brian?"

I was obviously more worried about the wedding banquet schedule than my coworkers. So looking around, I replied, "I think it might be a good addition to the summer schedule. That is, if we can organize the time to go."

"Of course we can," said our assistant manager, Brent. "We have plenty of noncommitted days to go to this conference. It'll be fun."

So as decided, we all went to the conference in June. And it was as big a headache as I had predicted. The preparation to arrange the banquet events around the conference forced us to work overtime. When we finally arrived in Phoenix for the conference, a heat wave descended on the city, making it unbearable to leave the hotel for the planned social events outside the conference center. And worst of all, the conference was not as educational as everyone had anticipated, and we gained nothing from attending any of the lectures or special events.

Four days later we sat silently in the Phoenix Airport, hot and miserable. As we waited for our flight home to begin boarding, I attempted to make the best of the situation. "It was an educational conference, don't you think?"

Everyone stared at me in silence.

Finally Brent said, with some frustration, "You know, I didn't really enjoy myself at all. I would rather have stayed home and kept the banquet schedule moving smoothly. I just went along with the rest of you because I thought you were all excited to go."

"Wait," I said, amazed, "I never wanted to go to the conference. Don't lump me in with the group. I would have been satisfied staying at the restaurant and preparing for the wedding receptions. I only came because everyone else wanted to."

Jen was stunned. "Don't make me part of the group," she said. "I knew the heat would be oppressive and the lecture schedule would be uninformative. I only said I wanted to go because the rest of you seemed so excited about the opportunity."

We all looked at Rob, who by now was chuckling to himself, rubbing his temples. "I never wanted to go to this conference," he said. "I just assumed you would all want to get away from the busy June schedule and try something new. I would have preferred staying at the restaurant preparing for July's wedding schedule."

There we were, four professionals, sitting in an airport in a scorching desert city, all with no desire to be there. We had taken a long plane ride to go to a conference we did not want to attend and ended up trapped in a hotel because of a heat wave. Basically, we had traveled hundreds of miles to do the opposite of what we had really wanted to do.

Answer the following questions:

1 What is the main problem the group in the story faced?

_____

_____

_____

_____

2 Why do you think none of them said what they were thinking?

_____

_____

_____

_____

3 Identify some symptoms of the group's problem.

_____

_____

_____

_____

4 How might a team break the cycle of wrong assumptions?

_____

_____

_____

_____

Review Your Learning

1 High-performing teams have which one of the following complementary skill sets?

A. Technical, delegating, interpersonal

B. Social, supporting, analytical

C. Technical, problem solving, interpersonal

D. Problem solving, coaching, motivating

2 If an employee is assigned to an interfunctional team, he or she is

A. already part of a group that now has expanded responsibilities.

B. selected to investigate other functional areas.

C. directed to be the primary connection among other groups.

D. rewarded with camaraderie.

3 A primary reason for creating teams is for employees to

A. get to know one another.

B. participate in achieving organizational goals.

C. have opportunities to advance.

D. grapple with quality-improvement issues.

4 Team members who have talents in interpersonal communication help the team to

A. identify conflict issues.

B. identify core competencies of each member.

C. determine its success level.

D. create an open and trustworthy team environment.

5 The major challenge to most teams is

A. promoting workplace diversity.

B. identifying stakeholder expectations.

C. balancing the amount of time it takes to make decisions.

D. prolonging team collaboration.

6 When teams are friendly and agreeable, which development stage are they most likely to be in?

A. Forming

B. Storming

C. Norming

D. Performing

7 Including teams in goal setting offers a major benefit of

A. building the team's strengths.

B. providing feedback and clarification of goals.

C. learning how to use goal-setting tools.

D. decreasing the length of time a team spends in the storming stage.

8 In the planning stage on a team project, the team can assist with

A. developing assumptions about the desired outcome.

B. determining the budget.

C. talking to stakeholders about their individual involvement.

D. monitoring each other.

9 The importance of a team discussing lessons learned is to

   A. point the finger at people who did not contribute.

   B. evaluate the strengths of the team.

   C. distribute and share this knowledge with others.

   D. measure how closely stakeholders and team members collaborated.

10 The leadership style that is the most inappropriate for highly effective teams is

   A. coaching.

   B. supporting.

   C. delegating.

   D. directing.

11 What activity should *not* be part of a debrief meeting?

   A. Celebrating accomplishments

   B. Recording lessons learned

   C. Assigning blame for mistakes

   D. Concluding the project

Notes

Dimensions of Problem Solving

9

Inside This Chapter

- The Importance of Problem Solving in Daily Activities
- Developing a Problem-Solving Model
- Potential Consequences of Improperly Solving a Problem
- Crisis Management
- Before a Crisis Strikes

After completing this chapter, you should be able to:

- Define the following terms: problem, problem solving, problem-solving model, root cause, alternative, action plan, documentation, crisis, preventable crisis, unpreventable crisis, evacuation, contact list, media policy, and spin.

- Explain the importance of applying a problem-solving model to daily operations.

- Describe and apply a problem-solving model.

- Give examples of consequences to a business of improperly solving a problem.

- Describe how different types of crises can be prevented.

- Create an evacuation plan.

- Describe the elements of an effective media policy.

Test Your Knowledge

1 **True or False:** A crisis is a question or situation that has occurred and needs a solution. *(See p. 213.)*

2 **True or False:** A solution to a problem normally takes place after the problem has occurred, while managing a crisis should be planned for in advance. *(See p. 213.)*

3 **True or False:** Doing nothing is always an alternative to be considered when solving a problem. *(See p. 203.)*

4 **True or False:** Following the problem-solving model is a "can't miss" proposition, since the outcomes will be logically decided. *(See p. 204.)*

5 **True or False:** A crisis should always involve an evacuation plan. *(See p. 215.)*

6 **True or False**: It is beneficial to invite the media into your restaurant after a foodborne-illness outbreak, since you will need the publicity to get back lost business. *(See p. 217.)*

7 **True or False:** Not all emergencies are preventable. *(See p. 213.)*

8 **True or False:** When solving a problem, time is not a factor to be considered. *(See p. 203.)*

9 **True or False:** A problem is a question or situation that has occurred and needs a solution. *(See p. 202.)*

10 **True or False:** A crisis, since it could happen instantaneously, cannot be planned for. *(See p. 213.)*

11 **True or False:** An unsolved problem could become a crisis. *(See p. 213.)*

12 **True or False:** One of the responsibilities of an evacuation plan is to secure the cash. *(See p. 215.)*

Key Terms

Action plan	Evacuation	Problem-solving model
Alternative	Media policy	Root cause
Contact list	Preventable crisis	Spin
Crisis	Problem	Unpreventable crisis
Documentation	Problem solving	

Introduction

Why does one operation run smoothly while another one struggles to stay organized and productive? The answer could lie in their management's ability to solve problems. In this chapter, you will learn how to handle problems. Put simply, a **problem** is a question or "situation" that needs an answer or a solution. Some problems require a simple answer, others require a reiteration of company policy, and still others require a more complex strategy. It is the latter situation that will be explored in this chapter.

Problems can come to light through statements made to management by employees, customers, or suppliers. In other cases, an unusual occurrence might uncover a problem. Whatever the source, it is management's responsibility to solve the problem effectively so it does not recur or turn into something worse that is even more difficult to fix.

Once you have learned how to solve problems, you will examine how to handle crises. Although a crisis is not an everyday occurrence, understanding the importance of being prepared and ready in the unlikely event one happens will be discussed in this chapter. Knowing the important elements of both effective problem solving and crisis management will help you to develop into an effective manager.

The Importance of Problem Solving in Daily Activities

Managers must handle any problem quickly and precisely. If left alone, a problem festers, gets worse, and becomes more difficult to solve. That is not to say that all problems require a complex solution. But it is imperative to know how to apply an effective problem-solving strategy. One important factor that management needs to weigh is the risk of the possible solution. Sometimes it is better to take action quickly, even though the solution may not be the most effective one. Sometimes managers need to take risks to ultimately put the restaurant on the right path. Managers rarely have enough information to be 100 percent certain of their decisions. However, becoming more comfortable with the uncertainty and risk associated with any decision, even the ineffective ones, is better than being immobilized by the risks. For the most part, a good rule of thumb to use is that the quicker a problem is solved, the better for the organization.

In rare cases, one possible solution to the problem is to do nothing. However, in most cases, a problem that is left unanswered, or worse yet, solved improperly, can wreak havoc on an operation. A problem that is either unsolved or incorrectly solved can:

- Cause poor employee morale and turnover
- Cause lost sales, increased cost, and decreased profits
- Continue to bother the operation

It is imperative that management recognizes a problem when it occurs, defines the problem, properly solves the problem, and quickly implements the solution.

Developing a Problem-Solving Model

Problems happen in every business, including those in the restaurant and foodservice industry. Restaurants with a large number of problems are most likely having a reoccurrence of the same problems that were not solved correctly the first time. Conversely, an operation with few problems probably solved its problems accurately and quickly.

Problem solving is not a haphazard occurrence—it is a thought-out process presented in a logical sequence, which must be followed to arrive at a reasonable conclusion. If done correctly, management will not have to deal with the problem again once it has been solved. It is therefore critical that you follow a **problem-solving model** to explore all of a problem's potential causes. There are several models available. The process model in *Exhibit 9a* is a compilation of some of the most common versions. Composed of seven major steps, each step provides input to the next until you reach the final phase, in which you document the outcome of your process.

1. **Define the problem.** Before a problem can be solved, it needs to be defined as precisely as possible. Misdiagnosing a problem will lead to a meaningless solution because the real problem has not been identified. You may have to ask numerous questions to find out exactly what is happening. Do not take a problem at its face value.

   ☐ **Identify who or what is affected.** Once the problem has been defined, you must then determine who or what is being affected by the problem. The answer to these questions could include one or more groups of people, including employees, management, owners, customers, or the public. It could also include one or more individuals within these groups and not necessarily the entire group. Asking these questions might also identify processes or systems within the restaurant that are not performing as well as they could, even though they may not be the source or the affected aspects of the problem.

2. **Determine the root cause.** Normally, one or two sources will be the cause of a problem. The **root cause** is the action or situation that initiates the problem. Typically, root causes are system breakdowns or human errors. Foodservice operations are made up of a series of systems, including those for purchasing, production, customer service, cash handling, cost control, scheduling, etc. Problems occur when one of these systems breaks down or was not built carefully in the first place.

Exhibit 9a

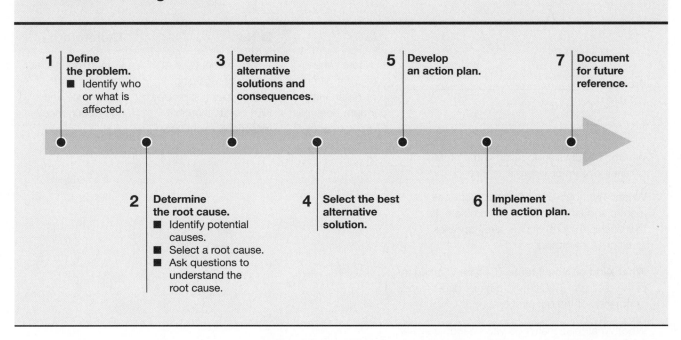

Problem-Solving Model

1 | Define the problem.
■ Identify who or what is affected.

2 | Determine the root cause.
■ Identify potential causes.
■ Select a root cause.
■ Ask questions to understand the root cause.

3 | Determine alternative solutions and consequences.

4 | Select the best alternative solution.

5 | Develop an action plan.

6 | Implement the action plan.

7 | Document for future reference.

When problems are caused by human error, you must question the people affected by the problem to determine its root cause. As you investigate, probe deeply to ensure you have identified the real root cause of the problem and not just one of the contributing factors or symptoms. You can use tools such as the matrix in *Exhibit 9b* on the next page, which will help you identify both the problem and its root cause. Be sure, however, to avoid accusations and blame when asking your staff these kinds of questions.

3 Determine alternative solutions and consequences.

An **alternative** is a potential solution to a problem. The list of alternative solutions should be as long as necessary. At this point, do not think about whether a solution is reasonable or workable; if it is a potential answer, put it on the list. One alternative that should always be investigated is "to do nothing." (Sometimes management comes up with elaborate resolutions for what ultimately is a non-problem. On the other hand, the action of "doing nothing" could have disastrous consequences.)

Exhibit 9b

The Is/Is Not Matrix

	Is	Is Not	Therefore
Problem: _____	Where, when, to what extent, or regarding whom does this problem occur?	Where, when, to what extent, or regarding whom does this problem NOT occur, though it reasonably might have?	What might explain the pattern of occurrence and non-occurrence?
Where: The physical location of the problem. Where it occurs or where it is noticed.			
When: The hour, time of day, day of week, month, and time of year of the problem. Its relationship (before, during, after) to other situations or activities.			
What Kind or How Much: The type of category of the problem. The extent, degree, dimensions, or duration of the occurrence.			
Who: What relationship do various individuals or groups have to the problem? To whom, by whom, near whom, etc., does this occur?			

Now that the list of alternatives is complete, you must analyze it for the consequences that each solution might have. These key questions should be asked for each solution:

☐ **What are the consequences of this action?** Who will be affected by this decision and how will they be affected? Will it be a positive or negative effect?

☐ **Is it cost effective?** Will the solution cost more than the problem? If so, is there a more reasonable approach? Can the solution be reconstructed to cost less money? All too often, management chooses a costly solution that is financially worse than the problem.

☐ **Is it reasonable?** Investigate the complexity of the solution. Does it have a chance to succeed, or is it so complex that people will ignore it, resulting in a reoccurrence of the problem?

☐ **Will it close the loop?** In the case of a problem caused by a system loophole, you must be sure the solution will address both the problem and the loop.

☐ **Will it be effective?** Finally, you must ask: will the solution work? Does it have a chance? Will everyone accept it as reasonable? Remember that a solution without acceptance will not be effective.

Exhibit 9c

Examining a Problem from All Angles

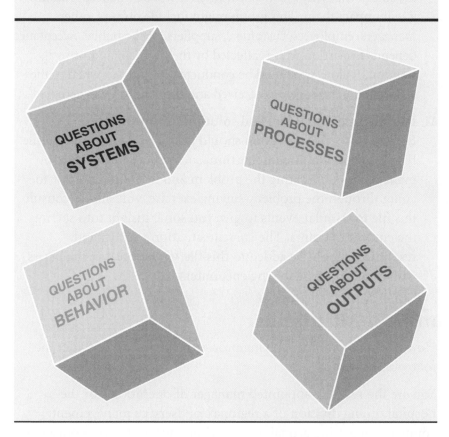

4 Select the best solution. Once you know the consequences of the proposed alternatives and have answered the questions in the previous step, your list of possible solutions narrows. Sometimes two or three alternatives are left. If so, they must go through this same scrutiny again. The problem and solution must be looked at from all angles, as though you are examining all six sides of a cube. (See *Exhibit 9c.*) Ask the tough questions and dig deep to find the correct solution. Do not rush the process. The correct solution will result in the problem going away. The incorrect solution will result in going through the entire process again.

5 **Develop an action plan.** After the solution has been chosen, an action plan must be developed. An **action plan** is a strategy of steps to carry out so that a problem does not recur. It must include exactly what should happen, step by step. (See *Exhibit 9d.*) This plan is very similar to a project plan, which you learned about in Chapter 2. The output from the action plan might take the form of a policy addition or change, an operational addition or change, or an employee handbook addition or change.

Exhibit 9d

Sample Solution Action Plan

Solution Action Plan

Task/Activity	Staff Responsible	Resources Needed	Due Date	Contingencies

6 **Implement the action plan.** The action plan and its outcome should be communicated to all individuals involved. Those who are involved in the problem and/or solution need to understand what the solution is, why it is needed, when it will be finalized, and how it will impact them. This group might include owners, other managers, employees, customers, suppliers, or the public. Acceptance depends in part on who is affected by the problem and/or by its solution. Follow-up should be conducted to find out whether the action plan's message was received and the solution was accepted.

7 **Document the problem and solution for future reference.** Every foodservice operation should have a problem/solution file. It should contain **documentation**, such as a report written by management reiterating the problem and its solution. Prior to going through the problem-solving exercise, you should consult this file for similar events to give you some insight into solving the current dilemma. The current situation's report and resolution should be added to this file to assist future managers with their problem-solving encounters.

Putting It All Together

How does this problem-solving process really work? Consider the following scenario:

You are the recently appointed manager of operations for the hospital dining division of a regional foodservice management company. In getting acquainted with your accounts, you notice that a particular hospital's food cost is higher than similar accounts' cost. Upon investigating further, you notice that this trend has been going on for quite some time. The cost is not exorbitantly high, just 2 or 3 percent, but it is consistent. You decide to see for yourself what is going on.

Upon arrival, you perform a complete analysis of the operation. Everything seems to be in order, and all company systems are being followed. You dig further by breaking down all purchases, finding that there is an unusually high purchase of meat. This does not make sense because all of your hospital accounts use the same menu cycles for their patients and cafeterias. You investigate the meat invoices and find some duplication of items between different purveyors. One company's invoices seem suspiciously sloppy, and upon further investigation you find out that the supplier does not even exist. You call your company's security department, and their investigation reveals that your organization's bookkeeper, who has been working there for several years, has set up a fictitious company. He processes the fake invoices and sends them to the home office for payment.

A check is sent to the fake company, which uses a post office box. The bookkeeper picks up the checks and cashes them himself. When confronted with this scenario, the bookkeeper admits to it.

Exhibit 9e highlights how the problem-solving steps were used in this scenario. You can see from this example how applying a systematic problem-solving process can ensure that a manager will make the best choices from the potential alternative solutions.

Exhibit 9e

Hospital High Food Costs

Define the problem	A particular hospital account has 2 to 3 percent higher food costs than those of similar accounts.
Identify who or what is affected	■ The foodservice company that was losing money ■ The manager who seemingly could not control costs
Determine the root cause	■ There was a loophole in the control system of the management company. ■ Invoices were signed by the receiving clerk and sent to the bookkeeper for processing. ■ The bookkeeper recorded the invoices and sent them to the home office for payment. ■ There was no control link preventing the bookkeeper from processing the fake invoices.
Determine alternative solutions and consequences	■ **Do nothing.** This is not a good solution. By doing nothing the problem could recur or it could expand to other units. ■ **Terminate the bookkeeper.** This will happen because the bookkeeper is guilty of theft. However, it does not solve the root problem. ■ **Have the unit manager sign off on the invoices.** This is a possible alternative. By having the manager sign off on the invoice, it will be recognized that the product was in fact purchased. By making this part of the process, it is a deterrent to having a fake company slip through the cracks. ■ **Set up a central commissary that would receive goods for all of the hospitals. The management company would then truck the requisitioned supplies to each hospital.** Due to the high cost of setting up this arrangement, this is probably not a viable alternative. While it would solve the problem, the cost may outweigh the benefit. ■ **Terminate the foodservice manager.** This is not a feasible alternative. The manager followed company policy and did not know that the bookkeeper had set up a fake company. ■ **Develop a list of approved suppliers that all hospital foodservice departments would use. Unit managers would order product only from these sources and invoices would be paid only to these companies.** This is a possible alternative. This would establish a list of reputable companies that the units could purchase from. By having accounting pay only those companies on the list, a fake company could not receive a check.

continued on next page

continued from previous page

- **Have the invoices sent to the vice president of operations, who would then sign off on them before forwarding them to accounting for payment.** This is probably not a practical alternative. Having the VP sign off would not prevent this from happening again. While the unit manager should know what is going on in the operation, the VP would have no way of knowing what is going on in every hospital. This step would become nothing more than a rubber stamp and would serve no purpose.

- **Have the hospital's accounting department pay the invoices rather than the home office of the foodservice management company.** This is another inferior alternative. Having individual units pay their own bills would reduce the economy of scale. It would serve no useful purpose to have one accounting department pay bills versus another. This step would not be a control mechanism.

Select the best solution	Choosing two of the viable options in combination would make for a good choice. - **Have a unit manager sign off on the invoices.** - **Develop a list of approved suppliers that all hospital foodservice departments within the company would use.** Unit managers would order product from only these sources and invoices would be paid only to these companies.
Develop an action plan	**Close the loop and make it difficult, if not impossible, to present fake invoices.** The foodservice company, its clients, and its management should all be happy with this solution. The action plan would include identifying and carrying out steps for an improved process to close this loop, as well as the creation of a new company policy.
Implement the plan	**Create criteria for selection of suppliers.** Evaluate a number of suppliers who will be placed on the list of preferred vendors. Conduct an information session for unit managers on the new process to use in ordering. A new company procedure might read: *A list of approved companies will be sent out from the home office. Individual units may purchase only from these suppliers. Invoices sent from companies not on this list will not be paid. All invoices presented for payment must contain the signature of the unit manager, indicating that these goods were purchased, and must also be signed by the receiving clerk, indicating that these items were received in good condition.*
Document for future reference	The vice president of operations should write a report on the problem and solution, and file it for future reference.

Potential Consequences of Improperly Solving a Problem

After using the problem-solving model several times, it becomes almost second nature. When a problem comes up, the process begins and solutions are identified. This method is much better than the alternative, which is to bypass the system and come up with a quick solution. All too often in the fast pace of the foodservice industry, a snap decision to a critical problem leads to a disaster. Consider the consequences of improperly solving a problem:

- **Problem gets worse.** Improperly solving—or not solving— a problem causes it to fester and eventually become a crisis.

- **Decrease in employee morale.** If the employees are a factor in the problem, it affects them emotionally. Improper solutions typically lead to frustration, damaging morale and giving management even more problems.

- **Employee turnover.** Employees spend a major part of their life at work. They want to be happy and enjoy it. Poor morale can compel an employee to look for another job.

- **Reduction of sales.** If the problem is related to sales, you must solve it as soon as possible, since diminished sales threatens the entire operation. Even if the problem is not sales related, it might damage morale, which could also result in lost sales.

- **Increased costs.** Many times, problems result in increased costs. This is normally due to a loophole in the control policies or processes, but could also be attributed to theft. Increased costs lead to reduced profit or, worse yet, a net loss.

- **Lost profit.** Most establishments cannot survive if their cash flow is affected drastically by lost profits. The first sign of reduction in profits is reduction in sales. Directly related to reduced sales are momentary increases in costs due to scheduling problems. This becomes a vicious cycle that if not caught immediately can leave a negative impact on the organization and its staff.

Take Risks

Not all decisions will be effective. Like everything else in life, we are rarely right all the time. Every conceivable effort, however, should be made to make the right decision. Sometimes risks must be taken, or tough choices and unpopular decisions must be made. Though they might not always be successful, your decisions should be made in the spirit of selecting the most appropriate solution at the time.

Activity

The Case of the Disappearing Liquor

You are the general manager of a trendy sports bar and grill located in an upscale suburb of a large metropolitan area. A popular sports talk radio show broadcasts live from your restaurant. You have a great crew that gets along and enjoys working there. Sales are good and all costs are in line except the bar cost, which is 1 or 2 percent high. You are not too worried about it because your strong sales give you a good profit and the owners are happy.

On a tip from an employee, however, you learn that a lead bartender is stealing wine and alcohol from the storeroom. You set up a hidden video surveillance camera. After a few nights, you catch the bartender on tape taking product from the liquor storeroom and going out the back door.

You do not know what to do. The lead bartender is very popular with your customers and the rest of the crew. Firing her would prove to be unpopular and could hurt sales and morale, but ignoring the problem would open the door to other employees taking product. Since you were tipped off, you know that at least some of the employees know what is going on.

In small groups, apply the problem-solving model to this situation and write down the responses to each step. Identify several alternatives, select the best solution, and write how you would implement the solution.

Some facts that might contribute to your problem-solving process are:

■ Lead bartenders have the keys to the storeroom, as the bar often runs out of product during a rush and management is busy with other problems.

■ Inventory is taken weekly.

Then in your group, discuss the following questions:

1 Should you terminate the lead bartender? Why or why not?

_____

_____

2 Discuss the ethics of setting up a hidden surveillance camera.

_____

_____

3 Is the cycle for inventory a problem? Why or why not?

_____

_____

Once you have presented your answers to these questions, choose a solution and discuss why it is the most effective. Walk through the problem-solving model for the class.

Also as a large group, talk about your opinions concerning the three questions.

Crisis Management

A **crisis** is a large problem—an event that happens without warning and normally affects a number of people. It is a crucial situation that must be handled carefully, or the outcome could include some terrible consequences. In the case of a restaurant, a crisis can affect the owners, managers, employees, customers, and the public (sometimes all at once). Quite often when a crisis occurs, the media arrives at the doors of the establishment to report on the event. If the emergency is handled properly, it will go a long way in determining whether the restaurant survives. In a severe crisis, proper reaction could even save lives.

One might assume that because a crisis happens without warning, it cannot be planned for. However, when a crisis does occur, the savvy operator can be prepared with a detailed plan to handle the situation. An organization's reaction to a crisis should be formulated prior to the catastrophe happening. When a crisis strikes, there is no time to sit down and think out a policy. Stress levels are high. Priority is, and should be, placed on action, be it saving lives, helping the authorities resolve the immediate problem, or calming the chaos at hand.

As you have already learned, an unsolved problem can become a crisis. For example, if management ignores the problem of an unsanitary condition in the kitchen, an outbreak of a foodborne illness could occur. An unsanitary condition is a problem, but an outbreak of a foodborne illness is a crisis. Every crisis, however, is not the result of an unsolved problem; sometimes it just happens. An out-of-control car crashing into the front of a restaurant and injuring several customers and employees is an example of a sudden crisis. Since a crisis, for the most part, is an unforeseen event, how it is handled becomes very important in minimizing the damage.

The key to crisis management is to have a plan formulated in advance and to practice, so that if a crisis should occur, it is second nature to handle it.

Types of Crises

Crises can be categorized into two broad groups: preventable and unpreventable. A **preventable crisis** is a catastrophe that can be precluded from happening, such as a fire or foodborne illness. An **unpreventable crisis** is a catastrophe that cannot be stopped from happening, such as an armed robbery. While it is impossible to list every conceivable type of crisis that could occur, the list in *Exhibit 9f* covers some of the more prevalent applications to the restaurant and foodservice industry. Along with the crisis is a summary of measures that can be taken to prevent an emergency.

Exhibit 9f

Types of Crises

Fire	In most cases a restaurant fire can be prevented. Proper installation of equipment and fire suppressant systems in the kitchen hood and appropriate placement of fire extinguishers can prevent most fires from spreading. Correct handling of ashtrays and smoking material, and periodic checks of the electrical and gas systems can prevent fires from starting. Only in rare cases, such as a lightning strike, can a fire not be prevented.
Foodborne illness	For the most part, foodborne illnesses can be prevented. Management should be trained and certified in food safety and should institute training programs for the staff in correctly handling and storing food. The establishment of a Hazard Analysis and Critical Control Point (HACCP) program within the restaurant is also beneficial.
Armed robbery	While an armed robbery cannot be prevented, it can be deterred. Most robbers are after a quick and easy strike and will survey a location before they rob it. They are primarily after cash; therefore, money should be handled properly. If a cashier collects cash from the customer, the cashier station should be away from the front door and periodic drops should be made into the safe. A video surveillance system is also a good deterrent.

A better control system would be having the servers collect from the guests and turn their receipts in after their shift. This way, the money is dispersed throughout the operation, as some servers will be in the dining room taking orders and some will be in the kitchen picking up orders. When turning cash in, it should be done in the back office and immediately put into a locked safe. ***Under no circumstances should any resistance be made during a robbery.*** Insurance will cover lost revenue, but it will not cover a lost life. |
| **Gas leak** | Although rare, a gas leak can be deadly, but it is also preventable. Gas equipment should be properly installed by a licensed technician. All gas lines and couplings should be inspected monthly. Pilot lights should be inspected daily to ascertain that they are working properly. |
| **Terrorist attack** | For terrorist attacks, there is concern about the water supply and/or the food chain being contaminated. The U.S. Department of Homeland Security has named restaurants and hotels as "soft" targets of terrorists. Regrettably, at this time, there is no way to prevent a terrorist attack or to know what form it will take. To deter such a thing from happening, management and staff should be alert and report any suspicious activity to the authorities.

You should also purchase only from reputable local suppliers that you know and trust. |
| **Natural disasters** | While you might receive notice for some types of weather-related events, many natural disasters will occur with little warning. You should take the time to learn if your area is prone to certain types of weather, such as hurricanes or tornadoes, and prepare as best you can if an event is imminent (e.g., boarding up windows or securing fixtures and furniture). Otherwise, you will have to rely on your crisis management plan to help you ensure the safety of your customers, employees, and establishment. |

Think About It...

Why is it important for every staff person to understand the importance of following crisis management procedures? Does each employee represent the organization in a time of crisis? What image do you want the public to have of your establishment?

Before a Crisis Strikes

When a crisis strikes, it happens fast. It could be instantaneous, such as a fire, explosion, or armed robbery. It could occur over several hours, such as an outbreak of foodborne illness. It could occur over many days, such as a lawsuit. The moment it happens is not the time to think about what to do. A plan should be made in advance and communicated to all involved. The plan should be a written policy that identifies clearly how to handle each type of crisis. The policy should cover the following:

- List of roles and responsibilities
- List of key contacts
- Sharing information
- Referring media to corporate offices, instructing employees not to talk to the media, and keeping media off the premises
- Filling out paperwork
- Incorporating the plan into training for all employees

Many emergencies will involve evacuating the premises. An **evacuation** is the process of removing customers and employees from the premises when a crisis occurs. Because everything is happening at once, management cannot do this alone. Responsibilities should be delegated by position and not by person. People change, especially with multiple shifts, while positions do not. To ensure that an evacuation is done successfully, the plan should include the following steps:

- A drawing should be made of the establishment showing all exits, routes to use to access those exits, and an alternate route in case a particular exit is blocked. The drawing should be posted throughout the building.
- A member of the management team should call 911 without delay when a crisis occurs and provide the location and explain exactly what the problem is and approximately how many people are involved.
- A member of management should be designated to secure all cash and other valuables.
- A member of management or a lead employee should be designated to meet the emergency personnel when they arrive and repeat what the problem is and how many people are involved.

■ A location outside the building should be designated for all evacuees to assemble. This should be located some distance from the building, perhaps in a neighboring establishment's parking lot.

■ Employees and customers should immediately be evacuated from the building. This should be done in a calm and orderly manner. Servers should be designated to lead customers seated at their stations to the assembly area outside the building. A chef or lead cook should be designated to make sure everyone is evacuated from the kitchen and back-of-the-house areas. Another employee should be designated to check the restrooms and assist anyone in these areas in the evacuation procedure.

■ All employees should practice the plan on a regular basis. It should be part of a sound training curriculum. As part of new hire orientation and other training programs, new employees should be made aware of the plan, including their area of responsibility.

Activity

Evacuation Plan Development

Find a restaurant or foodservice operation in your area. It could be where you are presently working or an establishment that you frequent. Get permission from the manager to draw up an evacuation plan. Remember to cover all threats and choose alternate routes in case the most obvious ones are blocked. After the plan is drawn up, ask the manager to review it. Bring the plan to class, exchange plans with another student, and give each other feedback.

Determining Roles and Responsibilities in a Crisis

As mentioned previously, a key component of any plan is to determine in advance who will do what. This will avoid confusion when a crisis strikes. It will also prevent two or more people doing the same thing when their presence is needed elsewhere. The roles and responsibilities should be in writing and listed by position, not person.

List of Key Contacts

There should be a list of key contacts next to every phone in the restaurant. A **contact list** includes key personnel to be notified in the event of a crisis, such as each member of management. Other useful contacts are city hall, the health department, an electrician, a plumber, and a security company, if applicable.

Sharing Information

Another policy to be determined in advance of a crisis is how information will be given or shared. It is always in the best interest of the restaurant or foodservice establishment to cooperate fully with local government officials. Sometimes management is reluctant to do this for fear of fines or other reprisals. The health department and code inspectors are there to protect citizens' interests. By cooperating with those officials and sharing information, they can complete their tasks quickly and efficiently. They will help the establishment correct a problem so that it does not recur.

Media Policy

Management should be careful about how much information is shared with the media regarding a crisis. Many larger organizations have media relations departments who will be called in to assist restaurant management in the event of a crisis.

Only one person should talk to the media. This person should be determined in advance and designated as part of the crisis or media policy. A **media policy** is a strategy developed in advance for dealing with newspaper, television, and radio reporters regarding the company's reaction to a crisis. The contact person would depend on the crisis. If the crisis is a lawsuit, then the legal firm representing the restaurant would be the logical voice. If the crisis is the destruction of property or patron illness, then one of the owners or management would be the most likely spokesperson. In no case should employees be allowed to talk to the media. They should be instructed to refer all questions to the appropriate person.

If at all possible, the media should be kept off the property. They should not be allowed to take photos or videotape. However, they have every right to do so from the street or other public space, but every effort should be made to secure the restaurant and grounds.

What to Say

When talking to the media, there are two words to remember: be brief. Do not ramble. Focus on the positive to get people into the restaurant and get sales back up to where they were prior to the crisis. In government and politics this is called **spin**—putting a positive thought into the public's mind following a negative situation. For example:

- After a fire, the quote might be, "We are going to rebuild, and when we are done, we will have a larger and finer facility for you to dine in."

Think About It...

Why would practicing how you communicate with the media before a crisis strikes be to your advantage?

■ After a robbery, it could be, "We have installed surveillance cameras and hired a security company to patrol the premises. Everyone should feel very safe here."

■ After an outbreak of foodborne illness, it might be, "We have spent a lot of time with the health department re-evaluating our food safety practices and procedures. As a result of this effort, our restaurant has to be the safest restaurant in the city for dining."

The way in which the designated spokesperson talks to the media will go a long way in the recovery effort to regain lost sales.

Incorporate Policies into Company Documents and Training

All of the above activities should be put in writing as part of company policy, and included in the employee manual and every employee's training. Various role-play activities and simulations can be utilized in management training to ensure that everyone is prepared to act in the event of a crisis. As part of employee training, it should be discussed and reviewed so that every staff person is familiar with the urgency to act in the event of a crisis. Employees need to know who is responsible for what, so they can help in gaining control of the situation. All staff should be trained to the point that they react and do not have to think about what to do. In a crisis, stress level is high and thinking is irrational. The better trained and prepared the staff is, the better off the establishment will be when dealing with a crisis.

After the Fact—Documenting and Completing Paperwork

After the crisis has subsided, there will be paperwork to complete. Forms from governmental agencies, insurance companies, and in the case of a chain operation, reports to the home office will all need to be completed. A meeting with all involved should also be held to ascertain how well the plan worked. Did things happen as expected? What did not work as well as it should have? What needs to be improved? Unfortunately, the effectiveness of a crisis plan, even practiced over and over, is unknown until it is needed. After the meeting, any policy that is affected by changes should be rewritten, based upon what was learned from the event.

Activity

Crisis in the Slaw

You are the general manager of a BBQ restaurant. Unfortunately, a large outbreak of foodborne illness has taken place with over two hundred of your customers becoming ill. The health department has investigated, and the cause was identified as improper refrigeration of coleslaw and potato salad. They have just completed an inspection of your restaurant and have cleared it to reopen. A local television reporter, known for asking probing questions, has requested an interview. As the spokesperson for the restaurant, you have agreed.

The following are some sample questions that the reporter might ask during the role-play. The person who is playing the reporter should also think of some other questions to ask. As the reporter, you do not have to ask every question; however, you should be tough. Think about a local reporter who is known for investigative reporting and try to emulate his or her style. Do not just ask simple questions—select those that you think would lead to a good story.

Sample Questions for Reporter:

1. Do you feel bad that your negligence caused over two hundred people to become ill?

2. What are you going to do about the lawsuits that are sure to follow?

3. An employee told me that your kitchen is filthy, and that it was no surprise that this happened. Are you surprised? Why did you allow for these conditions to exist?

4. Several employees told me that the walk-in refrigerator is always running warm, and that they told you about it. They also said it is too expensive to fix. Any comment?

5. You know you could have prevented this from happening—why didn't you?

Find a partner in the class and decide who will role-play the part of the store manager and the part of the reporter. Take about seven minutes to prepare yourselves, and about five minutes to role-play the interview between the manager and the reporter. Then switch roles and repeat the role-play. After the two role-plays, discuss the following questions as a large group:

1. How do you think the manager did in protecting the restaurant's interests?

2. Would you say that the manager used "spin" to keep the message positive?

3. How did you feel dealing with the reporter?

4. What kind of report would you write from this interview?

5. How could you have handled the interview differently?

Summary

Solving problems is something managers do on a daily basis. Some problems are simple, while some are more complex. It is the complex problems that are the most difficult to solve. They should not be taken lightly or answered by a snap decision. Rather, they should be analyzed using a problem-solving model similar to the one presented in this chapter. The steps that compose a problem-solving model can be helpful when problematic situations occur in the restaurant. Using this type of problem-solving methodology, an effective decision can be reached that is sound and, more important, will prevent the problem from recurring.

While problems occur on a daily basis, a crisis rarely happens. Many managers will go through their entire career without a crisis. This is not to say the possibility should be ignored—plans should be developed to prepare for a crisis, and opportunities to practice the plan should be scheduled. One never knows when a crisis will hit; therefore, management should always be prepared. Proper reaction can save lives or save the business. Establishing company polices for crisis response is crucial, including steps for handling interaction with the media. Written documentation and training are also important facets of crisis management.

Review Your Learning

1 In the problem-solving model, "identifying the player(s)" most nearly means

A. the person(s) affected by the problem and solution.

B. an individual.

C. a group of people.

D. All of the above

2 A problem could be caused by

A. one of the operational systems breaking down.

B. an improperly conceived system.

C. Both A and B

D. Neither A nor B

3 An action plan

A. details what is to happen step by step to correct a problem.

B. could take the form of a policy addition or policy change.

C. Both A and B

D. Neither A nor B

4 Which of these is *not* a consequence of improperly solving a problem?

A. Employee morale could decrease.

B. There could be a reduction of sales.

C. Costs could increase.

D. The problem goes away.

5 For the most part, which of the following emergencies cannot be prevented?

A. Armed robbery

B. Fire

C. Foodborne illness

D. All of the above can be prevented, in most cases

6 Evacuating the premises is best handled by

A. having specific people assigned responsibilities.

B. having specific positions assigned responsibilities.

C. Both A and B

D. Neither A nor B

7 Crisis management should be

A. company policy.

B. part of the employee training program.

C. practiced regularly.

D. All of the above

8 Which of the following is *not* part of the problem-solving model?

A. Developing an evacuation plan

B. Identifying the problem

C. Identifying the players

D. Determining alternatives

9 If a problem is improperly solved,

A. it could go away.

B. it could get worse.

C. Both A and B

D. Neither A nor B

Notes

Planning and Conducting Effective Meetings

10

Inside This Chapter

- Why People Dislike Meetings
- Planning Effective Meetings
- Conducting Effective Meetings

After completing this chapter, you should be able to:

- Define planning, meeting, information meetings, problem-solving meetings, brainstorming meetings, action meetings, call/emergency meetings, warm-up activity, facilitator, ground rules, parking lot, action item, next steps, and minutes.

- Identify different meeting types.

- Describe the steps in planning a meeting.

- Identify the components of an agenda.

- Develop an agenda for a meeting.

- Identify factors that lead to successful meetings.

- Describe the steps in conducting a meeting.

- Identify the parts of meeting minutes.

Test Your Knowledge

1 **True or False:** A meeting gives employees a chance to interact. *(See p. 226.)*

2 **True or False:** An agenda should be developed in advance of a meeting. *(See p. 233.)*

3 **True or False:** Meetings should have a clearly defined purpose. *(See p. 227.)*

4 **True or False:** Persons who attend meetings should receive any documents in advance of the meeting. *(See p. 231.)*

5 **True or False:** Meetings should end not more than ten minutes past the designated time. *(See p. 235.)*

6 **True or False:** Parking lot issues should be assigned to participants to lead discussions in the meeting. *(See p. 236.)*

7 **True or False:** Minutes are records of everything that happened in the meeting. *(See p. 238.)*

8 **True or False:** Ground rules create a participant contract of how people will behave during a meeting. *(See p. 235.)*

Key Terms

Action item	Facilitator	Next steps
Action meetings	Ground rules	Parking lot
Agenda	Information meetings	Planning
Brainstorming meetings	Meeting	Problem-solving meetings
Call/emergency meetings	Minutes	Warm-up activity

Introduction

One activity that has come to dominate today's business world is meetings. According to the National Statistics Council, 37 percent of employee time is spent in meetings. Nevertheless, conducting meetings tends to be a skill set that is often overlooked by leaders and managers.

From extremely formal procedures involving parliamentary rules of order to less formal staff updates, meetings are a way managers can keep channels of communication open with their staff. Meetings can also serve other purposes such as finding solutions to operational issues or brainstorming new ideas. The structure that a manager ultimately selects for meetings depends on a number of factors, including the particular culture of the organization.

Although every organization today conducts some type of meeting, there are times when employees do not appreciate them. This chapter

Think About It...

How are meetings viewed in the organizations you have worked for? Why do so many people think meetings can be a waste of time?

will look at reasons why people do not like to attend meetings and then suggest a number of ways to make your meetings effective.

This chapter will also examine the meeting process from planning a meeting through conducting and evaluating its effectiveness. Basic elements that are common to meetings will be reviewed. Suggestions on how to format meeting agendas will also be described. The flow of running a meeting is presented along with requirements for following up after the meeting.

Why People Dislike Meetings

A challenge for any manager who plans and conducts meetings is to change the perception people have of them. The reasons most people seem to dislike meetings can be as varied as those who attend them.

Some of the reasons people dislike meetings are:

- **Many participants do not take meetings seriously and are not prepared.** This is reflected in arriving late, leaving early, and spending a lot of time during the meeting not paying attention. Meetings that meander around topics—trying to figure out what the actual purpose is—drain participants who are prepared.

- **Just too many meetings.** People feel they cannot get their work done because of attending so many meetings. Too often the meetings seem to be unnecessary and a waste of their time.

- **Meetings are too long.** Too often meetings drag on because of lack of planning or lack of an effective facilitator who can keep things moving.

- **People are not focused at meetings.** Distractions and issues not related to the agenda often come up at meetings.

- **Some people dominate the meeting.** There are always a few people who want to be heard more than others. These people can intimidate others and suppress their ideas.

- **The information presented at meetings is confusing.** Many times people leave meetings with different views as to what happened; therefore, no productive results can be implemented.

- **Many people do not speak their mind in meetings.** Whether it is a facilitator who is not prepared to conduct the meeting to include participation, or attendees who dominate the discussion, a lot of people do not feel secure saying what they think.

■ **Meetings never seem to improve.** People have lost the expectation that meetings will ever improve and continue to believe that problems associated with meetings are never addressed.

Now that you know the reasons why employees become frustrated with meetings, you can take these factors into consideration when planning and conducting meetings at your own workplace.

Think About It…

Why is it important to know what type of meeting you are planning? What do you think is the most important contributing factor to badly run meetings? Why? What message are you sending to your staff if you are not prepared for a meeting?

Planning Effective Meetings

Meetings have come to decorate the organizational landscape of today's businesses. However, most workers would probably admit that one of their least favorite job-related activities is to attend meetings. Given the negative image that meetings have in the business world, how does a manager conduct meetings without perpetuating this image? The better prepared a manager is for conducting a meeting, the better chance everyone will find the meeting to be effective.

To be prepared, the manager needs to understand how to plan a meeting. **Planning** involves formulating the details of a meeting beforehand so you and the participants know what should occur during it. Planning also involves applying a standard methodology to the meeting process to ensure outcomes are achieved.

Types of Meetings

Meetings are held for all types of reasons. A **meeting** is an assembly of people for the purpose of discussing or making decisions about some topics. Knowing what type of meeting you want to plan and conduct is an important step. Most meetings can be sorted into four categories:

1. **Information meetings**—meetings that share communication, such as status reports, updates, orientation, and training.

2. **Problem-solving meetings**—meetings involving a group or team whose purpose is to tackle a problem. This meeting explores opportunities to solve problems and does not necessarily reach an immediate decision. The process is to gather information, analyze options, narrow the options, and then take action.

3. **Brainstorming meetings**—meetings in which the purpose is to generate a list of ideas or creative solutions to an issue confronting the organization. The purpose of this meeting is not to make a decision but to maximize creativity.

4 **Action meetings**—brief meetings, usually with just two or three employees, that address a problem to bring closure and take action immediately. The goal of the meeting is to decide and commit to action. A **call/emergency meeting** is a type of action meeting in which some type of crisis has occurred and immediate action must be taken.

Meeting Objectives

As part of the planning process, managers should identify any business objectives that need to be accomplished at the meeting and determine the appropriate type of meeting to accomplish those objectives. For example, discussing the yearly budget, staffing needs, turnover rates, special events, or promotions would be appropriate for an information meeting. An effective manager will also get input from the management team and employees who will be involved in the meeting. Getting feedback from these individuals in order to craft objectives helps everyone attending the meeting understand its specific purpose and reason. Contributing to the creation of the meeting, as well as understanding its purpose, helps employees become more interested in attending. Once the manager has clearly identified the purpose for a meeting and the appropriate meeting type, planning the meeting format and structure can begin.

Meeting Attendees

As you plan the meeting, you should determine who needs to attend the meeting, which is related to the type of meeting you are conducting and its purpose. Since meetings have such a poor image, it is important to invite and include only those people who are essential to the purpose of the meeting. Staff will grow to appreciate your leadership in meeting planning when they know that your meetings are focused, efficient and effective, and include only those workers who need to be there.

Meeting Frequency

For a meeting to be effective, it needs to follow a useful and comfortable process with established guidelines as seen in *Exhibit 10a* on the next page.

The type of meeting can dictate how often it is held. For example, managers will want to schedule staff meetings on a regular basis. These meetings tend to be information meetings that provide workers with timely updates—sales, promotional campaigns, customer-related issues, and company information. These meetings also offer an opportunity to recognize teams and individuals for work well done.

It is important for a manager to try not to mix too many types of meetings together. It is more effective to have shorter meetings that are focused on similar issues and objectives than to combine a number of items into one longer meeting.

Exhibit 10a

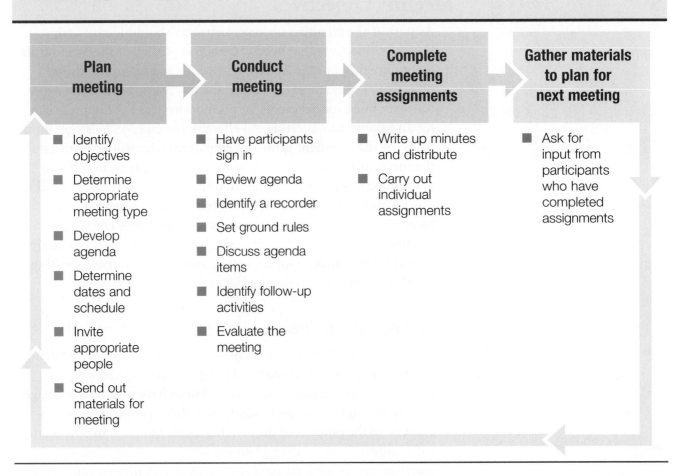

A Meeting Process

Plan meeting	Conduct meeting	Complete meeting assignments	Gather materials to plan for next meeting
■ Identify objectives	■ Have participants sign in	■ Write up minutes and distribute	■ Ask for input from participants who have completed assignments
■ Determine appropriate meeting type	■ Review agenda	■ Carry out individual assignments	
■ Develop agenda	■ Identify a recorder		
■ Determine dates and schedule	■ Set ground rules		
■ Invite appropriate people	■ Discuss agenda items		
■ Send out materials for meeting	■ Identify follow-up activities		
	■ Evaluate the meeting		

Developing the Agenda

The next step is to develop the meeting agenda based on the objectives. An **agenda** is simply a list of topics that will be reviewed or dealt with at a meeting. Agendas are created based on the objectives, purpose, and any feedback you have gathered from participants. The agenda becomes the roadmap for conducting the meeting. A sample meeting agenda is shown in *Exhibit 10b*. Following that is a list identifying the parts that should be included in all agendas.

Exhibit 10b

Sample Meeting Agenda

Weekly Preshift Staff Meeting

DATE October 11, 2006

TIME 4–5 p.m.

LOCATION Banquet Room

ATTENDING Jesus Fernando, Jorgé Herñandez, Eduardo Juarza, Kristy Lee, Lawrence Towns, Clayton Smith, Janet White, Tony Zardini

MATERIALS Ideas for new menu items

AGENDA TOPIC	PRESENTER	TIME
Introduction	Jorgé Herñandez	5 minutes
Ground Rules	Jorgé Herñandez	5 minutes
Warm-up Activity: Duck, Duck, Goose	Janet White	10 minutes
ITEM 1: Schedule for Wright wedding reception	Jorgé Herñandez	5 minutes
ITEM 2: New items for winter menu	Tony Zardini	15 minutes
ITEM 3: Vacation scheduling for November and December	Clayton Smith	20 minutes

NEXT STAFF MEETING: October 18, 2006

Parts of an Agenda

- **Name or type of meeting.** For example: staff, status, progress, or budget.

- **Date, time, and location**

- **People attending**

- **Materials to bring**

- **Meeting purpose/objectives**

- **Agenda topics.** Include a few sentences stating why this topic is being discussed.

- **Topic type.** Identify whether the topic requires discussion, a decision, or is just information.

- **If there are any presenters, associate them with the topic they will be presenting or facilitating.**

- **Time frame for each agenda item.** Determine a time estimate for how long you want to spend on each item. Sharing information that requires no discussion takes less time than an agenda item that involves discussions or activities for the participants. As you determine time limits for each item, consider including some time for any questions that participants might have. It is better to estimate a little extra time for agenda items than to run out of time.

- **Next steps.** Identify any assignments that need to be performed with specifics on who it is assigned to, what is supposed to be done, and by when.

- **Conclusion.** Always include a summary of the meeting, which reconfirms next steps and meeting dates.

- **Evaluation.** A variety of techniques can be used to determine the effectiveness of the meeting.

Warm-up Activities

Another important planning step is to determine any warm-up activities you might want to conduct at the start of the meeting. A **warm-up activity** is a quick, interactive activity that prepares people to focus on the meeting and its objectives. It is important to select an activity that is related to the meeting goals and agenda items to ensure that the activity has impact with the participants. The exception would be when you want to use a rev-up activity as a fun addition to the meeting.

A wide assortment of warm-up activities can be planned and designed into a meeting, including:

- **Introduction activities**—introductions in which participants pair up, ask each other a few questions, and then share this information with the group

- **Rev-up activities**—used to get participants enthused to participate. (See *Exhibit 10c.*)

- **Appreciative activities**—used at recognition and reward meetings to show employees that you are thinking about them

- **Competitive activities**—used at meetings involving sales campaigns or promotional contests in which you will reward an individual or team with a prize for winning the contest

- **Team-building activities**—used during various stages of team development to ensure the team is optimizing its performance

- **Training activities**—used to help staff understand the objectives of the meeting

Premeeting Activities and Assignments

As managers plan meetings, they need to determine whether there are any premeeting activities that need to be completed by the participants. These activities can range from reading materials that will be discussed at the meeting to completing some type of task and reporting their findings. If the manager determines that some type of premeeting assignment does need to be completed by participants so they are prepared to participate productively, the manager should answer the following questions:

- What pre-activity or assignment needs to be completed?

- Does the activity need to be completed before the meeting, or can it be done during the meeting?

- Does this activity support one of the objectives and purpose of the meeting?

Exhibit 10c

This manager uses humor to engage his staff in a preshift meeting.

- Will all participants need to complete the assignment? If not, who will be designated to complete the activity?

- How much time will it take to complete the pre-assignment?

- What materials do you need to put together for the pre-assignment?

- What instructions do you need to write to accompany the pre-assignment?

- Do you need to include a cover letter when you distribute the agenda and pre-assignment?

- Have you included the pre-assignment in the agenda?

Activity

No Time To Meet

You are the manager of a small sandwich restaurant. You have four employees. One of your concerns is that there is no time for meetings, yet you need to meet to discuss issues regarding new products, new customer focus programs, and training. The restaurant opens at 10:00 a.m. and closes at 10:00 p.m.

What strategy would you use to meet with employees at least once a week?

_____

_____

_____

_____

_____

Once the manager has settled on the need for a pre-assignment, it must be part of the written communication distributed with the agenda. The manager needs to clarify why the pre-assignment is needed and how the participant is supposed to complete it before the meeting. Always include contact information so that participants can call or email you if they have any questions.

Scheduling the Meeting

Once you have determined the objectives and set the meeting agenda, you need to schedule the meeting time and date. Since you have laid out the agenda with times for each agenda item, you know exactly how much time you will need to schedule for the meeting. You can look at your calendar as well as the schedule of participants to determine the best time for the meeting. Customer traffic might require that meetings be held before or after store hours. Another possibility for meeting times might be during times when customer traffic is slow. However, if there are some participants who absolutely have to attend the meeting, ensure that their schedules are free so as not to cause any unnecessary difficulty for them. Finally, add scheduling information to your agenda and distribute it promptly to participants along with any other meeting materials.

Activity

Plan the Meeting

You are a manager at the Chelsea Grill. The restaurant has been experiencing a lot of theft over the past month. The thefts started one month ago and have occurred during the busiest hours of operation. The items stolen were frozen meat items, pre-wrapped items placed at the register for guests to purchase, and items in a holding bin waiting to be placed in inventory. You currently have a system to track items taken from inventory. The items are matched with the orders that were sold, one week after a sale takes place. The pre-wrapped items are kept in inventory until placed on the counter, based on the par levels desired (the quantity of product a restaurant desires to keep on hand at all times). Employees enter and exit the premises through a special door. Employees are not allowed to bring packages to work, nor can they take any packages out. Personal items are kept in lockers.

An inventory specialist manages the inventory. She was the person who alerted you that items had been stolen. She provided you with the number of items stolen and the value of each item. Based on this record, you notice that in the past month, each week's theft total has increased by $20.00. You now have a total loss of $300.00. You must do something to stop theft in the restaurant.

You want to put a team of employees together to try to solve this problem. You want to conduct a meeting that helps identify where the problem originates and how to stop it. However, keep in mind that the problem may be caused by one of the participants that you want to attend the meeting.

As a group, complete the following tasks:

1. Identify objectives to accomplish during the first meeting. Identify at least three issues to discuss with the employees selected to help solve the problem.

2. Determine the most appropriate type of meeting for accomplishing these objectives.

3. Create an agenda for the meeting.

4. Identify employees to participate in the meeting.

5. Identify the length of the meeting.

6. Identify materials you would distribute either before or during the meeting, if any.

Conducting Effective Meetings

Since the key to running an effective meeting centers around the person who is conducting the meeting, it is important to understand the role that a facilitator can play. A meeting **facilitator** is someone who assists in making the meeting run easier. (See *Exhibit 10d*.) Whether you as the manager, act as a facilitator, or you decide to ask someone to play that role, a facilitator's major responsibility is to keep the meeting focused and moving.

Other responsibilities for a meeting facilitator are:

Exhibit 10d

This manager keeps the meeting focused.

- Determining whether any issues need to be tabled and reviewed later or in another meeting.

- Telling the group that time has expired on an agenda item.

- Intervening and refocusing the group if the discussion breaks into several different but related conversations.

- Managing the discussion of sensitive topics in a neutral manner.

- Preventing anyone from dominating the meeting or being ignored.

- Bringing closure to agenda points.

A few key objectives a manager can carry out to ensure a successful meeting include:

- **Arriving early**—to ensure the room is set up properly.

- **Having a sign-in sheet**—this creates a record of who attended.

- **Starting on time**—do not punish the people who show up on time. After missing the start of a few meetings, those who show up late will get the message and start arriving promptly.

- **Using and following an agenda**—meeting participants become discouraged when a lot of time and effort are put into the creation of an agenda, and then it is not used for the meeting. You should write the agenda on a flipchart or board and have extra copies for anyone who might have forgotten theirs.

- **Understanding the purpose and objectives of the meeting**—if there are other channels of communication that can be leveraged to get information out to the audience without sacrificing the goal, then a manager should consider using them.

- **Identifying action items and assignments consistently**—these should be indicated on the agenda. During the meeting, these items and assignments need to be discussed and given out.

- **Ending on time**—people will appreciate how well you are able to stay on track and bring a meeting to a timely closure.

- **Using evaluation information for improvement**—people appreciate a manager who is trying to become more effective and efficient at running meetings. This is a great source of information on how to improve the meetings you need to conduct.

The first part of the meeting should include:

- Explaining your role

- Reviewing the agenda to familiarize participants with the flow of the meeting

- Identifying who will be the recorder of the minutes of the meeting

Establishing Ground Rules

After these preliminary activities, a critical part to an effective meeting is establishing or setting ground rules. **Ground rules** are the norms regarding how meetings are run, how participants should interact, and what behavior is acceptable. Some organizations have company-accepted ground rules posted in all meeting rooms. If this is the case, you should refer to the rules, or have the group agree to and post their own. Ground rules may cover any of these behaviors:

- Promptness

- Conversational courtesies

- Breaks

- Interruptions

- Rotation or routine tasks—such as recorder or flipchart recorder

- Other norms the group wants to enforce

- Question and answer periods

A ground rule that is essential to an effective meeting is setting time limits for discussions and sticking to them. One of the reasons to include this item as a ground rule is that it ensures you will stay within the time limits of your meeting agenda.

Think About It...

What would you do if you were facilitating a meeting and realized you would not have time to cover the remaining agenda items?

Another rule should address parking lot issues. A **parking lot** is a visible space to write those ideas or topics that are important and brought up in a meeting, but that cannot be addressed because of lack of information or time, the right people not being present, or not directly relating to the agenda topic. Instead of wasting time on these items, they can be deferred to a meeting when they can be adequately addressed. These items should be placed on a flipchart and named as action items or included as future agenda items so they are not overlooked.

Activity

Setting Ground Rules

When a manager conducts meetings, it is important to establish ground rules with the staff. You will be divided into small teams to engage in decision making to reach consensus on a set of ground rules. The ground rules will be used during the case study in this chapter as well.

Individually, review the list of ground rules in the table below. Then rank the ten items in order, using the column "Your Ranking" to indicate which item is the most important to you (use 1 for most important and 10 for least important).

As part of the group to which you have been assigned, strive for consensus, and use the column "Group Ranking" to identify which rule is most important and which one is least important. If there is difficulty in reaching consensus, then majority vote will rule. Post your group ranking so the other groups can see them.

	Ground Rules	Your Ranking	Group Ranking
1	If we plan to be late or absent, we will inform the team facilitator, manager, or a group member at least a day in advance.		
2	We will come to the meeting prepared to work on the agenda and discuss issues.		
3	We will respect the opinions and feelings of all participants. Each person has equal participation in the meeting. When discussing issues, each person should expect to contribute to the discussion and be listened to with respect.		
4	We will avoid blaming people for shortcomings of the group. If the group somehow fails to do a task properly, we will examine the group process and attempt to improve it.		
5	We will support the decisions of the team after they have been made. Undermining group decisions and bad-mouthing the group and its work is unacceptable behavior.		
6	We will live up to our commitments, recognizing that failure to do so affects the whole group process.		
7	When faced with a decision, the process we will use is 1) state the problem, 2) discuss different ideas, 3) examine the benefits and risk associated with different methods, and 4) select an approach we can all support.		
8	We will deal with conflict in a productive way. Our general rule will be to understand the problem as best we can from each side's perspective. We will listen to all sides, looking for facts, and then help those in conflict create alternative solutions.		
9	We will not engage in sidebar conversations, whether or not they relate to the agenda topic.		
10	External interruptions will be kept to a minimum.		

As part of a large class discussion, each group will explain and answer the following questions:

1 How close were individual rankings in the group?

_____

_____

_____

2 How did you involve all participants in the discussion on group ranking?

_____

_____

_____

3 What lessons were learned from the process of group ranking?

_____

_____

_____

During the Meeting

Throughout the course of the meeting, each agenda item should be presented. Depending on the type of action the agenda item requires, the group should either discuss it, make a decision, or simply listen to the information being presented. Following each agenda item, a question and answer period should be allowed to ensure that everyone attending has gained an understanding of the item. If the question and answer time becomes too long, consider putting some of the questions on the parking lot. They can be further addressed at a future time to keep the meeting moving in a timely manner.

During each of the agenda items, you may identify one or more action items that need to be assigned. An **action item** is a specific point associated with an agenda item that needs some type of action performed. For example, an action item for a budget meeting might be to gather information from a vendor on the cost of new equipment, or obtain projections for remodeling parts of a restaurant. The action item would be identified and assigned to someone to complete for a future meeting. The person who is given the action item to complete would then gather the information in a report, based on the assigned deadline.

Closing the Meeting

Once you have gone through all the agenda items, you need to bring closure to the meeting. This phase of the meeting includes reviewing all the action items to ensure everyone understands what they are and who is responsible for carrying them out. Reviewing the action items also identifies what the next steps of the meeting should be. **Next steps** refer to identifying what tasks, actions, and other events need to happen as a result of the meeting, as well as setting a date and time for the next meeting.

Also, during the closure phase of the meeting, the manager should briefly summarize the meeting for the group. The manager should reflect on the decisions made, agenda items for the next meeting, and any issues that remain open. By doing this, the manager gives the participants a chance to indicate their consensus with what occurred during the meeting. Next steps also give the participants the opportunity to add any other information should the manager overlook some aspect of the meeting. Before ending the meeting, the manager should thank the participants for attending and for their contribution and remind them of the next meeting date.

After the Meeting

The only way to improve your ability to conduct meetings is to gather feedback from participants. The purpose of a meeting evaluation is to capture what worked well in the meeting and to change things in the future that did not work as effectively. The evaluation can either use a form that participants complete, or it can be a feedback session in which you ask them a series of questions and write down their responses. Whatever method you use, the evaluation should be short and concise. *Exhibit 10e* provides an example of questions you might ask in your meeting evaluation.

Once you have concluded the meeting, the person who was designated the recorder needs to write up the minutes of the meeting. **Minutes** are an official record of key points discussed or covered at a meeting, as well as anything that might have been decided or completed during the meeting. Minutes should not reflect the opinion of the person taking the notes. They should focus on three categories of information: decisions made, action items, and any open parking lot issues. The minutes should include the following:

■ Name of person who called the meeting, as well as those who were invited but did not attend

■ Date, time, and place of the meeting

■ Purpose and objectives of the meeting

Sample Meeting Evaluation Form

MEETING EVALUATION SURVEY

FOR Weekly Preshift Staff Meeting

DATE October 11, 2006

Please take some time to fill out this short survey about today's meeting. Your feedback and comments will help us improve future meetings.

The meeting today was:

Unproductive	①	②	③	④	⑤	Productive
Not focused	①	②	③	④	⑤	Focused
Pace was too slow	①	②	③	④	⑤	Pace was too fast
Blaming individuals	①	②	③	④	⑤	Looking for solutions
Unreceptive to questions	①	②	③	④	⑤	Responsive to questions

Did we do the right things? How effective was the meeting?

How productive was the meeting?

What could we do differently to make it better next time?

When you are finished, please return this form to Janet White.

- Each agenda item along with decisions made

- Action items

- Open issues

- Next steps

- Next meeting date and time

Ideally, the recorder should complete the minutes within a day or two and then distribute them to the participants. The minutes serve as a reference for participants to reconstruct conversations and discussions and to remind them of decisions made or actions to be taken. For those people who could not attend the meeting, it serves as a way to see what happened in their absence.

Summary

Managing effective meetings is a core skill all managers should develop. Meetings provide a venue to receive input from employees, inform and motivate them, and design solutions to problems and issues the organization faces.

Effective meetings are those with specific, measurable objectives that involve staff in their planning and implementation. Meetings should be scheduled regularly and fall into these categories: information, brainstorming, problem-solving, or action meetings.

Planning plays a critical role in how successful a meeting is. All meetings follow a general pattern, and establishing guidelines is essential to ensure that meetings are viewed as important to the organization. Another aspect of successful meetings is the importance of using and following agendas. An effective agenda and any premeeting activities should be distributed before the meeting.

An important element to conducting any meeting, especially those that are either team-based or recurring, is the use of ground rules. Ground rules are norms that dictate how meetings are run and what behavior is acceptable. Another tool that is helpful during a meeting is the use of parking lots. Parking lot issues are those that may be important, but are not necessarily related to the current issues of the meeting. As the meeting progresses, each agenda item should have some type of action associated with it. Action items are assigned to participants and then become part of the next steps of the meeting.

At the end of every meeting, the manager should evaluate the effectiveness of the meeting. This evaluation can either be a short feedback session addressing a few pertinent questions or a written form that is reviewed after the meeting. The evaluation is instrumental in improving the skills of the manager for continuous improvement in the organization. At the end of the meeting, the recorder should write up the minutes to summarize what occurred during the meeting. These minutes are documentation that should be distributed in a timely manner.

Understanding the key elements of running effective meetings will help managers improve their leadership and communication skills.

Review Your Learning

1 **When should you call a meeting?**

A. Whenever your staff need to share information

B. When a meeting is the best way to accomplish an objective

C. At least once a week

D. Infrequently, because other channels of communication work better

2 **What should an effective agenda include?**

A. The objective of the meeting, the time the meeting will begin and end, the location, and the participants involved

B. The issues to be discussed, the time the meeting will begin and end, and what is expected of the participants in terms of preparation before the meeting

C. The objective of the meeting, issues to be discussed, meeting times, location, participants involved, and premeeting activities

D. The objective of the meeting, the time the meeting will begin and end, and what food will be served

3 **Is it necessary for the agenda to be distributed before the meeting?**

A. Yes, the agenda should be distributed at least several days before the meeting, allowing participants enough time to prepare for the meeting.

B. Yes, the agenda should be distributed the day before the meeting, allowing participants time to review the agenda items.

C. No, the agenda should be distributed when the participants enter the meeting.

D. No, the agenda should be created at the meeting.

4 **What is the best way to evaluate the effectiveness of a meeting?**

A. Ask participants for their opinions throughout the meeting, after significant agenda items.

B. Get a show of hands at the end of the meeting as to whether they liked it.

C. Ask for feedback or written comments immediately after the meeting.

D. Several days after the meeting, once people have had a chance to think about it, have them leave you a voicemail with their thoughts.

5 **Which step is *not* part of the planning process?**

A. Determining objectives

B. Identifying a participant who will be a recorder

C. Determining any pre-assignment activities

D. Sending out meeting materials

6 **When is an action meeting called?**

A. A problem needs an immediate decision.

B. A significant announcement needs to be communicated.

C. A long-term problem needs to be addressed.

D. A creative solution to a problem needs to be identified.

7 **Which factors lead to successful meetings?**

A. Start on time, have food, and use the same process each time.

B. Start on time, use evaluations, and end on time.

C. End on time, use an agenda, and let key people dominate discussions.

D. Use action items, end on time, and allow for other issues to be discussed.

8 **Why are ground rules established in meetings?**

A. To agree on how participants should behave during the meeting

B. To agree on what kind of food to serve for snacks

C. To agree on who should be the facilitator

D. To agree on how long each agenda item should take

9 **The most effective way to handle a topic that is important, but not directly related to a meeting, is to**

A. make it a ground rule.

B. create an action item for the next meeting.

C. have the facilitator handle it.

D. place it on a parking lot.

10 **What is the purpose of recording minutes of a meeting?**

A. To recognize people who attended the meeting

B. To serve as a reference of what occurred at the meeting

C. To identify how efficient the meeting was

D. To create documentation for legal liability

Notes

Field Project

Becoming a Manager and a Leader

Managing a restaurant, foodservice, or hospitality operation and leading people are not easy tasks. Today, it is even more difficult due to the uncertainty of the economy, competition, and changes in the workforce pool. It takes leaders at all levels of the organization to determine how to best align what appear at times to be conflicting demands with various teams to achieve results, all while attending to and balancing personal and professional satisfaction. In addition, those in leadership positions must always evaluate these factors with the highest ethical standards.

The process of leadership and management development is greatly facilitated with feedback and coaching. Feedback is needed because it is often difficult for individuals to see themselves clearly and to honestly evaluate how they come across to others. Feedback that is solicited from those with whom you work or have a relationship with, and that is offered in a factual, noncritical way, is essential to determining those leadership skills that need the most development.

This field research project is designed to provide you with an opportunity to obtain feedback from others in the field, as well as to promote insight and to encourage you to ask questions. This guide focuses primarily on personal capabilities and competencies in becoming an effective manager and leader in the hospitality and restaurant industry. This project is designed to provide a composite picture of your current skill sets in areas discussed in this guide. In addition, it will also require you to reflect on this feedback, analyze it in terms of your strengths and weaknesses, and put together an action plan that can help you improve your leadership and management skills as part of your professional development.

Assignment

One of the most effective ways to learn about your skills as a manager and a leader is through feedback using a 360-degree feedback process. Successful leaders recognize that they must continually enhance and sharpen their leadership skills. They must focus their ability on achieving the organization's vision and mission through credible actions, authentic relationships, and clear communication of the company's strategic direction and goals.

1. Complete the "360 Shared Leadership Development Assessment Tool" on yourself.

2. Identify between five to seven individuals that you will ask to complete the same tool, providing you with feedback from their perspective. The individuals need to be in the following categories:

   ☐ Who is your supervisor/manager? Ideally, ask your current boss. If you currently are not employed, ask a past boss or a professor or instructor to provide you with feedback. This person should, however, know you beyond just general encounters as a student.

   ☐ Identify two to four other employees at your same level. These individuals should be your peers at your workplace. In most cases, they would be at the same level or perform the same functions as you do. If you are not employed, ask close friends who know you well.

   ☐ Identify one to two other employees who have reported to you in the past. These individuals are often classified as subordinates to your function. However, if you have not had anyone report to you either regularly or on a team, you could also ask someone who is fairly new in a similar position to yours who is familiar with your work. If you are not currently working, you can ask fellow students who know you to complete the assessments on you as well.

continued on next page

3 Make copies of the assessment tool and distribute it to the individuals you have asked and who have agreed to provide you with feedback. You should ask them to complete it as soon as possible, but no later than one week from when they received it.

4 Once you have received all the feedback tools back, use the "Individual Feedback Analysis Worksheet" to enter the raters' scores.

5 Add the scores across each row and enter the total. Then divide this total by the number of raters to get the average score. Enter the average in the appropriate cell on the worksheet.

6 Compare the ratings you have recorded (i.e., self versus others). Some questions you should ask yourself are:

☐ Is there congruity between the scores?

☐ How varied are the results?

☐ What four to five areas have the highest average scores? (Congratulate yourself on these scores and make a note to continue to engage in these successful kinds of activities or behavior.)

☐ What four to five areas have the lowest average scores?

☐ Prioritize the four or five areas in terms of relevance to what you currently do or aspire to do.

☐ Read the specific feedback for these ratings. You may want to go back to your raters and ask for more specific feedback (i.e., why they think you are a "1" or "2" in that particular area).

☐ Ask your raters for specific strategies or actions that you might take to improve in these areas.

7 Focus on two to three of the relevant areas that are in need of most improvement. Develop an action plan using the "360 Individual Action Plan Worksheet." This plan should include the area of improvement, the improvement goal you are setting for yourself, the strategy or action for improvement, resources needed, time frame, and method of evaluation.

☐ Use one action plan worksheet for each area you have selected. It is important that you use a systematic process to ensure you reach your improvement goals.

☐ Create a SMART goal for each of the selected improvement areas.

☐ Identify the strategies and actions you will need to take. You should be answering the following questions: What? When? Where? How?

☐ Identify the resources you will need.

☐ Identify a time frame for each action and a target completion date.

☐ Identify the measures you will use to evaluate your success.

8 Write a one- to two-page report that explains why you selected these two to three areas for improvement. Include your action plan along with this report and give it to your instructor for additional feedback. The report should include the following topics:

☐ Background information on who completed the assessments

　1. Not specific names, but positions, titles, or general categories such as close friend, fellow student, team member, supervisor, or crew member

　2. Number of years this person knows you

☐ Description of why you selected these two to three areas for your action plan

☐ Description of why these are important to your current professional development or work experience

☐ Explanation of how you will evaluate the outcome of your action plan. Be sure to include:

　1. What data you will collect to analyze?

　2. From whom?

　3. When?

　4. How?

5 What are significant milestones in the action plan?

360° Shared Leadership Development Assessment Tool

Name of person being rated:

Name of person doing the rating:

Date:

Following are twenty skill set areas that represent knowledge, skills, abilities and attitudes of successful leaders. Along with the skill set categories are several descriptions of what this skill set represents. Please read the description of each skill set, and then rate the individual identified above using this rating scale:

5 = Exceptional

4 = Very good

3 = Good

2 = Needs improvement

1 = Weak

Also, please provide any written comments that provide additional insights into your rating. These comments are very helpful in interpreting the scores.

360° Shared Leadership Assessment Tool		
Skill Set	Rating (1–5)	Written Comments
1 Vision ☐ Has a clear vision about what needs to be accomplished ☐ Understands an organization's deeper purpose ☐ Articulates the vision to others		
2 Mission and Goals ☐ Values and understands the mission statements of the company ☐ Sets realistic goals that reflect the mission of the company ☐ Communicates the impact of his or her job and that of others on the company's mission		

continued on next page

360° Shared Leadership Assessment Tool		
Skill Set	**Rating (1–5)**	**Written Comments**
3 Ethics and Personal Integrity ☐ Models integrity in daily interactions ☐ Asks questions to determine ethical decisions ☐ Says "thank you" for assistance ☐ Shows respect of others		
4 Written Communication ☐ Writes clearly ☐ Identifies appropriate channels to communicate written messages ☐ Documents problem solutions and policies		
5 Oral Communication ☐ Engages in open communication ☐ Informs others about the what and why of a message ☐ Communicates in a language the audience understands ☐ Uses appropriate telephone skills in dealing with others		
6 Communicating Expectations ☐ Provides advice or assistance to help me complete tasks ☐ Communicates expectations ☐ Keeps me informed related to our work together		
7 Active Listening ☐ Asks for input and is receptive to ideas ☐ Encourages other points of views to be shared ☐ Listens carefully and attentively to me		

360° Shared Leadership Assessment Tool		
Skill Set	**Rating (1–5)**	**Written Comments**
☐ Paraphrases or repeats points back to ensure they understand speaker's point		
8 Teamwork		
☐ Actively shares information with team		
☐ Does all possible to help team accomplish goals		
☐ Shares recognition willingly with team		
☐ Discourages we-they attitude		
9 Reliability		
☐ Consistently fulfills commitments made		
☐ Accepts personal responsibility and ownership for projects		
☐ Follows through with task in a timely manner		
☐ "Pitches in" when needed to meet deadlines		
10 Nurturing		
☐ Visibly shows they care about and are interested in others		
☐ Exhibits empathy for variety of personality types		
☐ Offers praise and positive feedback on work well done		
☐ Makes me feel like an essential member of the organization		
11 Interpersonal relations		
☐ Establishes trusting relationships, makes me feel comfortable		
☐ Treats everyone fairly		
☐ Delivers on promises and commitments		

continued on next page

360° Shared Leadership Assessment Tool		
Skill Set	**Rating (1–5)**	**Written Comments**
12 Motivating ☐ Creates a safe and fun environment for others ☐ Avoids embarrassing others ☐ Treats others with respect ☐ Recognizes others achievement		
13 Problem Solving ☐ Follows appropriate processes and systems to get at root causes ☐ Demonstrates flexibility in identifying solutions ☐ Selects best solutions based on facts and priorities ☐ Encourages risk taking		
14 Decisiveness ☐ Seeks input on decisions that others will be affected by ☐ Bases decision on facts and priorities ☐ Makes effective and timely decisions		
15 Conflict Management ☐ Tries to resolve issues in an objective open manner ☐ Handles complaints professionally ☐ Provides mediation, does not take sides		
16 Productivity/Contribution ☐ Adds overall value to company's products and services ☐ Uses time productively ☐ Produces results that need little revision		

360° Shared Leadership Assessment Tool		
Skill Set	**Rating (1–5)**	**Written Comments**
17 Delegating ☐ Understands the capabilities of others ☐ Empowers others after appropriate training ☐ Defines delegated task clearly ☐ Follows up and coaches as needed		
18 Feedback ☐ Manages by "walking around" to learn work status ☐ Solicits input from internal and external customers concerning satisfaction ☐ Provides appropriate and timely feedback to others ☐ Distinguishes between good and poor work and takes appropriate action		
19 Meetings ☐ Participates constructively in team meetings ☐ Conducts or facilitates meetings effectively ☐ Follows agenda items to keep focus		
20 Professional Development ☐ Stays knowledgeable of changes in industry to benefit organization ☐ Participates in various associations or industry organizations ☐ Networks with other professionals		

continued on next page

Individual Feedback Analysis Worksheet

Name of person being rated: _____   Date: _____

Instructions: Enter the numerical ratings for each of the raters. Total each row and divide by the number of raters to get an average score.

	Raters' Scores							Total	Average	Notes
Skill Set	1	2	3	4	5	6	7			
1 Vision										
2 Mission and Goals										
3 Ethics and Personal Integrity										
4 Written Communications										
5 Oral Communications										
6 Communicating Expectations										
7 Listening										
8 Teamwork										
9 Reliability										
10 Nurturing										
11 Interpersonal Relations										
12 Motivating										
13 Problem Solving										
14 Decisiveness										
15 Conflict Management										
16 Productivity/ Contribution										
17 Delegating										
18 Feedback										
19 Meeting										
20 Professional Development										

Individual Feedback Analysis Worksheet

Raters

1 _____

2 _____

3 _____

4 _____

5 _____

6 _____

7 _____

360° Individual Action Plan Worksheet

Name: _____

Area of improvement: _____

Goal for improvement: _____

_____

_____

Target completion date: _____

Strategy or Action to Take for Improvements			
Action	**Resources Needed**	**Begin Date**	**End Date**

Evaluation				
What data is collected?	**From whom?**	**When?**	**How?**	**Significance?**

Notes

Index